The Key
to
Mythic Victoria

Also by Linda Foubister

Goddess in the Grass: Serpentine Mythology and the Great Goddess

The Key
to
Mythic Victoria

Linda Foubister

Spirrea Publishing

Victoria, B.C.

Library and Archives Canada Cataloguing in Publication

Foubister, Linda, author
        The key to mythic Victoria / Linda Foubister.

Includes bibliographical references.
Issued in print and electronic formats.
ISBN 978-0-9868859-2-1 (pbk.).--ISBN 978-0-9868859-1-4 (pdf)

1. Victoria (B.C.). 2. Landscapes--Symbolic aspects--British
Columbia--Victoria. 3. Geographical myths--British Columbia--
Victoria. I. Title.

FC3846.36.F68 2013   971.1'28   C2013-903303-3
                                             C2013-903304-1

*Like the wave of a magic wand,
knowing the mythic heritage of a place
can re-enchant the landscape.*

.

CONTENTS

CHAPTER 1
Introducing Victoria

Where in the world would you find a Greek temple to Poseidon, the Holy Thorn Tree of Glastonbury, a seal harpooner transformed into rock and several fairy tale castles? Not to mention sea monsters, sea wolves and mermaids. The answer is Victoria, British Columbia, a seaside community located on the southern tip of Vancouver Island.

Victoria is situated in an area rich in contrasts. Formed millions of years ago from fire and ice, it is a land where volcanoes created mountains and where glaciers carved out valleys. Transformation is key in Victoria. Its foundations are granite and gneiss—rock that was created about 200 million years ago from magma deep in the earth and formed through the stress of high pressure and high temperature. Transformative pressures on the land continue today with seismic activity as energy is released periodically through earthquakes and volcanoes.

The area has a long history of human habitation, over four thousand years. The Coast Salish peoples lived in seasonal villages on southern Vancouver Island and nearby islands. European explorers began arriving as early as 1790. Hudson's Bay Company traders arrived on the island to find a site for a new trading post in 1842. The Fraser River gold rush of 1858 brought waves of miners to the small settlement, including Americans and Chinese people who travelled north from San Francisco after the 1849 gold rush. European settlers came to establish homes in the New World and the settlement grew to become a city.

1

Modern Victoria is built upon the layers of older cultures, from First Nations to gold-seeking Argonauts to settlers in the Victorian and Edwardian eras. The cultural layers can be seen in the shell middens and ancient artifacts found throughout the region, the tunnels running from the harbour to the old fort and the architectural features of each succeeding period.

Victoria's culture has been influenced by its geography. Travel writer Lawrence Durrell was fascinated by the spirit of place, writing in his novel, *Justine*, "We are the children of our landscape; it dictates behavior and even thought in the measure to which we are responsive to it."

In Victoria, much of its spirit of place reflects the sea. Victoria was founded by the Hudson's Bay Company on March 14, 1843 and, consistent with its marine influences, this makes Victoria a Pisces with Leo rising, astrologically. Pisces is a water sign ruled by the blue planet Neptune, named for the Roman god of the sea. As one of the farthest planets from the sun, Neptune rules dreams and illusions. Like the sea, Pisceans are shape-shifters. The symbol of Pisces is two fish tied together but swimming in opposite directions representing cooperation and opposition. Symbols relating to sea gods and the ideal of cooperation are found throughout Victoria, helping to communicate its spirit.

The boundary between land and sea is compelling both in terms of biological productivity and the symbolism that contrasts the land of the tangible with the sea of unconsciousness. Add the winds that allow hang gliders to soar above the cliffs off Dallas Road like Icarus flying to the sun, and you have the potent combination of land, sea and air. It has been suggested that the tension of the forces in Victoria has created its unique energy and perhaps has resulted in the psychic phenomena that many people experience in the area.

This book searches for the key to mythic Victoria—the key that opens the doors to its myths and symbols. Keys open locks, and as a symbol, they suggest the ability to gain access to hidden wealth, whether that wealth is material or spiritual. The Key Maiden is a compelling image related to this idea. Jacob Grimm described Key Maidens in his nineteenth century work, *Teutonic Mythology*. He recorded many accounts of maidens dressed in snowy white garments carrying a bunch of keys. They would appear to mortals and give them items such as grains of wheat, pods of flax or lilies. When the people returned home, they would find that the gifts had turned to gold. Just as keys provide access to treasure, the myths of Victoria provide access to a rich layer of meaning that enchants the landscape.

The focus of the book is not restricted to the City of Victoria, but includes the general area of Greater Victoria on southern Vancouver Island. Myths have arisen about geographical features, such as mountains and streams, about weather events, such as storms and comets, and about the plants and animals who share our environment. Indigenous myths link to life on the land for thousands of years, and immigrants brought stories and folklore from their home lands. Architects and artists wove symbolic messages and mythic references into their work. Much of the meaning in the sights, sites and symbols around us has become lost over time. This book seeks these meanings and explores how modern myth-making develops community spirit.

Generally, myths are stories, often about divine beings or heroes. They may be sacred stories with religious context and associated with rituals. They may explain the origin of life or natural phenomena. Most often, myths reflect universal or archetypal truths. Basically, myth is about the quest for meaning. Like myths, symbols have a diversity of meanings; some represent deep archetypal values, others work by association.

Psychologist Carl Jung delved into the use of symbols and their implication of something vague and hidden. He believed that the world has become dehumanized with the growth of scientific understanding, observing,

> *Man feels himself isolated in the cosmos, because he is no longer involved in nature and has lost his emotional "unconscious identity" with natural phenomena. These have slowly lost their symbolic implications. Thunder is no longer the voice of an angry god, nor is lightning his avenging missile. No river contains a spirit, no tree is the life principle of a man, no snake the embodiment of wisdom, no mountain cave the home of a great demon.... His contact with nature has gone, and with it has gone the profound emotional energy that his symbolic connection supplied.*

Myths give expression to our unconscious processes and retelling them brings them to life. People have always been story-tellers. Many cultures recognized the group value of story-telling. In Western Africa, the Griots are recognized as a special caste responsible for maintaining an oral record of tribal history in the form of music, poetry and storytelling. Like the Celtic bards, the story-tellers of Africa performed traditional stories, incorporating current events and observations into their stories, acting as myth-makers. Skalds performed a similar function in the Viking Age, composing and performing poems that exalted the deeds of their kings. The poems often had mythological content, incorporating stories about the gods. Myths have a particularly powerful effect as they have evolved to meet the needs of audiences over thousands of years. In the telling and re-telling of myths over time, the elements change to reflect the present while preserving the essence of shared human experience. Myths come alive when they help to relate personal experience to the broader context, providing a powerful tool of social identity.

Retelling myths can serve to re-enchant the landscape. Paul Devereux warned in his book, *Re-visioning the Earth*, "If the full, rich, mythic sense of place is finally taken out of our cultural compass, then we will mentally inhabit a spiritual wasteland." Conveying a sense of place and the idea that divinities energize every stream, hill and tree provide a connection to the land that can counteract the destructive forces that lead to a wasteland.

The idea that the landscape is a place of supernatural powers can be found in the worldview of the local Songhees people who identified a strong interconnection between people, nature and spirituality. To them, nature was a source of spiritual power and food, a gift from the spirit world. Accordingly, they performed rituals to ensure that the natural world was treated with due respect.

Land or sea, mountains or meadows, wild or cultivated, Indigenous or immigrants, Victoria is a study in contrasts and textures. The mythology of the area is rich with meaning because of the contrasts. With these ideas in mind, here are the stories of Victoria.

CHAPTER 2
FINDING EDEN

Southern Vancouver Island has been a land of mythic attraction for hundreds of years. Explorers were drawn to the area in search of the fabled Northwest Passage. Hudson's Bay Company traders came to establish a trading post and found an Eden. Miners arrived to search for their own El Dorado or city of gold.

Juan de Fuca Strait

The Juan de Fuca Strait dominates the southern outlook of Victoria. Over 128 kilometres long (80 miles), the Strait is bordered by Vancouver Island on the north, the Olympic Mountains on the south and the Pacific Ocean to its west.

Even the name of the Strait reflects a mythic tale. Who was Juan de Fuca? He was not Spanish, but Greek. His actual name is not certain. Some scholars even doubt that he existed. His story starts in Venice. One day in 1596, an English merchant named Michael Lok met an old man called Juan de Fuca who told him an exciting tale of maritime adventure. He said that he had sailed for forty years as a mariner and a pilot in the service of the Spaniards. Because the Spaniards could not pronounce his real name, Apóstolos Valeriános, they called him Juan de Fuca. Alternatively, some scholars say that Juan de Fuca was a Spanish version of the Greek name, Ioánnis Fokás.

The search for the mythical passage linking the Pacific and Atlantic Oceans had started with Christopher Columbus in 1492. It is believed that the name, the Straits of Anián, was based on an account by Marco Polo published in 1559 which mentioned Ania, a province in China. The route began appearing on maps starting in the 1560s.

In 1592, the Spanish Viceroy of Mexico sent Juan de Fuca to find the Straits of Anián. Juan de Fuca sailed north from Acapulco and found an inlet located between 47 and 48 degrees of latitude. He noted a high pinnacle or spired rock at the entrance to the inlet. When he went ashore at various places, he found people clad in the skins of beasts living in a land rich in gold, silver and pearls. He reported that he sailed for 20 days up the inlet and believed that he had found the North Sea. He returned to Acapulco, then Spain, hoping to be rewarded but his hopes were in vain. Four years later, he told his story to Michael Lok in the expectation of financial support from England. Michael Lok had a strong belief in the existence of a Northwest Passage and he was a keen supporter of the explorations of Martin Frobisher. Juan de Fuca's story would have piqued his interest, reflecting his belief in the existence of a passage, so he championed Juan de Fuca's interests in England. On the mariner's behalf, Lok wrote to Her Majesty Queen Elizabeth of England offering Juan de Fuca's services to find the fabled passage but no monies were sent. In 1602, Lok wrote to Juan de Fuca in Greece and, as he did not receive a reply, he believed that the old man had died.

Lok's account of the story was published in 1625 in Samuel Purchas's book, *Purchas Pilgrimes*, a collection of voyages by explorers, and it caused a stir. The existence of a sea passage to China was of great interest to people at that time. Such a route would have provided a shorter trade route to China. Spanish tales of El Dorado, the land of gold, further spurred interest in such exploration.

Over a hundred years later, Charles William Barkley, captain of the *Imperial Eagle*, recognized the inlet as the strait described by Juan de Fuca and in 1787, named it in his honour. The latitude of the inlet described by Juan de Fuca corresponds with the present Juan de Fuca Strait, and Fuca Pillar at Cape Flattery fits his description of the rock pillar. However, the only record of Juan de Fuca's discovery is the account written by Lok. Although the pilot was in the service of the Spanish king, there is no record of his name or voyages in Spanish archives.

We'll never know if Juan de Fuca did discover the strait bearing his name. But the story of the naming of the Strait shows the power of belief in mythical quests, such as the searches for the Straits of Anián and El Dorado. Juan de Fuca's story included both the legendary passage and a bountiful land of gold, silver and pearls, representing a grail quest for actual or spiritual riches that one spends a lifetime seeking.

A Perfect Eden

When James Douglas, Chief Factor of the Hudson's Bay Company, arrived at southern Vancouver Island in 1842, he saw a headland knee-deep in red clover, grasses and ferns. He wrote to his friend, James Hargrave, "The place itself appears a perfect 'Eden,' in the midst of the dreary wilderness of the Northwest Coast, and so different is its general aspect, from the wooded, rugged regions around, that one might be pardoned for supposing it had dropped from the clouds into its present position." Douglas named the headland Clover Point.

The Hudson's Bay Company had sent Douglas to Vancouver Island to find a suitable place for a trading post. After exploring several harbours, he selected the one called Camosack because of its meadows and grasslands, rather than the more densely forested Esquimalt or Sooke Harbours. In 1843, Fort Camosun was built and renamed Fort Victoria in honour of Queen Victoria.

Victoria has been described as an Eden or a paradise by many of its notable visitors. When Francis Rattenbury first saw Victoria 1892 as he entered the Inner Harbour by steamer, he envisioned a future city with monumental architecture, like an imperial Garden of Eden. In 1933, Canada's first all talking motion picture, *The Crimson Paradise*, filmed at Hatley Park and the Cowichan River, featured the forests of B.C. as a paradise. When Canadian Prime Minister Mackenzie King visited Victoria on July 1, 1941, he wrote in his diary, "The beauty of the city is beyond all description. The luxuriance of the growth and vines, the variety of shrubs, flowers, etc., surpasses imagination— Victoria, indeed, is a little paradise."

For millennia, people have longed for the land of plenty where food is abundant and life is easy. Some people believe that it only exists in the afterlife; others think that paradise can be found on earth, either as a mythic concept or as an actual place. Myths of an island paradise with temperate weather date back to antiquity. Homer described the Elysian Fields as early as the eighth century BCE in his epic, the *Odyssey*, writing, "No snow is here, no winter long, no rain, but the loud-blowing breezes of the west the Ocean-stream sends up to bring men coolness."

The mythic name *Elysium* has also been used to describe Victoria's climate. In 1843, Hudson's Bay Company factor Charles Ross was transferred to Fort Victoria and found the sunny days a welcome change from the rains of his previous post further north. When Hudson's Bay Company Governor George Simpson read letters from Ross describing the climate, Simpson pictured "a very Elysium in point of climate & scenery." Ross wrote that the landscape was beautiful and the climate "perhaps too fine." Indeed, Victoria beckons to visitors with its boasts of having the mildest climate in Canada, with warm, dry summers and mild, wet winters. Lying within the rain shadow of the Olympic Mountains, Victoria receives less rain than neighbouring areas with a yearly average rainfall of just over 60 cm, and the least snowfall in all of B.C.

The Elysian Fields were also known as the Islands of the Blessed or the Fortunate Islands. In some traditions, the northern paradise of Hyperborea was described as an island. Hyperborea is a place of harmonious music where the people do not suffer from illness, old age, war or labour.

Pliny the Elder linked the mythical Fortunate Islands to the existing Canary Islands in his encyclopedia, *Natural History*, published in the first century CE. He described the islands as abounding in fruit and birds of every kind. However, the islands "are greatly annoyed by the putrefying bodies of monsters, which are constantly thrown up by the sea." The bodies of sea monsters on shore seem to plague many island paradises, including southern Vancouver Island. In 2010, the carcass of a gray whale washed up on the shores off East Sooke Park. Then in 2009, a brown cow nicknamed Cuddles was thrown up by the sea near Clover Point, to the consternation of many.

In Celtic mythology, heroes would venture to magical island paradises inhabited by supernatural beings. The Irish mythical island of Mag Mell was such a paradise. Some adventurers found the mythical Irish island of Tír na nÓg far to the west of Ireland where there was no sickness or death, only eternal youth and beauty. The hero Oisin visited it on a magic horse that galloped over the waves. When he returned to his home, he found that 300 years had passed. The Celtic belief in magical islands likely contributed to the idea that Avalon was an island paradise where King Arthur went to die and be reborn as a future king.

Promotional material to encourage tourism furthered the image of Victoria as a paradise. A 1909 pamphlet by the Tourist Association of Victoria described Victoria as "the holiday seekers' paradise." It quoted the Prince and Princess of Wales saying in 1901 that Victoria was the most beautiful city they had seen in their trip around the world. The pamphlet went on to note that Rudyard Kipling described the climate as the "most perfect in the world." Many descriptions of Victoria included references to a fairyland and this pamphlet continued this practice, stating "No more delightful trip can be imagined than the one to 'the Gorge,' with its unique 'reversible falls,' at the head of Victoria Arm. On a summer evening, when the stately residences that adorn the banks are brilliantly lighted up, and the fires of the campers grow red through the trees, while sweet music steals oe'r the waters from the numerous boating parties, it seems like a glimpse of fairy-land."

Paradise is often envisioned as a place filled with happy people, dancing, singing and in love. Using picturesque metaphors drawn from classical mythology, the *British Colonist* newspaper described Victorians as "worshipping at the shrine of Terpsichore." The paper reported in July 1867 that at Cadboro Bay where people were celebrating the fourth of July, "the dancing platform was monopolized by the devotees of Terpsichore." Other references over the years mention "worshippers at the shrine of Terpsichore" and invited "all who enjoy playing tribute to Terpsichore" to attend a dance. Terpsichore was one of the nine muses, the muse of dance. Her name means "delight in dancing." In the Victorian era, knowledge of classical mythology was helpful in reading the paper. Newspaper reports of police raids of brothels in Victoria described the women in the sex trade as "Cyprians," referring to the ancient worship of the goddess of love, Aphrodite, rising from the sea foam off the island of Cyprus in the Mediterranean.

Although the Garden of Eden was not located on an island, it was a paradise with abundant food, including every tree that is pleasant to the sight and good for food, every beast of the field and every fowl of the air. The concept of a land of plenty became associated with the Garden of Eden. The early visitors to Victoria saw the abundant vegetation on the lands cooled by ocean breezes and the myths about island paradises and Eden came to mind.

El Dorado

Victoria's significant growth in 1858 was influenced by the legend of El Dorado. With the discovery of gold in the Fraser Canyon, over 20,000 people arrived in Victoria, which had a European population of about 500 at the time. Most of the gold-seekers had sailed from San Francisco, still suffering from gold fever even though the California gold rush was over. The miners had to purchase a mining licence and supplies in Fort Victoria before travelling on to the Fraser River. In mere months, Victoria was transformed from a village to a major commercial town.

Accounts of the gold rush included references to the miners as modern Argonauts and to the gold fields in British Columbia as the New Eldorado. When gold was found in California in 1848, newspapers of the day made similar references to El Dorado and the Argonauts. In fact, the area in which gold was discovered in California was named El Dorado County in 1850.

The references to El Dorado and the Argonauts inspired a bank clerk in Boston, Thomas Bulfinch, to start writing about the ancient myths. Bulfinch read newspaper accounts about the California gold rush that stated that the old myth of El Dorado had come true. California was described as a magical land where you could pick up lumps of gold off the ground. Bulfinch thought that ordinary people would like to know the origin of such stories and so wrote an article about the myth of Jason and the Argonauts. His article was popular, leading to more articles and a three-volume collection entitled *Bulfinch's Mythology*. The first volume, published in 1855, sold out in two months. Bulfinch believed that mythology allows us to understand literature and literature can make us happier; his passion was to entertain and educate. He wrote, "Without knowledge of mythology much of the elegant literature of our own language cannot be understood and appreciated." As examples, he included Lord Byron's reference to Rome as "the Niobe of nations" and descriptions of Venice as "a Sea-Cybele fresh from ocean." He noted,

Our work is not for the learned, nor for the theologian, nor for the philosopher, but for the reader of English literature, of either sex, who wishes to comprehend the allusions so frequently made by public speakers, lecturers, essayists, and poets, and those which occur in polite conversation.

The Argonauts were the sailors on the ship, the *Argo*, who accompanied Jason on his search for the Golden Fleece. The Greek myth of Jason's heroic quest was an ancient story, known in the time of Homer in the eighth century BCE and detailed in the epic *The Argonautica* written by Apollonius in the third century BCE. The ram with the Golden Fleece had been sacrificed to the sea god Poseidon. Its fleece hung on an oak tree in a grove sacred to Aries, the god of war, where it was guarded by a dragon that never slept. To help Jason, the princess Medea put the dragon to sleep with a song and sleeping potion so that Jason could grab the fleece and return home with it. Jason had met many challenges during his quest to prove that he was the rightful king and once home, he took his place on the throne. There are a multitude of interpretations suggesting what the fleece symbolizes, such as that it was a magic talisman bestowing kingship on its possessor, or it was used in placer mining, or it represented a psychological quest for inner meaning. The ram became the constellation, Aries, illustrating the astrological association of Aries with the ram.

The *British Colonist* newspaper also included mythological references in its reports from the gold fields. An article in November 1863 reported, "The future of the mines affects the success of the colonies. The power of gold is as great now as it was in the days of Horace who tells a naughty story about Jupiter and his transformation into a shower of gold to seduce the lady named Danae."

In 1858, Kinahan Cornwallis wrote *The New El Dorado (or British Columbia)* to inspire immigration to British Columbia, enthusing, "The magic spell of the discovery is being felt throughout the world, and nations have been awakened to the knowledge of another—a new—El Dorado, outvying all beside. And this land, upon which nature has so lavished her treasures, in inviting prodigality, rests beneath the sway of the British sceptre, and its riches are open to all."

El Dorado was the mythical lost city of gold. The source of the El Dorado legend was a collection of several accounts written as early as 1536 by Spanish explorers describing El Dorado as either a place or a person.

The name *El Dorado*, or *The Gilded One*, referred to a high chief of the Muisca people who lived in the area of present day Colombia. When the Spanish first arrived in South America, the Indigenous people told them stories about a city of immense wealth and gold. A few reports described *The Gilded One*. According to the accounts, a new high chief of the Muisca people would be covered with gold dust and carried on a raft of reeds to the center of Lake Guatavita to offer gold and emeralds to the goddess of the lake. As an initiation rite, *The Gilded One* would jump into the lake, washing off the gold. To the Muisca, gold was a sacred metal, capturing the light of the sun. It was not used in trade or as a measure of wealth but as an offering to the gods. A votive offering made of gold may represent the raft used in the account of El Dorado. The piece, dating from 1200 to 1500 CE, is now in the Gold Museum, Bogotá, Colombia. The small raft carries a large central figure surrounded by twelve smaller figures, perhaps the chief with his subjects.

The Spaniards first tried to drain Lake Guatavita in search of gold in 1545. The lake has been drained several times since then, damaging its ecology. However, no significant amount of gold has ever been found. Regardless, the legend of the lost city of gold grew and became very popular in Europe. Explorers, such as Sir Walter Raleigh, launched expeditions to find it. Often the expeditions cost more than the amount of gold that was found. The geographical location of the lost city of gold became generalized and the myth became associated with any region of untold wealth in the Americas. The city of gold became the mythical ideal, like the Holy Grail, that fires people's imaginations and attracts seekers.

Edgar Allen Poe published his poem *El Dorado* in 1849, at the time of the Californian gold rush. It was about a knight who spent his life seeking El Dorado but grew old without finding it. The poet advises the knight to "ride, boldly ride" if he seeks for El Dorado. The quest can be summed up by Poe's poem which suggests that we may never find the Land of Golden Dreams, but it is the search that matters.

CHAPTER 3
SEEKING THE SEA GOD

Among the many features that make Victoria special is its proximity to the sea. Edged by water on three sides, Victoria has a natural harbor. The interface where land meets water speaks to the connection of opposites. The ocean produces mists and fogs which create an air of illusion and hidden things.

The Mystery of the Ocean

After his visit in 1907 to Victoria on a speaking tour, Rudyard Kipling noted that no place in England was so fully charged as Victoria with the mystery of the ocean. He praised Victoria in his letters to the family, writing,

> To realize Victoria you must take all that the eye admires most in Bournemouth, Torquay, the Isle of Wight, the Happy Valley at Hong Kong, the Doon, Sorrento, and Camps Bay; add reminiscences of the Thousand Islands, and arrange the whole round the Bay of Naples, with some Himalays for the background. Real estate agents recommend it as a little piece of England—the island on which it stands is about the size of Great Britain—but no England is set in any such seas or so fully charged with the mystery of the larger ocean beyond. The high, still twilights along the beaches are out of the old East just under the curve of the world, and even in October the sun rises warm from the first Earth, sky and water

wait outside every man's door to drag him out to play if he looks up from his work; and, though some other cities in the Dominion do not quite understand this immoral mood of Nature, men who have made their money in them go off to Victoria, and with the zeal of converts preach and preserve its beauties.... I tried honestly to render something of the color, the gaiety, and the graciousness of the town and the island, but only found myself piling up unbelievable adjectives, and so let it go with a hundred other wonders.

Myths present the ocean as mysterious, both dangerous and generous. In psychology, the ocean symbolizes the depth of the unconscious. It is ever changing, from placid glass surfaces to wild wave-arousing storms. The ancients saw the sea as an animate being and identified many divinities to represent its various aspects. It was important to show respect for the gods of the sea, both for protection and for their gifts.

In Greek myths, the ever changing aspect of the sea was personified by Proteus, the old man of the sea. Homer described Proteus as a sage old god who knows the sea throughout its depths. He is unerring and deathless. He left the ocean every day to sleep among the seals which he tended as a shepherd looking after his flocks. When Odysseus sought an oracle from Proteus, he had to capture the god first and hold on to him as he changed from one shape into another—from lion to snake to panther to boar water and finally, to tree before he tired and gave his prediction. It is easy to understand how the name of Proteus came to be used for the adjective, *protean*, meaning the ability to assume different forms.

The overarching Greek god of the sea was Poseidon who ruled with his queen, Amphitrite. They lived in a grand palace on the bottom of the sea. Phosphorescence in the sea is said to be the shine of jewels from underwater palaces. Poseidon can be recognized by his trident, a three-pronged spear, used for both fishing and combat. He used his trident to shatter rocks to release water, to call forth or subdue storms, and to create the horse. When Poseidon struck the earth with his trident, he would cause earthquakes and for this reason, he was often referred to as the "earth-shaker." He would ride over the sea in his chariot drawn by his golden-maned horses, and as he travelled, the seas would become calm and sea monsters would cavort around his chariot. Poseidon's association with horses perhaps predates his association with the sea. Horses were sometimes sacrificed to gain his favour. As Poseidon rode over the sea, the power of waves became identified with the strength of horses, their manes billowing out like the white caps of the waves.

The seas off the coast of Victoria can be violent, more in keeping with the sea gods of the Norse. The Norse identified the sea in its dangerous aspect with the sea goddess, Rán. Rán had a net with which she caught the men who went to sea. Sailors brought gold with them on any voyage, so that if they drowned while at sea, Rán would be pleased by their gift. The attributes of the gods were used by Old Norse poets in their kennings or metaphors. In poetic terms, the sea was referred to as "Rán's mouth" and gold as the "brightness of Rán."

In many cultures, the varying forms of ocean waves were personified as spirits. In Greek mythology, the Nereids were sea nymphs in Poseidon's entourage. Several represented different aspects of waves. Hipponoe was the Nereid who knew about horses, or waves; Hippothoe represented swift horses (i.e., swift waves), and Menippe was the Nereid of strong horses, or strong waves. In Norse mythology, the sea divinities Aegir and Rán had nine daughters. Each was named to capture a different aspect of waves—billowing, pitching, surging, light-reflecting, chilling and finally, the blood-red waves that result from a naval battle.

The Irish sea god was Manannan mac Lir, whose name means "son of the sea." Like Poseidon, he galloped over the waves on horseback or by chariot. He had the ability to cast spells, and he taught this to the Druids. He could create a mist to render himself invisible. His magical attributes included an enchanted sword, a magical cloak and a bag that held his possessions, including language. His magical cloak reflected the light, taking on the many colours of the sea. When he waved his cloak, he would change destinies. Fishermen prayed to him for a bountiful catch.

Fogs arise from the seas and cover the landscape with a thick cloak. There are days when Victoria is hidden in a fog. In Irish folklore, the Druid's fog was a magic mist that rendered those under it invisible. The Irish 'grey man' or *far liath* is believed to appear as a fog, obscuring rocks so that ships crash on them and hiding roads so that travellers lose their way and stumble over cliffs to their deaths.

Undutar was the goddess of fog and mist praised in the epic poem of Finland, the *Kalevala*. She lived in the highest regions of the heavens and passed fogs and mists through a silver sieve before sending them to the earth. The line of silvery mist that Victorians can see edging the ocean off Dallas Road suggests the work of Undutar.

The story of Jason and the Argonauts includes a reference to the use of light to guide their ship through darkness. On their return voyage, Jason and the Argonauts became scared by a night so dark that they did not know if they were in Hades or on the waters. Jason called upon Phoebus Apollo, the sun god, who shot an arrow from his golden bow. The arrow flashed a dazzling ray which gleamed of light allowing the crew to see their location. They landed on an island and created an altar for Apollo, whom they called "Phoebus the Gleamer."

The antidotes to the dangers of fogs and mists, as well as darkness, are lighthouses with their dazzling lights and booming voices. The prototype for lighthouses was the Lighthouse of Alexandria, built in the third century BCE on the island of Pharos in the harbour of Alexandria in Egypt. The lighthouse served as a symbol of Greek maritime power and helped guide ships safely into the harbour. In ancient times, Proteus, the old man of the sea, was believed to dwell in Pharos. A statue of a god, either Poseidon or Zeus, dominated the structure, standing at its top, and statues of the god Triton decorated the four corners of the tower.

In Victoria, the Fisgard lighthouse, built in 1860 was the first lighthouse on Canada's west coast. It is located on Fisgard Island at the mouth of Esquimalt Harbour. The Race Rocks Lighthouse was also illuminated in 1860. Both were funded by the British government, symbolizing the government's commitment to the Colony of Vancouver Island. The image of the old man of the sea, Proteus, looking after the seals on Pharos is captured by pictures of the Race Rocks Lighthouse surrounded by a variety of seals. The mythic treasures of the sea came into play about 1885 when Thomas Argyle, Chief Keeper at the lighthouse, started to pay for his supplies with gold sovereigns. It was speculated that he had discovered sunken treasure and kept the secret close.

A scientific study to explore the mystery of the ocean off Vancouver Island is being conducted by Oceans Networks Canada. The names of its two underwater networks are derived from the

Roman deities, Neptune and Venus. NEPTUNE (North East Pacific Time-series Undersea Networked Experiments) is transforming ocean science with its 800 kilometre network of instruments which connects the ocean floor live to the Internet. VENUS (Victoria Experimental Network Under the Sea) collects data from its nearly 50 kilometre network in the coastal waters of the Salish Sea. Already the first function of mythology identified by Joseph Campbell, to reconcile us with the nature of life—that life lives on life—is being played out in the abyss for the world to see. In January 2013, a teenager from the Ukraine made news with his observation from the NEPTUNE video feed of a "monster" eating a fish in the ocean depths. Scientists determined that the video showed an elephant seal eating a hagfish. Although many aspects of the depths of the sea can be measured scientifically, the magic of the sea's lure continues in the rich mythological themes of the ocean.

Victoria Harbour

Victoria is favoured with a beautiful natural harbour. The harbour is approximately four kilometres long. It is well protected because of its shape and has the added buffer of a breakwater from winter storms.

The Songhees people consider the harbour sacred. Their traditional name for Songhees Point at the northern entrance to the Inner Harbour was *Pallatsis* meaning "place of cradle," where parents would place the cradles outgrown by their children so that the spiritual power of the water would ensure a long life. As well, dancers' staffs were placed on the site and young men on vision quests would perform cleansing rituals by diving into the water. Purification by immersion in water was an important practice for the Indigenous people of southern Vancouver Island.

Portunus, the Roman god of harbours, was celebrated as the gateway to the sea and invoked by sailors for the boon of a safe return. The word, *opportunity,* evokes his name. The harbour was one of the reasons that Sir James Douglas selected the site for Fort Victoria. It became an excellent port and provided the opportunity for economic growth. Accordingly, the harbour became a hub of commercial activity. Its ship building industry began in 1863 with the start of Albion Iron Works. Ships carrying gold miners, settlers and visitors entered the harbour as the economy grew. In 1880, nearly 500 sea-going vessels arrived at the Port of Victoria.

At the entrance of Victoria's harbour to its south stands a beautiful temple for the Greek god of the sea, Poseidon. Like the ancient Temple of Poseidon (ca. 440 BCE) overlooking the sea at Cape Sounion in Greece, it is rectangular in shape with free standing Greek columns. It also resembles the well-preserved Temple of Hephaestus in Athens which is believed to have been built about the same time at the temple at Cape Sounion and by the same architect.

Ionic Columns on the CPR Building

Carved heads of Poseidon and related iconography such as crowns and crossed tridents leave no doubt that the building in Victoria is dedicated to the god of the sea. Dolphins flank a cartouche identifying the building as the "CPR BC Coast Service Office." As a symbol of Poseidon, dolphins are often shown accompanying the sea god. In Greek myth, Delphin was a dolphin who served Poseidon. When the god wished to marry Amphitrite, the goddess of the sea, Amphitrite fled to avoid the union. It was

Delphin who found her and persuaded her to marry Poseidon. As a reward, Poseidon put the dolphin in the sky as constellation Delphinus. A third century Greek poet noted that there is no sea without dolphins for Poseidon loves them exceedingly.

Frances M. Rattenbury and Percy L. James designed the building in 1923 as a new terminal for the Canadian Pacific Railway steamships. Rattenbury's choice of a Neoclassical temple spoke to the importance of the maritime influence on Victoria, paying homage to the god of the sea. In the early 1900s, the steamship terminal was the gateway to Victoria where visitors arrived and departed. Princesses came daily to pay homage to Victoria's temple of Poseidon since the terminal was the base of the "Princess fleet." These ships carried passengers daily on the Triangle Route between Victoria, Vancouver and Seattle. One of the earliest steamships was the Princess Victoria. The Princess ships were called "pocket liners" because they were small versions of the ocean liners in the CPR's Empress fleet that sailed across the Pacific and Atlantic Oceans. The service continued until 1963 when the CPR moved its head office to Vancouver.

History came to life in the building when the Royal London Wax Museum moved into the main floor in 1971. The Museum had nearly 350 wax figures depicting royalty, politicians and historic figures. Its chamber of horrors was particularly eerie. Over 300,000 visitors a year came to see the iconic figures of the present and the past, including Queen Victoria, Queen Elizabeth, Princess Diana, Marilyn Monroe, Captain Cook and Julius Caesar. Wearing historical costumes, the figures impressed the visitors with their realism. The Royal London Wax Museum closed its doors in 2010 after nearly 50 years of operation in Victoria.

In addition to the notional temple of Poseidon, Victoria has an active temple to the Chinese sea god, Tam Kung. The Tam Kung Temple is the oldest Chinese temple in Canada. According to legend, a gold seeker from China brought a statue of Tam Kung to Victoria in the 1860s. Tam Kung is the god of seafarers and sacred to the Hakka people of south China. He could calm storms by throwing peas into the air or cause them by throwing water. As he could forecast weather, he was popular with fishermen. He remains popular with sailors in Hong Kong and Macau and his birthday on the eighth day of the fourth lunar month (around May) is celebrated to bring good luck to sailors over the coming year.

Boat races take place in Victoria harbour, usually without divine help. Portunus, in an account by the Roman writer, Virgil, favoured one of the boats in an ancient race and gave it shove.

Annual Dragon Boat Festivals have been held in mid-August in Victoria since 1995. In Chinese mythology, dragons are associated with water. They rule moving bodies of water, such as rivers and seas. With this symbolism, what could be more appropriate than a flotilla of dragons racing around the inner harbour? Dragon boat races have a 2,500 year history. They celebrate the Dragon King, hoping to encourage him to bring rain for the crops. Traditionally, the races were held on the fifth day of the fifth month, a time when special care had to be taken to ward off evil. The races also commemorate the suicide of the poet Qu Yuan who, in the third century BCE, sacrificed himself in a river to protest corruption. Mythic rituals surround the dragon boat races. At the start of each race, the dragon is awakened when a Taoist priest dots the pupil of its eyes with red paint. The drum on board represents the beating of the dragon's heart and helps pace the paddlers. Children may wear fragrant pouches of herbs to protect them from summer illnesses and people may eat special foods, such as rice dumplings, in recognition of Qu Yuan.

Clover Point

The knee-deep red clover that impressed James Douglas with the fertility of the land and led to him calling the headland Clover Point is no more. But in modern times, fertility rituals take place on this point. Every year on May Day, Morris dancers gather at Clover Point before sunrise to wake up the sun and keep it coming back. The Maypole dance is an old British tradition. Dancers dressed in costume and incorporating items such as sticks, ribbons and hankies perform rhythmic dances to live music. Characters such as the Hobby Horse and Dragon perform antics to amuse the crowd. In a local tradition, Caddy, the sea monster who lives in Cadboro Bay, has been known to leave the sea and join the dancers. The Maypole is a phallic symbol complete with two balls, as well as a garland at its top symbolizing the female element. After sun-up, the entire audience joins in a whirling spiral dance to the Maypole at the center of the circle and then back out again, confident of the returning fertility of the land.

Not only has Clover Point served as a site to restore the fertility of the earth, but it has also been the site for final farewells. It was used for Sikh cremations until about 1920. Cremation symbolized the need for the soul to move on, and the ashes were thrown into flowing water to disperse.

Esquimalt Harbour

Esquimalt Harbour is another sheltered natural harbour in the Greater Victoria area. Coast Salish peoples lived around Esquimalt Harbour for thousands of years. Their name for it, Esquimalt, means "place of shoaling waters."

The earliest European arrival was in 1790 when Lt. Don Manuel Quimper of Spain landed in Esquimalt Harbour and named it Puerto de Cordova (later applied to Cordova Bay).

The harbour has had a strong naval presence since 1865, when it became the Royal Navy Headquarters in the Pacific. Today, Esquimalt Harbour is the home of Canada's west coast navy at the Canadian Forces Base (CFB). Naval symbolism can be found throughout the base. The anchor is a popular symbol, found in coats of arms, signs and ship badges. Several anchors are displayed on the base, including one that is a sailors' memorial. Dolphins are featured on many of the displayed coats of arms. Even the ghosts reportedly spotted on the base reflect the naval history of the place. The oldest building, the Commodore's residence, which dates to 1879, has a resident ghost. It is the ghost of Royal Navy Lt. Reginald Scott who was shot by a sentry on April 4, 1900. He was carried to the nearby Commodore's residence until he could be taken to the hospital where he died seven days later. It has been said that bloodstains appear on the porch occasionally and electronic devices may turn on and off mysteriously. Another spirit haunts what was once the Royal Navy Prison. A man named George hung himself in his cell in the early years of the base. George's cell is now a women's washroom where doors do not stay closed.

The maritime symbolism continues in the corporate logo for the Township of Esquimalt. The logo features a wave to reflect Esquimalt's seaside location and naval roots and to suggest forward movement and progress. Esquimalt's coat of arms references Poseidon's trident, held aloft by an arm, symbolizing defence against enemies at sea. It includes a depiction of the Naden Raven of the Haida people of the Raven crest who lived along the Naden River in Haida Gwaii, recognizing the importance of the H.M.C.S. Naden shore facility on Esquimalt Harbour.

Ships

The canoe was vital to the survival of the Coast Salish people of southern Vancouver Island who relied on canoes for fishing, transportation and trade. They carved dugout canoes from Western red cedar. The canoe featured prominently in the myth of the Great Flood. In order to survive the rising waters, the people sought safety in their canoes. Spiritually, canoes represented transport to otherworlds. Shaman might travel to the land of the dead in a spirit canoe to recover souls that had been stolen. When a warrior died, he may have been laid to rest in his canoe surrounded by his belongings. Such canoes were seen among the arbutus trees at Laurel Point in the nineteenth century.

The selection of the cedar log for the canoe and its carving involved spirit guides and rituals, many of which remain secret because of their spiritual importance. The sides of canoes were often decorated with paintings illustrating the family crest of the owner and images for protection and success. The Nuu-Chah-Nulth canoe was built to withstand the surging ocean off the West Coast of Vancouver Island. Its prow was carved in the shape of the head of a wolf. Through trade, it became adopted by the Coast Salish people. As valuable trade items, canoes symbolized wealth.

In the nineteenth century, canoes became popular for inter-tribal racing. From the 1860s to the 1890s, canoe racing was a regular event on the Gorge Waterway. The canoe culture almost disappeared in the early twentieth century, except for racing events. It was revived in the 1970s with the influence of artists such as Victoria-born Bill Reid, himself a mythic figure in that he was an artistic genius who shone in public but had a shadow side replete with contradictions.

The image of mythological creatures paddling together in a canoe was captured by Bill Reid. His bronze sculpture, the *Spirit of Haida Gwaii*, completed and installed in 1991 outside the Canadian Embassy in Washington, DC, features a canoe carrying thirteen mythological Haida figures. The paddlers include the Bear Mother, the Beaver,

Dogfish Woman, the Eagle, the Wolf, and a reluctant human. It is not harmonious in the canoe. The Wolf is biting the Eagle's wing while attacking the Bear's paws. The Frog is half out of the canoe. The canoe is steered by the trickster, Raven, who may change the course of the canoe by whim, reflecting that life is unpredictable.

The importance of the canoe as a symbol continues to the present day. Steven Point became B.C.'s first Aboriginal lieutenant governor in 2007. One day, he found a partially carved log on Gonzales Beach. Together with carver Chief Tony Hunt, he carved a traditional inland river canoe in the shape of sea monster with a shovel nose and scales on the sides. The canoe was named *Shxwtitöstel*, meaning "a safe place to cross the river." The symbolic importance of the canoe is illustrated in Steven Point's words:

> *I've had this belief for some time that if people see our world like a canoe—like we're together—we're not individuals in separate canoes. We're in the same canoe—it's called the Earth, the world. It's like we're travelling through space. We have to try and work together, paddle in the same direction. Maybe we can accomplish something.*

Later in 2010, Point, his brother, Mark, and Tony Hunt carved a second canoe from a 15 1/2 foot red cedar log and named it *Sea Raven on the Salish Sea*. It featured prominently in a historic event, being launched on July 15, 2010 at a ceremony to name the Salish Sea, a composite body of water encompassing Juan de Fuca Strait, Georgia Strait and Puget Sound, named in honour of the Coast Salish people of the area. The canoe was presented to the Canadian Navy to celebrate its one-hundredth anniversary.

The traditional use of the canoe is undergoing a modern revival. Following the naming ceremony of the Salish Sea, almost twenty canoes were welcomed by the Songhees First Nation. The canoes were participating in the 2010 Tribal Journeys, an annual event involving Indigenous people from Canada and the U.S. that pays tribute to Aboriginal canoe culture. The sight of canoes being paddled across the Salish Sea recalled the days when canoes were an integral part of daily life and a common sight.

At the time of the 1858 gold rush, ships arrived in Victoria Harbour carrying modern Argonauts seeking gold. The ancient

Argonauts sailed in the *Argo*, a forty-oared ship. Its construction had been overseen by the goddess Athena. She had brought an oak beam from the sacred oracle at Dodona and fitted it in the middle of the ship's stern. As a result, the *Argo* had the power of speech and prophecy. When it was time for her to set sail on her maiden voyage, she called to the sailors to get onboard. On the return voyage, an angry Zeus sent a storm to drive the *Argo* off course. The ship began to speak in a human voice in the darkness, telling the Argonauts about Zeus's wrath and advising them that the storm would not end until they went to see Circe, Medea's aunt, to be purged of the guilt of a ruthless murder. They followed the ship's direction, passing safely through dangerous shores hidden in a mist created by Hera. The storm abated and the heroes proceeded on their way home. At the end of the adventures, the talking ship, the *Argo*, was dedicated to the god Poseidon. Today, with electronic technology, ships entering Victoria Harbour do have the ability to speak and prophesize the weather.

In ancient times, ships were named after goddesses to incur their favour. It may seem that several places in Victoria have names derived from mythology. However, often place names in Victoria were named for ships, and the ships are named after figures in mythology. For example, Pandora Avenue recalls the Greek myth of Pandora. Pandora was the first woman, created from clay and endowed with gifts from each of the gods. She was made to punish man because Prometheus stole fire from the gods to give to man. It was the beautiful Pandora who opened a jar containing evil, releasing misery into the world. However, the street is named not after the Greek Pandora but a ship. The *HMS Pandora*, under Lieutenant Commander James Wood, carried out the first hydrographic survey of Esquimalt Harbour in 1846 and determined that it would be ideal for use as a British naval port. The Royal Navy often used the names of mythological figures for ships. The name Pandora was popular and the Royal Navy named ten ships after Pandora. One of the Pandora ships was sent out in 1791 to apprehend the sailors who had mutinied on the *HMS Bounty*. Herald, Cormorant and Fisgard Streets were also named after Royal Navy ships that were sent to protect British interests in Canada.

In Greek mythology, the Nereids were sea nymphs. Depicted as beautiful young women, they were considered good luck for sailors.

As such, the British Royal Navy often named ships after the Nereids, and in turn, the names of ships were applied to geographical locations. For example, Thetis Lake and Thetis Lane in James Bay were named after a ship named for Thetis, leader of the fifty Nereids. The *HMS Thetis* was a 36-gun frigate assigned to Esquimalt from 1852 to 1853 as part of the Royal Navy's Pacific Squadron. Twelve ships of the Royal Navy have borne the name *HMS Thetis*. Showing respect to the divinities of the sea was important in ancient times. The Persians made sacrifices to Thetis and the Nereids to calm the seas.

The role of the Nereids as protectors of sailors was illustrated in the *Argonautica*. In the myth, Thetis and the Nereids were sent to help the Argonauts sail safely between the clashing rocks. After frolicking like dolphins for awhile, the Nereids ran along the top of the angry waves, passing the *Argo* from one wave to the next, until the ship reached safety.

Like other sea goddesses, Thetis had the ability to change shape. She was forced to marry a mortal king, Peleus who was told to ambush her and bind her tightly to keep her from escaping. She shifted shapes, becoming flame, water, a lioness, and a serpent, but in the end, she married Peleus and bore him a son, Achilles, the famous warrior of the Trojan War.

The Queen of the Sea and consort of Poseidon was Amphitrite. Named for the sea goddess, the *HMS Amphitrite* was a twenty-four-gun vessel stationed in British Columbia from 1851 to 1857. The ship gave its name to the Amphitrite Point Lighthouse in Ucluelet, a wise choice for a lighthouse that served to protect the ships that sailed over the Graveyard of the Pacific, the treacherous stretch of sea along the west coast of Vancouver Island that resulted in numerous ship wrecks.

CHAPTER 4
Needing the Naiads

In ancient Greece, waterbodies were considered to be sacred. It was believed that every stream, spring, well, fountain and lake was inhabited by a water nymph known as a Naiad. Worshipped as the spirits of springs and streams, the Naiads were not immortal, but they did live for thousands of years. However, their lives depended upon the survival of their associated waterbodies. If the waterbodies were lost, the Naiads were lost. To secure their protection, people sacrificed lambs and goats and offered honey, wine and olive oil. Supplicants asked the Naiads for wealth, poetic inspiration and good health. But the Naiads could be dangerous. When one of Jason's Argonauts, Hylas, went to get water, he was kidnapped by the Naiad of the spring who fell in love with the beautiful young man. He was never seen again.

Springs and Wells

We can live several weeks without food but only a few days without water. Our survival depends upon clean, fresh drinking water, which is why ancient people came to venerate springs and wells. Wells date from the Neolithic period. Some of the oldest wells in the world were found on the island of Cyprus, dating from 9,000 to 10,500 years ago and in Israel, from 8,500 years ago.

Before he took on the aspect of Poseidon, the Roman sea god, Neptune ruled the inland springs, rivers and waters. His festival, the

Neptunalia was held around July 23 at the height of summer when rivers ran low. The Romans would build huts of laurel branches in fields where they would drink spring water and wine and eat, offering sacrifices to gain the Neptune's protection for their irrigation water.

Water was a key consideration in James Douglas' decision to locate the new Hudson's Bay Company Fort on Victoria harbour rather than Esquimalt Harbour with its dry streambeds.

In Victoria, summer drought is a problem and water use is controlled. In early Victoria, the chief source of freshwater was springs and wells. The original well for Fort Victoria was located across from the Inner Harbour. In 1978 when a restoration of the Rithet Building at 1117–1125 Wharf Street was undertaken, the old well was rediscovered and made into a fountain in the lobby of the building. It is believed that pipes from the well crossed the street to the wharf to carry fresh water to the ships in the harbour in the 1840s and 1850s.

Emily Carr wrote in *The Book of Small* that three springs provided "sparkling deliciousness" in pails for Victoria. One spring was located on Spring Ridge, one in Fairfield and one at Beacon Hill. The spring at Spring Ridge, located near the intersection of Denman Street and Spring Road in Fernwood, provided water to Victoria for over 30 years. In 1864, the Spring Ridge Water Company was formed. Initially, water was carried in horse-drawn carts down Chambers Street to Victoria, and later it was piped to town through wooden pipes. An 1862 article in the *British Colonist* noted that an average of 140 loads of water was brought into town every day but a more abundant supply of water was needed. Elk Lake was suggested as a good source and the article invoked the image of the aqueducts of ancient Rome as inspiration for piping water to Victoria. In 1875, the residents of Victoria began to receive water via cast iron pipes from Elk-Beaver Lake. In 1915, the Sooke Lake Reservoir replaced Elk-Beaver Lake as the water source for the city.

Public use of the water from the spring at Spring Ridge became a major controversy. In 1858, Governor James Douglas declared the spring waters to be a public resource. However, in 1861, Attorney General George Hunter Cary bought the well and surrounding land and announced that the water was private. He and the other owners would charge the public $80 or more for the water from Cary's Springs. People became outraged and burned down the barrier fence.

The *British Colonist* described Cary as "shallow beyond belief; conceited beyond conception; untruthful and unscrupulous." The case went to court and the court confirmed that the water was indeed public. The right to the water was included in the 1866 statute unifying the colonies of Vancouver Island and British Columbia that surrendered the Island to the larger colony except for "one well set apart and appropriated to public use."

As in the 1860s, modern communities unite to protect water sources. The Fernwood Community Association rediscovered the 1866 statute and created the Community Well Project to restore the well water to public use again. In 2008, a well was drilled in William Stevenson Memorial Park in the 1200 block of Pembroke Street, striking an aquifer.

In September of 2008, the public well in the park was dedicated in a ceremony that celebrated the symbolism of the connectedness of the community to the flow of water. Water was pumped from the well and the participants tasted its freshness as children danced to the music of a pan flute. Representatives of Catholic, Buddhist, Jewish and Wiccan faiths blessed the well and the Aboriginal Unity Drummers provided the heart beat of the ceremony. The restoration of spring water to the public is a powerful statement about the value of water—too precious to sell. Clearly, modern people understand the importance of wells. There is something very special about drinking water that comes deep from underground in your own neighbourhood.

The ancients associated certain wells with healing and with eternal youth. In Glastonbury, England, the famous Chalice Well has iron deposits in the water which may have cured pilgrims with iron deficiencies. The reddish hue of the waters suggested the blood of Christ springing forth from the ground when the Holy Grail was washed in the spring. It was believed that the waters of the Chalice Well brought eternal youth to whoever drank from it.

Throughout Great Britain, people still frequent "clootie wells" to tie a piece of cloth to a tree by the well to heal ailments. As the cloth rots away, so does the illness. St. Madron's Well, a "clootie well" in Cornwall, is believed to have not only healing powers, but the power of divination. One researcher theorized that radioactive properties of the water may relate to sacredness of the site.

Throwing coins in a wishing well to attract good fortune likely originated in the worship of goddesses or nymphs of springs. Archaeological evidence suggests that Coventina's Well in northeastern England by Hadrian's Wall was used as a religious shrine dedicated to the nymph Coventina for over two centuries until 388 CE. Thousands of coins were found at the site together with other offerings such as brooches, rings, pins and pottery. At the hot springs at Bath where the Romano-Celtic goddess, Sulis, was worshipped, over 12,000 Roman coins were found together with pleas for her intervention on behalf of the petitioner. In the modern day, people throw coins into local wishing wells for good luck, a tradition that continues in Victoria with the coins thrown into the iconic fountain in Centennial Square. Good luck symbols were popular in the 1950s when Macdonald's Furniture-T.V. on Fort Street gave away little envelopes, each containing a penny that "was mailed to Ireland, placed on the Blarney Stone, returned to Victoria, placed on a bed of four leaf clovers, and hung in the Wishing Well at Cadboro Bay."

The Watercourses

Over 150 years ago, numerous streams flowed across the meadows and woodlands of Greater Victoria. During the winter rains, they would often overflow their banks, flooding nearby areas. As urbanization increased, many of these streams were forced into culverts and the wetlands were drained. Thus, the streams were lost to the daylight world.

In 2003, Jennifer Sutherst produced a map of the *Lost Streams of Victoria*, showing the locations of the lost and altered streams, wetlands and shorelines. Many of the lost steams flowed through urban Victoria. For example, a lost creek ran north from Harris Pond near Stanley and Vining Streets through Fernwood to drain into Rock Bay. Another creek collected the waters from a wetland under the present day intersection at Vancouver and View Streets and proceeded along Pandora Avenue to the harbour. Two or three creeks flowed through Fairfield into Ross Bay. During winter storms, First Nations people would paddle up these streams to the Inner Harbour with only a short portage. James Bay was filled in to form the foundation for the Empress Hotel.

In ancient Greek art, Naiads were shown as beautiful young women, often with flowing hair and carrying water jugs. In contrast, rivers were personified by river gods known as the Potami, depicted as muscular male figures with beards, denoting wisdom and maturity. The river gods often sported the horns of bulls or took the form of bulls with men's faces, suggesting the roaring of the river and the horn-shaped meanders of the watercourses. As rivers flowed horizontally, the river gods were often shown reclining. Images of the ancient river gods were captured in fountains such as the *Fountain of the Four Rivers* in Rome designed in 1651 by Bernini for Pope Innocent X. The Nile of Africa, the Danube of Europe, the Ganges of Asia, and the Rio de la Plata of the Americas are shown in the form of powerful bearded river gods semi-reclining on the rock base.

The gentle and small streams of Victoria call for the concept of protective Naiads, rather than the stern and powerful river gods. The Fraser River on the mainland is more like a formidable river god in its life-giving power and destructive force. One of the names used for Bowker Creek from the 1860s to 1912 was the Thames, a name that seems at odds with the small stream that flows from the grounds of the University of Victoria to Oak Bay. The Thames River, the longest river entirely in England, is personified as Old Father Thames. A statue created by sculptor Raffaelle Monti shows the Thames as an intense bearded Greek god, bare-chested and reclining. Yet, the Thames River in Oxford is known as the Isis, an Egyptian fertility goddess. Henley Bridge built over the Thames River in 1876 features sculptures of the face of Isis looking upstream and of Old Father Thames looking downstream. Celts often worshiped the spirits of streams in the form of goddesses, whereas the Romans favoured river gods.

Suppressing water spirits leads to problems. The bog located under the intersection of Vancouver and View Streets formerly drained into a lost creek, but it began to dry up and become compressed under heavy pavement, resulting in a huge sinkhole at the intersection. In 2007, the City of Victoria had to spend just over $4 million to replace storm drains, refill the peat bog with water and lay a base of a lightweight concrete. The cost can be high for failing to live in harmony with nature.

Major sections of watercourses such as Cecelia, Bowker and Douglas Creeks were channeled to flow underground. In a Greek myth, the Baphyras River in Macedonia sank underground to maintain its purity when the women who had killed the hero, Orpheus, wanted to wash his blood off their hands in the river. But ensuring the purity of a stream was not the rationale for sending Victoria's lost streams underground.

Cecelia Creek was likely the most polluted lost streams in early Victoria. For over one hundred years, most of the creek was diverted through underground culverts, yet it still carried its contaminated waters to the Gorge Waterway. In recent years, public interest in restoring the stream has increased. In 2000, a 133 metre section was restored to daylight and efforts were made to reduce the sources of pollution. The 2011 Cecelia Ravine Park Management Plan noted that one of the factors that indicate the health of a stream is the presence of Stonefly and Mayfly naiads. Derived from the name for the Greek spirits of the stream, the term *naiad* refers to the immature form, or nymph, of some orders of aquatic insects.

Bowker Creek once supported salmon in a watershed graced by the Garry oak ecosystem unique to this area. As development increased, 70 per cent of the stream was confined to pipes and culverts and the salmon became a ghost run. In the last several years, the community started to come together to revitalize the urban watershed, to restore Bowker Creek to health and to create a greenway that connects neighbourhoods.

If a stream disappears, its resident Naiad dies. But according to Homer's *Odyssey*, Naiads do spend time in a sacred cave, suggesting that they may be able to survive for a time underground. Although many of the lost streams in Victoria will never again see the light of day, some can be saved. Watershed management plans on altered streams such as Bowker, Cecelia and Douglas Creeks are leading to changes that revitalize these watercourses and restore the ailing Naiads, both insect and spirit, to health. As the Naiads are revived, they inspire the creativity of a community when events such as the annual Bowker Creek Brush Up are held, featuring art, music and storytelling as people rejoice in the beauty of the creek.

Mystic Vale

On the eastern grounds of the University of Victoria campus lies a forested ravine called Mystic Vale. The very name evokes mythical connections. *Mystic* is defined as inspiring a sense of mystery and wonder. *Vale*, a shortened form of valley, evokes the mortal world, as in the phrase "this vale of tears."

The actual place, a 4.7 hectare area in the Hobbs Creek watershed, does feel otherworldly. Tall Douglas firs and big-leaved maples cling to steep slopes that descend to the valley carved over the eons by Hobbs Creek. The dappled light, the sentinel trees and the energy of flowing water give visitors a sense that this is a sacred place.

Mystic Vale

The name, *Mystic Vale*, is likely derived from a story, "The Mystic Spring" written by D.W. Higgins and published in 1904. Higgins wrote that the spring was located at the foot of a magnificent maple tree. Its waters were as clear as crystal and as cold as ice in the summer as well as in the winter. Higgins noted that the local Indians were proud of the spring and used its water freely, advising that it possessed medicinal properties and was bewitched. According to Higgins' story, one of the chiefs told new arrivals about the spring, saying,

> *If a woman should look into the water when the moon is at its full she'll see reflected in it the face of the man who loves her. If a man looks into the water he will see the woman who loves him and will*

marry him should he ask her. If a woman is childless this water will give her plenty. The tree is a god. It guards the spirit of the spring, and as long as the tree stands the water will creep to its foot for protection and shade; cut down the tree and the spring will be seen no more.

Higgins wrote that he first saw Mystic Spring in 1860 and visited it often with friends. They named the maple tree *Father Time* because of the "old man's beard" lichen that hung from a branch and they called the spring *Undine* after a famous water sprite in fairy tales by Jean de La Fontaine.

One evening on a full moon in August 1862, Higgins joined two men and two women at the spring, when its waters "glistened like molten silver." When he looked into the waters hoping to see the face of his future wife, he saw only his own "ugly" face. However, when Annie, one of the women, looked in, she saw a face so horrible that she fainted.

Higgins included in his story another event about a mysterious woman wearing a turban with a bright green veil who asked for directions to the magic spring on the afternoon of April 21, 1868. She joked about seeing her future husband in the spring. In the middle of the night, a family living nearby heard a wail. In the morning, they discovered the body of Julia Booth lying face down in the water. Bits of torn paper were found near the spring.

Twenty years later, Higgins noted, the Father Time tree was felled with an earth-shaking crash and, as prophesized, the spring disappeared. Higgins added that Annie, the woman who had seen the spirit face in the waters, actually did marry a good man, not a monster.

Higgins' story made the area even more popular. In 1938, a man named William Inglis built a pool, added a water wheel, and operated the area as a tourist attraction featuring the healing waters of *ye Olde Mystic Spring*. Hundreds of people came to visit it and dozens went regularly to collect the healing water. Places like Mystic Lane and Mystic Vale were named after the spring.

However, it is doubtful if Mystic Spring ever existed. In 1922, the Victoria Chamber of Commerce tried and failed to find the original spring. Higgin's work is fictional and it is likely that Higgins, himself, coined the name *Mystic Spring*.

Higgins ascribed the legends associated with the Mystic Spring to Indigenous folklore. It is likely that Higgins incorporated oral legends that he had heard into his story. Ponds and streams were sacred to the Coast Salish. No doubt ephemeral ponds appeared in the creek when log jams slowed the flow of water, and these reflective ponds may have been used for spiritual purposes. Canoe Pond, located at the base of the stairs down to Hobbs Creek, was not one of these ponds as it was believed to have been dug out by heavy machinery in the last 70 years.

Scrying, a method of divination which includes using a reflective surface to see the face of a future spouse is found in traditions around the world. Halloween cards from 1904 often illustrated a girl looking into a mirror to see the face of her future husband. Like Mystic Vale, a natural pond on Smith Hill, now in Summit Park, was said to be used for divination by local Indigenous women to see the reflections of the faces of their future husbands.

Much of Higgins' story reflects European traditions, such as naming the maple tree Father Time and the spring Undine. Father Time represented the constant flow of time, which cuts down all things only to be replaced by the next generation. Undine is a water nymph, usually found in ponds or waterfalls. In many legends, Undine is one of the supernatural female spirits who lose their immortality if they fall in love with a mortal man and bear a child, the price to pay for being human.

Higgins' story also included elements from an actual event—the death of Martha Booth. The *British Colonist* reported on April 22, 1868 that the body of a young lady had been found floating in Cadboro Bay. The body was identified as Miss Martha Booth and it was speculated that she threw herself from the water into the rocks. She had been seen the previous day wearing a black turban hat with a green veil. A scrap of paper with words from a popular song about farewell was found near her body; Higgins repeated the words in his story. Edgar Fawcett, who was the last person to speak to Miss Booth, suggested that she had killed herself due to unrequited love. It is interesting to note that David Higgins was a publisher of the *British Colonist* newspaper at that time.

Over the years, urbanization put pressure on Mystic Vale. In 1993, it was purchased by the University of Victoria in response to the imminent threat of development of the area. Today, the Vale receives many visitors who take pleasure in the natural environment so close to the urban setting.

Higgins' story about the Mystic Spring adds to the allure of the place and hopefully, heightens people's interest in the preservation of Mystic Vale. That it needs to be protected is apparent. The watershed has been severely altered since the middle of the nineteenth century by logging, farming and development and has been classified as a sensitive ecosystem. The watershed suffers from seasonal run-off from parking lots and culverts, bank erosion, poorly placed trails and bridges, and trampling by dogs and people. The slopes are unstable and the water polluted. No fish live in Hobbs Creek. Invasive species such as ivy threaten to choke out the trees.

Like the warning in Higgins' story, not respecting the spirit of the place can lead to its destruction. The University of Victoria is taking remedial action to protect and restore the woodland, such as planting vegetation to stabilize the banks, fencing off areas and sandbagging to prevent undercutting. A fifty year restoration plan is being put in place to repair the degradation that has occurred over the last 100 years. But the restoration effort will require the cooperation of the community. The techniques used to restore this special site are being applied to similar problems globally as we all need to respect the Naiads in the face of increasing urbanization.

CHAPTER 5
Respecting Gaia

The ancient Greeks worshipped the earth as the goddess, Gaia. She appeared at the start of creation, immediately after the emergence of chaos, and independently created the heavens, the mountains, and the seas. She then gave birth to the god, Uranus, and with him, bore the Titans and other divinities. With Pontus, she bore the divinities of the sea. She became known as the nourishing mother of the gods. She also gave birth to monsters. The concept of the earth mother is found in many mythologies. She is known as Terra to the Romans, Jord to the Norse and Pachamama to the Inca. Modern people refer to Mother Nature as the personification of the earth.

The face of Gaia in the Victoria area has been sculpted over the millennia by water in various forms. Glaciers scoured the area about 29,000 to 15,000 years ago, carving striations on the rocks and depositing large boulders known as erratics. Since the retreat of the ice about 10,000 years ago, erosion has worked its changes on the landscape.

Myths about the land serve to establish a sense of place and connectedness. The myths may serve as mnemonic devices to help in way-finding and suggest timing of seasonal harvest of food. Myths may include stories about the origin of specific geographic or geological features or serve to explain events such as storms, earthquakes and volcanoes.

Stone

Areas of Victoria are built on bedrock of granite and gneiss, providing a stable foundation for a town. However, our appreciation for rock goes beyond its structural elements. People have ascribed magical properties to rock for eons. Granite commonly has a high content of radioactive elements. Studies have shown that sites of megaliths in Europe tend to be built mainly where granite or gneiss occurs and it has been suggested that granite megaliths evoke heightened consciousness due to granite's radioactivity. Perhaps the granite foundation of Victoria contributes to its spiritual energy.

In the Victoria area, Coast Salish traditions include stories about transformer rocks of great spiritual significance. Salish myths refer to a mythic time before the Great Flood when people and animals were the same and could speak to one another. Once the flood waters had subsided, Hayls the Transformer travelled the world and provided order, giving everyone and everything its rightful use and place. In many legends, Hayls transformed people into rock as a reward for their good behavior, giving them immortality. Other times, the transformation was a punishment for not following the proper order.

A large erratic boulder stands just off Harling Point. With its vertical orientation, it could be seen as a large man. In 1952, Songhees elder James Fraser told anthropologist Wilson Duff the story about the origin of this boulder. One day, two harpooners were hunting seals off the point when Hayls the Transformer and his two companions, Raven and Mink, paddled in, frightening the seals. One of the harpooners was annoyed and scolded the gods. In response, Hayls transformed the harpooner into the rock, saying, "You'll be the boss of the seals from Sooke to Nanaimo." The area was known as *Sahsima*, meaning "harpoon." The Salish name for the nearby Trial Island was *Kikwaynan*, meaning "lots of seals," suggesting that the harpooner was in a good location to oversee the seals.

Harpoon Rock at Harling Point

The story that science tells about glacial erratic rocks is interesting. The wandering rocks had been plucked by moving glaciers and then dropped as the glaciers retreated at the end of the last glaciation about 15,000 years ago. The erratics at Harling Point are comprised of Saanich granodiorite, a crystalline igneous rock, whereas the glacially scoured bedrock takes the form of bands of sedimentary rock and metamorphosed basalt. Distinct against the sea and the underlying rock, erratic rocks draw photographers with their changing beauty, celebrating that which is different in a natural landscape.

Nearby in Gonzales Bay, a horizontally oriented erratic appears just off the shore. It was known as the Devilfish Rock, named for the octopus found in the bay. According to James Fraser, if a person walked out to the rock at low tide and touched it, the devilfish would rise to the surface and then could be captured for food or bait. The octopus found off Vancouver Island is the Giant Pacific Octopus that averages 50 kg (110 lbs) in weight, providing a valuable food source.

The Gorge Waterway runs from Victoria's Inner Harbour to Portage Inlet. It is famous for its reversing waterfall. A shell midden at Gorge Narrows reveals that the area has been occupied for over

4,000 years and that the early people enjoyed a diet of shellfish such as oyster, mussel, clam and crabs, as well as fish, deer and seals.

The rich bounty of food relates to one of the earliest known myths about the Gorge – the Songhees story of the maiden, Camossung. James Fraser related the story to Wilson Duff. One day, Hayls the Transformer found Camossung crying because she didn't have anything to eat. He offered her sturgeon, berries and other food items that she refused, which is why those food items are not found along the Gorge to this day. When Hayls offered her duck, herring, Coho salmon and oyster, she accepted, and this is why these food sources are abundant on the Gorge. Hayls told the girl that she would control the food sources for her people and then he transformed her into stone. To keep her company, Hayls also transformed her grandfather, Snukaymelt (meaning "diving"), into stone as well. Camossung and her grandfather protect the abundant food resources in the "Canal of Camosack", as it was known in the 1840s. This mythical maiden gave her name to the original Fort Camosun, and her name is still common throughout Greater Victoria.

Believers would dive into the rapids at Gorge Narrows and hang onto the sacred rock to receive powers and spiritual guidance from Camossung. However, in 1960, a large portion of the rock was blasted away to make the narrows safer. The spirit of Camossung lives on in a sculpture created by artist Fred Dobbs and unveiled in the Gorge Waterway Park in 2010. The sculpture shows the maiden with the duck, herring, salmon and oyster from the story.

The idea that people can be transformed into stone is common in folklore worldwide. These stories explain the origin of prominent rocks and provide memory devices for wayfaring. In Greek mythology, a glance from the Medusa could turn men into stone, a deathlike state. Stories about some standing stones in Cornwall tell how dancing maidens and their pipers were transformed into stone as punishment for breaking the Sabbath. The Sto:lo people of the Fraser River had a tradition that the Creator transformed people into rocks where their souls would survive forever. This must have happen often as chain of transformer rocks extends up the Fraser Valley.

Another transformer rock is Siwash Rock, a basalt sea stack off Stanley Park in Vancouver and its related myth provides a context for the stories about transformer rocks. Poet Pauline Johnson recorded legends told to her by Chief Joe Capilano of the Squamish Nation, including the story of Siwash Rock. Thousands of years ago, a young warrior was swimming in the water to purify himself for the birth of his baby. Parents imminently expecting a baby were required to cleanse themselves so that a wild animal could not find their scent. The young chief was so dedicated to his ritual preparation for fatherhood that he defied the four gods in a canoe who ordered him out of their way. Impressed, the gods transformed the warrior into a rock as an indestructible monument to "clean fatherhood." Hayls then transformed the warrior's wife and baby into smaller rocks (which were later destroyed to make way for the Stanley Park seawall). The story is commemorated in a plaque located in Stanley Park that states, "Siwash Rock - Indian legend tells us that this 50 foot high pinnacle of rock stands as an imperishable monument to 'Skalsh the Unselfish' who was turned into stone by 'Q'uas the Transformer' as a reward for his unselfishness."

Settlers who came to Victoria brought their own heritage. In ancient times, standing stones such as Stonehenge provided sacred space for seasonal rituals throughout Great Britain and Europe. In the Victoria area, a stone circle can be found in Vantreight Park in Gordon Head. These days, New Age sacred ceremonies are performed in this park, taking inspiration from the mystical alignments called ley lines running through the circle.

Stone was associated with destiny or kingship. Various myths reflect the belief that a special stone recognizes the king. King Arthur established his sovereignty by pulling a sword from a stone. In Ireland, kings were crowned on the Stone of Destiny, the *Lia Fáil*, until 500 BCE. According to legend, the stone roared with delight when the rightful King of Ireland put his feet on it. The magical stone served to rejuvenate the king. Some historians suggest that this stone was carried to Scotland where it became known as the Stone of Scone and was associated with the crowning of Scottish kings since 847. Understanding the power of the Scottish legend, King Edward I of England captured the Stone of Scone in 1296 and fitted it into the coronation chair on which English sovereigns were crowned for 700 years. The Stone was returned to Scotland in 1996 on loan until it is needed for the coronation of the next British monarch. The Stone, made of sandstone and weighing 152 kg, was last used at the 1953 coronation of Elizabeth II. In Sweden, the same tradition existed. Swedish kings in the twelfth to fourteenth centuries were crowned by standing on the Stones of Mora. The link between stones and ruling is also evident in the Salish tradition of transformer stones ruling over the seals or the bounty of the Gorge.

Mountains

The view from Victoria across the Juan de Fuca Strait is dominated by the Olympic Mountains. Mount Olympus, multi-peaked and luminous with glaciers, is the highest in the range.

In Greek mythology, Mount Olympus was the home of the gods. Here the twelve principal gods and goddesses lived in crystal mansions, eating nectar and ambrosia to preserve their immortality. Entry to Mount Olympus was gained through a gate of clouds guarded by the goddesses known as the Seasons. The mountain peaks formed the throne of Zeus and gave him the height from which to hurl his lightning bolts to earth. It was believed that Mount Olympus reached up into heaven itself.

The ancient Greeks identified many mountains as Olympus. Over time, Olympus became generalized as the home of the gods, wherever it was located. However, the mythological Mount Olympus is most often associated with the highest mountain in Greece situated in northeastern Greece on the border with Macedonia and Thessaly.

Today, mountains named Olympus are found not only in Greece, but in many places, including Washington State. In fact, the use of the name Olympus is not confined to mountains on earth. The tallest known volcano and mountain in the solar system is located on the planet Mars and is named *Olympus Mons*, Latin for Mount Olympus.

In 1788, the English explorer, Captain John Meares, named the Washington State mountain "Olympus" because it was beautiful enough to be the home of the gods. The term "Olympics" soon came to include the rest of the peninsula.

Mount Olympus in Greece and Mount Olympus in Washington have many similarities. Both are the highest in their respective ranges, although both are less than 3,000 metres in height (they are 2,917 metres and 2,432 metres, respectively). Both have several peaks and when those peaks are covered in snow, the light bouncing off the snow gives them a special luminosity. It is easy to see how people could visualize the mountains as reaching into the clouds as the gate of the gods.

Mount Olympus in Greece was first climbed in 1913 and the first ascent to the highest peak on Mount Olympus in Washington was in 1907. According to Greek mythology, any mortal who tried to climb Mt Olympus was guilty of hubris and would be punished for it. In one myth, the hero Bellerophon flew on the winged horse, Pegasus, to the top of Mount Olympus only to be thrown down to earth by Zeus for his attempt to reach the home of the gods. Today, climbers still risk their lives to reach the peaks.

Has reaching its pinnacles de-mystified Olympus? It has not reduced the popularity of the mountains. About 250,000 people, including 20,000 climbers, visit Mount Olympus in Greece every year. The Olympic National Park in Washington records over two million overnight visits annually. The climbing community considers the ascent of the American Mount Olympus a northwest rite of passage.

The popularity of both of the mountains has necessitated state protection. In 1937, Mount Olympus in Greece became the first national park to be established in Greece. The Olympic National Park was established in 1938 to protect the Roosevelt elk, old-growth forests and the grandeur of the mountains. In 1988, the park became the Olympic Wilderness, the largest wilderness area in the US outside of Alaska.

As for the continuing appeal of the mountains, writer Hugh Elmer Brown raved in his 1913 "Melodious Days" essay that his trip to Washington's Mount Olympus allowed him "to ponder the solemn wonder and beauty of existence." Today, as in 1913, "the Olympics with their untrodden solitudes and spiry summits have much to teach the inquiring spirit."

The mythical Thunderbird lives in a cave on Mount Olympus in Washington, according to local tribal mythology. The Squamish people have a similar legend that the Thunderbird makes its home in a prominent mountain; in this case, it is Black Tusk. Their name for the mountain is "Landing Place of the Thunderbird" and they believe that the black colour and jagged peaks of the mountain result from the lightning fired out by the Thunderbird. As a symbol of power, strength and nobility, it is fitting that the Thunderbird lives in the dominant peak in the land.

Mount Newton

The highest mountain on the Saanich Peninsula is Mount Newton, called *Lau Wel New* by the Saanich people. It has been speculated that the sight of this mountain looming up from the sea suggested the name of Saanich, which means "rising." The mountain has spiritual significance. Early records describe the rings of white stones placed on the mountain. *Lau Wel New* figures prominently in the flood legends of the Saanich people. According to the legend, the people anchored their canoes with a long cedar rope to this sacred mountain and this allowed them to survive the Great Flood.

Stories of great floods appear in mythology around the world. In 1873, Scottish explorer Robert Brown reported that a friend of his, an eminent ethnologist, told him about an interview with a native Northwest elder about the Great Flood. He asked the elder the name of the man who got away with his wife in a big canoe. The elder could not remember the name, so went to ask another man. The two men came back with the answer—the man's name was Noah. It seems that this part of the myth reflects accounts by missionaries of the Biblical flood. This story illustrates how aspects of myths can spread from culture to culture, especially when they have critical elements in common.

Mount Douglas

Mount Douglas is a hill carved by glacial ice. The Songhees people called Mount Douglas the "hill of cedars." One day in 1843, James Douglas travelled to the Lekwungen village at Cadboro Bay and announced that he was building a fort. He offered to pay one 2½ point blanket for every forty pickets of 22 feet by 36 inches brought to the fort. The people cut down the trees and transported them to the fort along what is now Cedar Hill Road. Soon Fort Victoria took shape with the cedars from Cedar Hill.

Scottish author Robert Brown explored much of Vancouver Island in the 1860s and recorded many of the myths he heard. He wrote that Indigenous story-tellers said that Cedar Hill (i.e., Mount Douglas) was once the highest peak in the district but it quarreled with Point Roberts on the mainland. They threw stones at each other until Cedar Hill was lowered. A few of the stones came more than halfway, accounting for the islands in Haro Strait. The highest point in an area has long held symbolic significance since the days of the Sumerian ziggurats reaching for the heavens to the medieval cathedrals to the present day race to construct the tallest building on earth.

Mount Douglas was named after Sir James Douglas, Governor of the Colony of Vancouver Island. In 1859, Captain G.H. Richards, Hydrographer of the Royal Navy, wrote that although he referred to any rise under one thousand feet as a hill, he made an exception for Mount Douglas as he did not wish to "'lower' the Governor and partly because Douglas Hill does not sound well." Emily Carr commented on the name change in *The Book of Small*, observing "Cedar Hill lying to the north of the town went 'snooty'; elevating her name to Mount Douglas, she became a Public Park, smug with tameness."

Emily Carr felt the attraction of Mount Douglas. In 1942, Carr had a vision that inspired her to go to Mount Douglas Park where she felt that woods still had something to say to her. Her series of oil paintings of the forest of Mount Douglas were mystical and enchanting, capturing the spirit of the forest.

Mount Tolmie

Mount Tolmie, a 120 metre hill, was known by the Songhees people as *Pkaals*. According to oral legend, Hayls the Transformer landed on *Pkaals* and changed some people to the oak trees on the hill. About 1845, the hill was named after Dr. W. F. Tolmie, a surgeon with the Hudson's Bay Company.

Malahat Mountain

North of Victoria, Malahat Mountain rises to a height of 356 metres (1,158 feet) above Saanich Inlet. The mountain is known to the Salish people as *YAAS* and it is one of the most sacred sites on southern Vancouver Island. A legendary rainmaker made his home on the mountain and the people believed that if one pointed at the mountain, it would rain. The Thunderbird also lived on the mountain and is represented as a pole located at a viewpoint off the Malahat Highway.

Summer drought has always been challenging in the Victoria area. As recently as 1951, a rainmaker was called in from Saskatchewan to try to make it rain. The attempt required special apparatus—rather more complicated than simply pointing at the spirit of *YAAS*.

Earthquakes

Victoria is located in one of the most seismically active regions in the country. Off the west coast of Vancouver Island, the Cascadia subduction zone separates the Juan de Fuca Plate from the North American Plate. The Juan de Fuca plate is sliding beneath the continent at a rate of about 4 cm/year. As these two plates adjust, earthquakes result. More than 100 earthquakes of magnitude 5 or greater have occurred during the past 70 years in the Cascadia subduction zone. In addition to the large subduction earthquakes located offshore which occur about every 500 years, Victoria experiences ruptures of local shallow faults.

Poseidon, the Greek god of the sea, was also called the "earth-shaker". When he struck the ground with his trident, he would create earthquakes. Here in Victoria, with major earthquakes coming from the Cascadia subduction zone, you can believe that the god of sea sends earthquakes from the sea.

Earthquakes can cause great destruction. The Cascadia earthquake, which occurred on January 26, 1700, was one of the largest in the world. The ocean floor rose about 20 feet followed by a giant wave that hit the shore. The tsunami destroyed the winter village of the people of Pachena Bay and collapsed houses of the Cowichan people.

Seismologist Ruth Ludwin searched for native tales and legends that related to the earthquake and tsunami of 1700 and found a set of related stories that suggested that a strong shaking was felt accompanied by coastal flooding. She found that there was an intermingling of the actual event with stories about a mythical battle between supernatural beings. In some accounts, the battle took place between the Transformer and the Thunder god. The Hoh people of the Olympic Peninsula told about a battle between the Thunderbird and the Killer Whale. The Killer Whale was slaughtering other whales and so the Thunderbird flew from its mountain top and seized the whale in its talons. The Thunderbird set down on land where a terrible battle ensued between the Thunderbird and the Killer Whale. The Thunderbird prevailed. The ripped pieces of the whale turned to stone and can be seen today in the landscape. The Thunderbird also won a battle with the son of the Killer Whale. Following this battle, there was a shaking of the earth and rolling up of the waters.

In Nuu-chah-nulth mythology, the Earthquake mask is named Tagit, an ancestor who lives on the mountainside. He caused tremors or major earthquakes when he felt nature had been disturbed or abused by humankind.

The ancient Greeks also attributed earthquakes to mighty battles between supernatural beings. An example is the myth of Typhon, the monstrous son of the earth goddess, Gaia. When Typhon challenged Zeus, a mighty struggle erupted. Zeus hurled thunderbolts at Typhon; Typhon hurled mountains at Zeus and caused storms. Finally, Zeus crushed Typhon with Mount Etna. Mount Etna, located on the island of Sicily, is one of the most active volcanoes in the world. To this day, islanders believe that the flames and steam coming from the crater are caused by the buried Typhon, whose movements produce earthquakes. Indeed, scientists tell us that earthquakes are one of the indicators of increased volcanic activity which leads to eruptions.

Early people often conceptualized earthquakes as the movements of creatures under the earth. In the myths of ancient India, earthquakes resulted when the eight elephants that held up the earth shook their heads. In Mongolia, it was a giant frog. The ancient Japanese spoke of a giant catfish that lived in the mud under the earth. When the catfish moved, earthquakes resulted.

The Okanogan people of Washington State told a myth that the earth was once a woman. The Creator changed her into the earth to be the mother of all people, with the soil as her flesh, the rocks as her bones, the winds as her breath, and the trees and grass as her hair. Her movements were earthquakes.

Volcanoes

Victoria is located within the Pacific Ring of Fire, a 40,000 kilometre (25,000 miles) horseshoe-shaped area around the basin of the Pacific Ocean where large numbers of earthquakes and volcanic eruptions occur. With over 450 volcanoes, the Ring of Fire is home to over 75% of the world's volcanoes and 90% of the world's earthquakes.

A strikingly beautiful snow-capped mountain can be seen in the east from Victoria on most days. Mount Baker, located in Washington State, is an active volcano, with its last eruption in 1870. It has been described as the volcano with the greatest potential hazard to British Columbia. Early settlers in Victoria witnessed its minor eruptions in the nineteenth century. The *British Colonist* reported on October 31, 1864 a shock from an earthquake, saying that it felt like travelling a full speed in a railway carriage. The article noted that the summit of Mount Baker had undergone considerable change in the last several years. When it had last erupted, a dense volume of smoke and a bright flame had issued from the fiery furnace.

Since 1975, emissions of steam have been increasing from one of the craters. Combining the opposites of fire and ice, the volcanic Mount Baker is one of the snowiest places on earth, setting a world record for snowfall in 1999 with 29 metres (95 feet) of snowfall.

The Indigenous peoples of the Pacific Northwest had many names for the mountain. *Kulshan* was the name used by the Lummi people, referring to the wound, or crater, in the mountain caused by lightning bolts shot from the eyes of the Thunderbird, or as punishment by the Great Spirit. The Nooksack name was *Kweq' Smánit*, simply meaning "white mountain."

Mount Baker was named by Captain Vancouver in 1792 for his third lieutenant, Joseph Baker who spotted the peak. In 1853, American Theodore Winthrop visited the Northwest and noted *Kulshan* as the Indigenous name for Mount Baker. In his 1862 book, *The Canoe and the Saddle*, he wrote that Kulshan is "worthy to stand a white emblem of perpetual peace between us and our brother Britons," referring to the border between the United States and Canada. He wrote about an eruption in 1852, "There is fire beneath the Cascades, red war suppressed where the peaks, symbols of truce, stand in resplendent quiet." According to Winthrop, mountains are "our grandest emblems of divine power and divine peace." He believed that Kulshan was best seen from Vancouver Island.

The view of Mount Baker rising up on the eastern horizon captures the imaginations of Victorians as it heralds the daily approach of the sun and flares red as it reflects the rays of the setting sun. Paintings and postcards over the last 100 years often feature views of Mount Baker from Victoria. The first successful ascent of Mount Baker, made on August 17, 1862, was led by Victoria resident Edmund T. Coleman and included another resident of Victoria, David Ogilvy. Coleman moved to Victoria for the purpose of climbing the peaks of the West. In an interview published in the *Daily British Colonist*, Ogilvy noted that during the ascent, the Lummi climbers who accompanied them would not go any further than the line of vegetation. The Indigenous people of the Northwest were concerned about angering the powerful spirits who lived on the tops of the highest mountain peaks.

Mt. Baker

As a prominent peak, the mountain features in flood myths. During the time of the Great Flood, the men of the area built a giant canoe and the women made a long rope to anchor the canoe. The children were put into the canoe, along with the bravest warrior and newest mother as guardians. One morning, they spotted land—the peak of Mount Baker—and it was here they landed. It is said that the outline of a canoe can still be seen in one of the mountain's crevices.

In many myths, volcanic eruptions are ascribed to the actions of the gods. In Greek mythology, the blacksmith Hephaestus was the god of volcanoes. Some myths told how Hephaestus or his Roman counterpart, Vulcan, caused the eruptions of Mount Etna on Sicily. Whenever his wife, Venus, was unfaithful, Vulcan would stoke his forge under the mountain so strongly that smoke and fire would issue from the mountain until it erupted. In another tradition, it was claimed that Mount Etna is the place where the goddess Athena buried the giant Enceladus, who breathed out fire as he died. In Hawaiian mythology, volcanoes are personified as the goddess, Pele, who created Mount Kilauea on the island of Hawaii as her home. Sometimes appearing as a beautiful young woman, other times as a crone, she would erupt in jealous rages.

The most destructive volcanic eruption in the history of the United States was the eruption of Mount St. Helens on May 18, 1980. A total of 57 people were killed, as well as about 7,000 big game animals and 12 million salmon fingerlings in hatcheries. The blast was heard in Victoria and later, debris rained down on Victoria.

Mount St. Helens is less than about 37,000 years old, but it has been especially active over the last 4,000 years. Since about 1400 BCE, eruptions have occurred at a rate of about one per 100 years. Over 100 years had passed since the 1980 eruption. Canadian artist Paul Kane witnessed an eruption of the volcano when he visited the area in 1847. He painted the eruption at night, showing a red plume of smoke and ashes issuing from a side vent in the mountain rather than its summit.

Before the 1980 eruption, the snow-covered peaks of Mount St. Helens were so symmetrical that the mountain was nicknamed the Mount Fuji of America. Mount Fuji was an active volcano considered sacred by the Japanese. After his visit to the Northwest, Theodore Winthrop praised the beauty of the mountain in *The Canoe and The Saddle*, writing "Dearest charmer of all is St. Helens, queen of the Cascades, queen of Northern America, a fair and graceful volcanic cone."

The tribal lore of the Pacific Northwest peoples includes many legends to explain the eruptions of Mount St. Helens and the other volcanoes in the Cascade Range. The most famous legend was the Bridge of the Gods. Mount St. Helens was a beautifully symmetrically snow-capped mountain that stood between two mountains with jagged peaks, Mount Hood and Mount Adams. The story holds that the beautiful mountain was once a lovely maiden named Loowit. Mount Hood (called Wyeast) and Mount Adams (called Klickitat) were once sons of the Great Spirit and their land was joined by the Bridge of the Gods so they could visit more easily. In some versions, Loowit served as the guardian of the bridge.

49

When two sons of the Great Spirit fell in love with Loowit, she could not choose between them. They fought over her, burying villages and forests in the process. The earth shook so violently that the bridge fell into the river. The Great Spirit was furious. He killed the three lovers and erected a mighty mountain peak where each fell. The beautiful Loowit became Mount St. Helens, Wyeast became the proud and erect Mount Hood and Klickitat, who bowed his head in mourning, became Mount Adams, asymmetrical with a flat summit. This legend combines the themes of transformation and a mythic battle causing earthquakes.

A tribal legend of the Cowlitz Tribe of Washington State tells of a time when Mount Rainier had an argument with his two wives, Mount St. Helens and Mount Adams. Mount St. Helens became jealous, blew her top, and knocked the head off Mount Rainier. The Cowlitz name for Mount St. Helens was *Lavelatla*, meaning "smoking mountain."

The image of Mount St. Helens as a beautiful, but explosive woman is intriguing. Captain Vancouver, however, did not name the mountain for a lovely woman named Helen or for a saint, but rather for his friend, British diplomat Alleyne Fitzherbert, 1st Baron of St. Helens.

Victoria lies on the edge of the vast Pacific Ocean in a region of earthquakes and volcanoes. Life in paradise is heightened by the tension of living in an earthquake zone within the range of several active volcanoes—a life on the edge where the favour of Gaia is critical.

CHAPTER 6
Forecasting the Skies

In the beginning, according to some ancient Greek myths, the mother goddess, Gaia, created the starry heavens as her equal to cover her on all sides. When ancient people looked up at the skies and saw the celestial bodies in motion, they personified the objects as gods, heroes or ancestors. They linked events on earth to the appearance of phenomena in the skies such as comets and they attributed severe weather such as storms to mythical creatures and sought their favour. Winds may be caused by the flapping of the wings of the Thunderbird. Or storms may be conjured up by Scottish storm witches.

As scientific knowledge grew, and humans began to study other planets, we learned more about the earth in comparison. When scientist James Lovelock was investigating the lack of life on Mars, he saw photographs of Earth taken from space and had a revelation about this blue planet. His revelation was that Earth could be considered to be a self-regulating living being, able to maintain its climate and chemical composition. His Gaia theory, proposed in the 1970s, established the metaphor of the earth as the Greek earth goddess, Gaia. According to Dr. Lovelock, the Gaia theory embraces the intuitive side of science as well as the rational. The concept of earth as Gaia speaks to processes that are hidden and can not be reduced to mathematical expressions.

The goddess Gaia was both nurturing and fierce. It is easy to see the increasing intensity of tropical storms as Gaia's response to attacks on her body. Global warming is a controversial theory. However, some scientists, including Dr. Lovelock, believe that global warming is resulting in an increase in the frequency and intensity of storms. Mother Earth is turning on us. Lovelock's 2007 book, *The Revenge of Gaia*, captures the beliefs of the ancients that treating the earth without due respect will lead to her punishing humans. Dr. Lovelock warns, "We are at war with the Earth itself. We are Gaia's target now."

Stars

Worldwide, people ascribe meaning to the stars. The Sumerians associated the planet Venus, the brightest star in the sky, with the goddess Inanna, and their myth, *The Descent of Inanna*, reflects the movements of Venus across the sky, setting as the evening star and rising as the morning star. Venus itself is named after the Roman goddess of love and beauty. Many Greek myths tell how humans and animals were transformed into stars by the gods. Nowadays, numerous stars and planetary bodies are named for figures in Greek and Roman mythology, and more recently, for figures in the mythologies of other cultures. The belief that the movement of constellations can predict the future led to the development of astrology thousands of years ago. Asteria, the Greek goddess of the stars, sent prophetic dreams and was linked to astrology. A bright star led the Magi to Bethlehem for the birth of Jesus.

The stars at night are so beautiful that they have spawned myths where women fall in love with the stars and marry them. There are several local variants of the Star Maidens myth. Robert Brown recorded a version in his 1873 book, *The Races of Mankind*. It begins a long time ago when the heavens were nearer to the earth and the gods were more familiar. Two Songhees girls were gathering camas near Elk Lake during the day and camping at night. One night, they lay awake looking at the stars. Brown wrote, "The Indians suppose stars to be little people and the region they live in to be much the same as this world down below." One girl looked at Aldebaran, the star known as the red eye of the bull, and wished that he was her lover (in Greek mythology, Aldebaran was the eye of Zeus transformed into Taurus the bull). The other girl said that he was too angry-looking and preferred a nearby pale, gentle-looking star, Sirius.

The girls fell asleep and the two stars came down to earth. When the girls awoke in the morning, they were in Starland with their lovers. Eventually they grew homesick and missed their friends at the Gorge and Esquimalt. While their husbands slept, they twisted a rope from cedar bark long enough to drop to earth. Using a pointed stick, they dug a hole in the vault of heaven. Then they tied the rope to a stick and slid down but the rope was not long enough. Satitz, the east wind, took pity on them and blew them to earth. They found themselves near the valley of the Colquitz River, with the rope beside them. They coiled the rope and Hayls transformed it into Knockan Hill as a monument to remind mortals not to wish for the stars. The girls became great medicine women but remained single for love of the little people above. When the sun had ended his travels across the earth, their star husbands often visited them. They can still be seen as falling stars. Knockan Hill is now a park located north of Portage Inlet. The Songhees people referred to it as *Nga'kun'*, meaning "coiled up" and the Scots called it *Gnocan*, Gaelic for knoll or hill. The rock formations on the hill can appear to be a coiled rope.

Many Coast Salish peoples believed that they had descended from the stars. As guardian spirits, stars convey healing power. Stars survey the whole world and with this all-revealing view, they can identify the causes of various ailments.

Comets

The appearance of comets in the night sky was seen as an omen by early people. For millennia, people have feared comets as messages from the celestial gods. Comets were usually thought to be harbingers of misfortune, such as death or catastrophes. Roman astrologer Marcus Manilius wrote about comets in the first century CE, stating, "Heaven in pity is sending upon Earth tokens of impending doom." The fear inspired by Halley's Comet was captured on the Bayeux Tapestry that recorded the Norman conquest of England in 1066. The omen seemed predictive since the invasion of the Normans resulted in the death of King Harold and defeat of the English Army.

When Sir James Douglas made a second visit to Victoria in March of 1843 in the steamship, the *Beaver*, he saw a luminous streak in the heavens. He could not account for it, but thought that it might have been a reflection from the waters of the Juan de Fuca Strait. The streak appeared for five consecutive nights. In fact, the streak was the Great Comet of 1843 which was very bright in March of that year. Its tail was over 300 million kilometres long. Throughout the world, this comet inspired a fear that judgment day was imminent.

For the native people in the area, the coincidence of the comet together with the arrival of the *Beaver* must have seemed significant. It tied into their beliefs that the first human fell from the sky to earth as a meteor. Other stories told how Hayls the Transformer took the form of a meteor as he travelled through the sky.

A meteor forecast an important birth in March of 1768. It streaked across the sky over the present-day Ohio, leaving a greenish-white fiery light. The Shawnee people thought that it heralded the panther spirit and that it was good sign. Then the cry of a newborn baby was heard. The baby was named Tecumseh, "The Panther Passing Across" or "The Shooting Star." The meteor did indicate an important birth because Tecumseh grew up to become the legendary warrior who participated in the War of 1812.

Early observers, such as Aristotle, described comets as "stars with hair"; the name comet means "long-haired." As they move through space, comets leave a trail of solid debris. Meteor showers can be seen when the earth passes through the debris.

About August 12th of every year, Victorians can enjoy the Perseid meteor shower which can be seen as the earth passes through the orbit of the Swift-Tuttle comet. On a dark night, 60 or more meteors an hour can be seen streaking across the sky. The Perseid meteor shower is so named because the meteors come from the constellation Perseus, itself named for the hero in Greek mythology.

Comets portend doom and were also linked to sacrifice. A Greek myth about the Coronides tells how two sisters offered themselves in sacrifice to save their land from a plague. They killed themselves with the shuttles they used for weaving. As a reward, they were transformed into comets.

The Sun

As the sun travels across the sky from east to west, it was pictured by many cultures as a god driving a chariot. For the ancient Egyptians, it was the sun-god Ra who rode the chariot across the sky.

The Greeks envisioned the god, Helios, crowned with the rays of the sun, driving a chariot drawn by four winged horses across the sky. One day, Helios let his son, Phaethon, drive his chariot but the young man lost control of it, setting the earth on fire. Zeus killed the boy with a thunderbolt and brought the sun back to its rightful course.

In a similar tradition, Robert Brown recounted that local native people described the sun as a great chief driving a fiery sledge. Some myths told how the raven married the daughter of the sun. Their son attempted to drive his grandsire's chariot across the sky, setting fire to some mountains, including Mount Baker. Brown noted that chariots were unknown among the Cowichan and Fraser people at this time and he thought the myth may have been more recent. Perhaps it was inspired by stories of the Greek myth of Phaethon.

The sun often appears in Northwest Coast art and features prominently in myths, often as a benevolent spirit. In one myth, the Sun Chief was released from a box by Raven. He lived in the sky and people could reach him by climbing a chain of arrows. The native people believed that the long rays of the sun allowed travel between earth and sky. In carvings, the sun usually has the face of the hawk with its re-curved beak touching its mouth. Every morning, the Coast Salish people of Vancouver Island directed their prayers to the rising sun, to animal spirits and to Hayls the Transformer.

The Moon

The moon is luminous in the night sky. The Greek goddess of the moon, Selene, was radiantly beautiful, with long wings and a golden crown. Like her brother, the sun, Selene drove a chariot across the sky. Freshly bathed in the world ocean, she would emerge from the world ocean to guide her silver chariot drawn by two horses across the night sky.

The moon has great influence on the lives of people on Vancouver Island. Robert Brown reported that in Alberni, Indigenous people looked at the moon and said, "Life, life." Brown noted that the Cowichan tribes believed that the moon has a frog in it. In Songhees carvings, the moon represents the Grandmother and acts a protector and guardian. Carver Butch Dick added an image of Grandmother Moon in his Spirit Pole in Centennial Square's Spirit Square as a reminder to people to be respectful in a way that is fitting to their family and community.

Grandmother Moon on Spirit Pole by Butch Dick

The Rainbow

Rainbows appear when sunlight hits droplets of moisture in the atmosphere to produce of an arc of the colours in the spectrum. Rainbows in Victoria are particularly spectacular over the Juan de Fuca Strait.

The Greek goddess of the rainbow was Iris, a messenger of the gods. The ancient Greeks occupied coasts and commonly saw the arc of the rainbow reaching between the clouds and the sea. As a result, they believed that Iris gathered water from the sea and refilled the clouds.

Rainbows are often associated with floods. The *Epic of Gilgamesh* describes how the goddess Ishtar wears a rainbow necklace of jewels to remember the great flood that killed her people. After the Biblical flood, God set his bow in the cloud as a covenant between himself and all living creatures that he would never again send a flood to destroy all life.

The Songhees people believed that the elements of the natural world were beings with certain powers. Songhees elder Jimmy Fraser said that he had learned to sing and bring out the rainbow spirit. As a result, the rainbow saved him once when he fell out of his boat.

Winds

The winds off Victoria support a variety of activities, such as sailing, windsurfing and kite-flying. In many cultures, the winds were personified and identified based on the direction from which they came.

Aeolus was the ruler of the winds in Greek mythology. In one tradition, he was the son of Poseidon. Poseidon, too, could rouse the winds and storms. In the *Odyssey*, Aeolus gave a sealed bag of the winds to Odysseus to release as needed. But his men, thinking the bag contained gold and silver, released the winds, blowing the ship off course.

Aeolus kept the wind in caves on the mythical island of Aeolia. He would release the winds, called the Anemoi, as ordered by the gods. The north wind was Boreas, who brought winter gales with his cold icy power. Notus was the south wind, the wind of fog and mists, bringing danger to people on mountaintops and sailors at sea. He carried a vase from which to pour rain. The gentle Zephyrus was the west wind with light spring breezes. The east wind, Eurus, brought rain and was considered to be unlucky. Sometimes the winds were depicted as winged men and other times as horses. Aeolus was titled Hippotades, the reiner of horses, just as Poseidon had symbolic links to horses.

Many of the early wind gods were depicted carrying large bags of wind over their shoulders. Boreas wore a billowing cloak; bags of wind in Greek mythology may have been derived from this. The Japanese god of the wind, Fūjin, is shown as a demon carrying a large bag of wind over his shoulders. The Chinese god of the wind, Feng Bo, carried the wind in a goat skin.

Winds can be helpful spirits, such as Zephyrus who carried Psyche to Cupid's cave to unite the lovers. The Finnish goddesses of the winds include Suvetar, the goddess of the south-wind, a kind-hearted deity who healed the sick. Or winds can be very destructive, causing ship wrecks. Herodotus wrote about how the Athenians were advised to invoke Boreas, the north wind, for help in defeating the Persians led by King Xerxes in the fifth century BCE. The resulting storm lasted for three days and 400 Persian ships were sunk. The Athenians built a sanctuary to Boreas whereas the other Greeks thanked Poseidon for the victory. The wind god was considered to be a powerful ally.

Robert Brown noted in his 1873 book, *The Races of Mankind*, the natives of the Northwest believed the winds came out of large boulders that had once been people who had been transformed into stone. They thought of the south wind as an old woman who lived in the south. When they wanted a south wind, they would throw stones at her. Brown reported that there were some large rocks between Victoria and Cowichan that were supposed to be "Eolus-like hags." One day, he saw some people slapping and throwing water on the rocks. When the afternoon breeze came up, the people believed that the breeze was due to their attention to the hags who controlled the winds.

The power of the hags recalls the Scottish tradition of storm witches. In north Scotland, people believed that some women had the power to conjure up storms. For example, on November 11, 1629, Janet Forsyth was put on trial in Kirkwall, Orkney for calling forth a treacherous fog. She was found guilty of witchcraft and sentenced to death.

Rituals to honour a family of sacred stones take place to this day near Glen Lyon in Perthshire, Scotland. The stones are believed to represent the storm witch known as the Cailleach and her family. The stones are taken out of their rough house in May of each year and returned at the end of October to spend the winter. At a ritual on May 1, 2012, people sung to the sacred stones in Gaelic and splashed them with river water.

People's belief in the entities that control weather can change the course of history. When King James VI of the Scots was returning from Denmark in 1590 with his bride, Anne of Denmark, they encountered storms so fierce they almost drowned. The Admiral of the Danish fleet accompanying the royal party said that witches had caused the storms. As a result, witch trials took place in Denmark and Scotland and many people were executed as witches. King James presided over the trial of the North Berwick witches, accused of causing the storms and wrote a book about witchcraft and punishment. He persecuted witches. Over the years, thousands of people were tortured and executed as witches.

In the Coast Salish worldview, winds could be guardian spirits. Anthropologist Diamond Jenness visited a reserve on the Fraser River in 1936 and interviewed a shaman named Old Pierre. Old Pierre said that the northwest wind had been one of his guardian spirits and it had saved him in a terrific storm. He noted that the northwest wind was linked to the warrior spirit. The northeast wind conferred the power to handle fire without injury on a person seen by the wind purifying himself, but this power was taken away in the summer. The west wind allowed a person to calm storms and to bring good weather, and the south wind enabled a person to run over the surface of the water like a rain-squall. In Iroquois mythology, the god Gaol personified the wind. The north wind was personified by a bear spirit named Ya-o-gah who could destroy the world with his fiercely cold breath.

The Esquimalt and Songhees peoples called the area *Lekwammen* or "the land of the winds" because of the wind storms in winter. In tribute to the winds, a spirit pole was carved by Coast Salish artist, Richard Krentz and eleven others. *The Spirit of Lekwammen*, or "The Land of the Winds," was unveiled on April 8, 1994 on Songhees Point. The pole, carved from a Western red cedar tree that was over 500 years old, was the world's tallest totem pole until its height was reduced in 2001 due to air navigation concerns.

Storms

Victoria has spectacular storms. Storm watching is a popular tourist event with the storm season extending from November to March. Victoria's winter storms are influenced by two phases in the temperature cycle of the Pacific Ocean, the warm, dry *El Niño*, or "Little Boy" and the cold, wet *La Niña*, or "Little Girl." *El Niño* occurs on average every three to five years and *La Niña* usually half as often. As *El Niño* often appears around Christmas time off the coast of South America, its name refers to the baby Jesus. The opposition of the warm dry cycles versus the cold wet cycles illustrates the mythic concept of duality.

In many myths, sky gods controlled the weather and sent lightning and thunder. Teshub, a Bronze Age god of the Hurrian people, carried a triple thunderbolt and an axe. Zeus, the Greek sky god, was in continuous contact with humans through the thunder and lightning he sent and the flight of birds he controlled. Like many of the Indo-European sky gods, his symbols were the thunderbolt, eagle, bull and oak. Thor of the Norse pantheon created lightning with his magical hammer, *Mjöllnir*. Perun, the Slavic god of thunder and lightning, would sit on top of the world oak tree in the form of an eagle and survey the world. He subdued his enemies with lightning bolts, returning order to chaos. Indra, the Hindu god of thunderstorms and war, used the *vajra* or thunderbolt to kill his enemy, releasing the waters of the world that Vritra had confined. In Japanese mythology, Raijin is the god of lightning, thunder and storms. He is typically depicted as a demon beating drums to create thunder.

First Nations peoples attribute storms to the mythological Thunderbird. When the Thunderbird flapped his wings, thunder was produced and when he blinked, lightning flashed from his eyes. He carried lightning snakes under his wings and used them to hunt his enemy, the Killer Whale. Sometimes lightning snakes had the heads of wolves, enhancing their ability to hunt. These lightning snakes were often painted on the sides of canoes and then covered up by another coat of paint. The power emitted from these snakes would help the native whalers in their hunt. As the Thunderbird was so powerful, care had to be taken not to get the Thunderbird angry.

Some First Nations, such as the Cowichan, believed that the Thunderbird could shapeshift into human form. Thunderbirds married into human families and as a result, some families could trace their lineage to a Thunderbird.

People in the ancient world both revered and feared the weather gods. We, too, are in awe of the power of storms and other weather extremes. Whether winter storms are caused by the rage of Zeus, the thunderbolts of Thor, or differential atmospheric pressures, we can only prepare to withstand them and hope that we can make peace with Gaia.

CHAPTER 7
Stalking Flora

Flora, the plant life of a region, is named after the Roman goddess of flowers, Flora. She lived on the Blessed Islands and could transform people into flowers. It was she who called the bees to violets, clover and thyme to make honey. The Romans honoured Flora in the spring with a festival called the Floralia that started on April 28 and lasted until May 3, essentially an early May Day festival to petition the goddess for protection. People wore floral wreaths in their hair as a tribute to Flora.

Early European visitors to Victoria mentioned the abundance of its flora—its oak and pine trees and meadows. Berhold Seeman was a German botanist who was appointed as the naturalist on the voyage of the *H.M.S. Herald* exploring the west coast of North America. In 1846, the *H.M.S. Herald* arrived in the harbour of Fort Victoria. Seeman described the area around Fort Victoria as

> *a natural park; noble oaks and ferns are seen in the greatest luxuriance; thickets of the hazel and the willow, shrubberies of the poplar and the alder, are dotted about. One could hardly believe that this was not the work of art; more particularly when finding signs of cultivation in every direction-enclosed pasture-land, fields of wheat, potatoes and turnips.*

Root Gardens

The Europeans believed that the meadowlike appearance of the Victoria area was a natural condition. However, the meadows were created by the Coast Salish people as they cultivated the landscape to support root crops such as red clover and camas. They used specialized digging sticks to aerate the soils, undertook selective harvesting and initiated periodic burns to revitalize the land. The new life born of fire has mythic significance, recalling the Phoenix rising from the ashes as a sign of rejuvenation.

Springbank clover, a species of red clover, was once abundant along Victoria's coastline. Its rhizomes were an important food source for Indigenous people. When James Douglas landed at Clover Point in 1842, he described the vegetation on the headland in a letter he wrote to James Hargrave, saying, "I was nevertheless delighted in ranging over fields knee-deep in clover, tall grasses and ferns reaching above our heads, at these unequivocal proofs of fertility." In folklore, the rare four-leaved clover is considered to be good luck, perhaps because clover indicates fertile soil. Springbank clover is characterized by its three toothed leaflets. Scientists have searched for springbank clover along Dallas Road and other places where it was abundant, but due to habitat changes over the years, virtually no plants remain.

The camas bulb was an important food for the Salish people on southern Vancouver Island before European contact. The women cultivated the camas in April and May when the plants were in flower. At this time, they were able to separate out the white flowered "death camas" from the blue-flowered edible camas. The death camas had a similar bulb but it was toxic. For such an important plant, there are few known myths about the camas. As it was a living thing with a spiritual essence, the women would have sought the permission of the plant for its harvest. Likely a ritual, possibly singing, would have taken place as the plant was harvested, but little information is available on this. The constant threat of eating the bulb of the white-flowered death camas rather than that of the blue camas likely would have called for proper rituals to ensure protection.

The camas does figure in the legend of the "Wives of the Stars," collected in 1895 by anthropologist Franz Boas. The story is similar to the tale of the Star Maidens recorded by Robert Brown. The myth tells how two sisters made a wish to marry two stars in the sky. They got their wish and the stars became their husbands. Their husbands told them to collect camas but unlike on earth, they could only cut off the stalks rather than dig up the bulbs. The elder sister began to long for the taste of the camas bulb so one day, she dug one up. And to their amazement, the hole she dug allowed them to see down to earth. The sisters made a rope in secret and used that rope to climb down to earth through another hole. When their husbands found the rope, they cut it so it fell to earth. When the sisters arrived home, they found that their mother's hair had turned gray and their sister's hair had been cut short in mourning. The star wives had powers of rejuvenation, and when they stroked the hair of their mother and sister, the colour and length were restored. As for the coiled rope on Mount Nga'k'un (now known as Knockan Hill), it was said that only a young man who obeys the laws, purifies himself frequently and has never touched a woman can see the rope.

City of Gardens

Victoria is known as the City of Gardens. Thanks to its mild climate, gardens flourish. Gardens and garden-lovers are plentiful in the city. As early as 1890, the *Victoria Daily Colonist* suggested that Victoria was "the Garden City of the West." An enduring emblem of Victoria is its distinctive flower baskets which the City has displayed on its lamp posts every year since 1937. Gardens were particularly important for early settlers in Canada as they were seen as defences from the wildness of nature.

Gardening began in the Neolithic era. Over the ages, gardens have been created with special meanings, often using mythological themes. There are gardens in myths and myths in gardens. One of the oldest stories in the world, the *Epic of Gilgamesh*, describes how Gilgamesh journeyed to the Garden of the Gods where trees grew jewels instead of fruit. In Greek mythology, the golden apples that grew in the garden at the end of the world were guarded by a trio of nymphs known as the Hesperides. After Hercules stole the apples, the despairing nymphs were turned into trees.

As for myths in gardens, Renaissance gardens featured a language of symbols based on mythology. The sixteenth century Italian garden of Ville d'Este at Tivoli highlighted the myth of Hercules and the garden of the Hesperides. Golden apples were incorporated as design elements and statues and other symbols of Hercules abounded, supporting the claim of the d'Estes family that Hercules was their ancestor. The garden became a model for European gardens.

Statues of the Greek Sun God, Apollo, became popular in the Garden of Versailles in 1664. The Apollo Fountain showed the sun god driving his chariot to light the sky. The solar imagery of Apollo was evoked as a metaphor for the French sun king, Louis XIV, around whom the court revolved like the planets around the sun.

Victorian-era gardens showcased statues and fountains inspired by mythology. The Halifax Public Garden is one of the best examples of a Victorian garden in North America. Its imagery included statues of three Roman goddesses: Flora, goddess of spring; Ceres, goddess of harvest; and Diana, goddess of the forest. The *Nymph Jubilee Fountain* incorporated the image of the nymph Egeria, who, according to myth, wept so much upon the death of the king that she became a spring.

Butchart's Gardens on the Saanich Peninsula attracts over a million visitors a year. The garden itself is like the Cinderella fairy tale. In 1904, it became a quarry when Robert Pim Butchart removed its rich limestone deposits for the manufacture of cement. When the limestone ran out in 1908, Butchart's wife, Jennie Butchart, was challenged to turn the quarry into a garden. Over the next nine years, she supervised the work to create the "Sunken Garden" which was finished in 1921. The ugly quarry was transformed into a world-class garden just as the kitchen maid became a beautiful princess with Jennie Butchart in the role of fairy godmother.

The garden displays a bronze statue known as Tacca the Boar, one of five copies cast in 1962 by a foundry in Florence, Italy, based on the work of the seventh century Florentine sculptor Pietro Tacca. The statue is very popular, its snout rubbed shiny by visitors seeking good luck. Why a boar? Boars and gardens often feature in myth, such as the cautionary Greek myth about the Calydonian boar. When the king did not sacrifice the first fruit of his orchard to the goddess of the hunt, Artemis sent a fierce boar to ravage the orchards. Only the king's son could kill the boar. Its hide was dedicated to Artemis and hung from a tree in a sacred grove. Statues of boars in gardens can symbolize the need to live in harmony with nature, as well as testifying to the destructive power of nature unleashed.

The Greek hero, Adonis, was born when a wild boar opened up a myrrh tree that was really Smyrna, Adonis's mother, transformed by the gods. Myrrh, the precious resin that flowed from a wounded myrrh tree, was said to be the tears of Smyrna. Adonis was beloved by the goddesses Aphrodite and Persephone and lived with each for a different part of the year. When he was killed by a wild boar at a young age, Aphrodite established a funeral ritual for him. Each spring, his followers would grow plants, called "Gardens of Adonis", which grew quickly then died, symbolizing his fate.

Trees

"God is the experience of looking at a tree and saying, *Ah!*" said mythologist Joseph Campbell. Myths and folklore celebrate the interconnectedness of humans and trees. In mythological terms, trees represent the human spirit. As goes the spirit of the tree, so goes the life of the human connected to it. A version of the Cinderella fairy tale implies that Cinderella's good fortune is linked to a hazel tree that she plants on her mother's grave, capturing her mother's spirit.

Tree spirits are common in many mythologies. The ancient Greeks believed that female spirits, or dryads, inhabited trees as the entity of the tree. When the tree dies, the dryad dies. However, a few dryads lived on in immortality. The nymph Daphne was transformed into a laurel tree and remains as the spirit of the tree. Different tree species supported specific dryads. For example, the dryad of nut trees was Karya, the dryad of acorn-bearing trees was Balanos, and the dryad of the fig tree was Syke. Figs were so delicious that the ancient Greeks viewed them as gifts from the gods, created by the goddess Demeter as a reward to man for his hospitality.

Related to the need to protect the spirit of the tree, many traditions hold that if a person harms a tree, they will come to harm. A modern example is the Devil Tree of New Jersey. Locals believe that anyone who harms this old oak will suffer harm, possibly a car accident, possibly injury caused by a phantom black car. New Jersey's Devil Tree is now protected by chain link fencing to prevent anyone from trying to cut it down, although attempts are still made.

Tree spirits appear in many images from popular culture. The menacing trees in the Forest of No Return in Disney's *Babes in Toyland* have human features and sing. In Tolkien's *The Lord of the*

Rings, talking trees, known as Ents, serve as protectors of trees. In many cultures, rituals were followed when trees were cut down to apologize to the spirit of the tree.

Reverence for trees has been with us since time immemorial. Why did the ancients revere trees? In temperate areas, deciduous trees symbolized rebirth, shedding their leaves in the fall to appear dead over winter only to be reborn in the spring. Conifers are green year round, symbolizing immortality. Coast Salish people believed evergreen trees retained their vitality more than deciduous trees and evergreens are used in rituals to transfer vitality to people and increase their strength.

Many cultures conceptualized the world tree. Yggdrasil, in Norse mythology, was the tree of the cosmos, joining heaven and earth. In China, the Fu Sang tree was the abode of the gods. Archaeological findings from ancient Mesopotamia and India show images of the tree of life.

The rustling of leaves in the wind sounds as if the trees are whispering. Locally, the aspens at Government House can be heard telling their tales during a light breeze. The ancients believed in oracular trees. At Dodona, the oldest oracle in Greece, seekers' questions would be answered by the rustling of the leaves of the sacred oak. In ancient Scythia, soothsayers would twine linden leaves around their fingers to predict the future. The laurel was also considered to be a plant of divinity and prophecy. The leaves of the laurel tree were eaten by priestesses at the oracle at Delphi. Similarly, Druids ate acorns to prepare for prophetic utterances.

The linkage between the health of trees and the well-being of people has a scientific basis. Trees absorb carbon dioxide, filter pollutants and provide oxygen. According to Tree Canada, one large tree can provide a day's oxygen for up to four people. Trees reduce run-off and erosion, act as windbreaks to reduce residential heating costs and provide wildlife habitat. Urban trees convey emotional and health benefits. Studies have shown that people are friendlier, happier and more assertive when looking at scenery with urban trees. Hospital patients recover faster if they have a view of trees. Retail centers benefit when trees are part of the streetscape.

As important as the scientific benefits are, the deep emotional ties between people and trees cannot be explained solely by increased property values, reduced air pollutants and temperature moderations.

This is shown by the extraordinary measures people take to preserve special trees.

The mythological spirit of the greenwood is perhaps best captured by Robin Hood's Sherwood Forest—a tribute to freedom from oppression. Still popular today, Sherwood Forest Country Park receives about 500,000 visitors each year. In Sherwood Forest there is a large tree called the Major Oak which is said to have sheltered Robin Hood and his men in its hollow trunk. It was voted Britain's favourite tree in 2002. The English oak is thought to be around 800 years old and it is showing some decay. In order to preserve this important tree, conservation measures have been undertaken since 1908, including using a network of support poles to prop up its heavy branches and checking its health regularly. In England, oaks were considered sacred to Druids and later they became associated with woodland spirits.

Trees can live to thousands of years. Sequoia trees, in particular, are praised for their size, age and eternal youth. They can live over 3,000 years, contributing to the belief that they are immortal. Described as the Titans of trees, the largest sequoias in the world are found in the secret Grove of Titans in northern California. The tallest tree in the world, Hyperion, is named after a Titan in Greek mythology. Ancient trees are story-tellers with stories of the world's climate found in their rings. Victoria is home to several sequoia trees from California. The largest and oldest resident in Fairfield is the 48 metre (157 feet) sequoia on the corner of Moss and Richardson Streets. Sequoia trees can be found in Irving Park in James Bay and in Beacon Hill Park. A sequoia planted in the 1800s on the lawn of the Parliament Buildings serves as the official provincial Christmas tree. Every December, the 30 metre (100 feet) tall tree is decorated with thousands of lights, a reminder of the coming increase in daylight.

Victoria's urban forest is one of the rarest and most threatened in the Pacific Northwest. Its principal trees include the Douglas fir and western red cedar. Named after botanist David Douglas, the Douglas fir is the second tallest tree species in the world. A myth associated with it explains the origin of the bract in its cone. According to a First Nations legend, a mouse hides in Douglas fir cones during winter. Its legs and tail protrude from the cone as the three-pronged bract that characterizes a Douglas fir. Further, if the tail and legs stick up, the cone is from the interior species, whereas in the coastal species, they face downwards.

The cedar tree is sacred to the Coast Salish people. It provides the material for houses, canoes, hats, clothing and baskets. Called "the tree of life," it is held with the highest respect by all Northwest Coast peoples for its healing and spiritual powers. A Coast Salish myth says the Great Spirit created the red cedar in honour of a man who was always helping others. A cedar tree grew where he was buried, helping the people who used the roots for baskets, the bark for clothing and the wood for shelter.

Municipal governments in Greater Victoria recognize the value of neighbourhood trees and most have enacted tree protection bylaws. The bylaws protect native trees, heritage trees, landmark trees and trees deemed significant by the community. The recognition of these trees serves to build community with residents coming together to identify what trees are "significant." Municipalities like Victoria and Saanich hold annual tree appreciation days when volunteers come out to plant native trees and shrubs.

Despite their longevity, we continue to lose trees. In Victoria, winter storms destroy hundreds of trees each year. Even Sherwood Forest is losing oaks at five each year. Contrasted with the desire to preserve our trees is the fear of falling trees during storms, resulting in the removal of more trees. The silver lining is that the strong interconnection between trees and people means that we will continue to value the spirit of the greenwood.

Boulevard Trees

The City of Victoria manages over 40,000 trees within its parks and boulevards, including over 17,000 boulevard trees. In March and April of every year, Victorians delight in the clouds of pink blossoms that appear on many streets. In the 1930s, the Parks Department brought flowering cherries from Japan to plant on boulevards, planting over 5,000 trees. The local Japanese community donated over 1,000 trees, purchased with money from the first place prize for their float in the 1937 Victoria Day Parade.

The Sakura or cherry tree is a key symbol for the Japanese, denoting their national character. The Japanese tradition of picnicking under blossoming cherry trees started in the eighth century. In the eighteenth century, cherry blossoms came to symbolize the ephemeral nature of life. The blossoms are beautiful but short-lived. During World War II, the cherry blossom became associated with dying an honourable death, like the falling of beautiful cherry petals. Kamikaze pilots would paint cherry blossoms on their planes before they went on suicide missions. The symbol came to be considered lucky and it is common in art and branding. Cherry blossoms festivals celebrate the blooming of the cherry trees not just in Japan but in many places in the world. The blossoms also symbolize the coming of spring and rebirth. After the earthquake in Japan on March 2011, the 1,000-year old Miharu-Takizakura cherry tree in Fukushima survived the earthquake and blossomed in April. Over 60,000 people visited the tree as a symbol of hope.

The Chinese also celebrate cherry and plum blossoms. Cherry blossoms represent feminine beauty. Plum blossoms indicate perseverance in the face of difficulties as they blossom at the end of winter.

Victoria Blossoms

Memorial Trees

Trees are often planted to commemorate events and people. The Mayor's Grove was established in 1927 in Beacon Hill Park to allow for commemorative trees. Winston Churchill, then a former Chancellor of the Exchequer in the United Kingdom, planted a hawthorn tree in the grove in 1929. King Prajadhipok of Siam planted an oak in 1931 and Lord Baden-Powell came to the grove in

1935 and planted another oak. Over thirty trees have been planted in the grove, including oaks, maples, Douglas fir, ash, hawthorns, and other ornamentals. The trees provide a spot for people meet to commemorate the person associated with the tree. For example, people gather by the Churchill hawthorn to celebrate the life of Sir Winston Churchill around the anniversary of his death on January 24, 1965.

Coronation Oaks were planted around the world to commemorate the coronation of King George VI in 1937. Over 240 seedlings from the English oak were sent to Commonwealth countries for the celebration. A Coronation Oak planted in Esquimalt's Memorial Park in 1937 is deemed to be a significant tree to the community. Other Coronation Oaks can be found in the Victoria area and along King George Highway in Surrey. The source of seedlings was Windsor Great Park in England. An oak tree in Windsor Great Park figures in the legend of Herne the Hunter. Herne hung himself from the oak tree. An early reference is found in the play *The Merry Wives of Windsor* in which William Shakespeare describes how Herne the Hunter, with antlers on his head, walks around an oak at midnight in the winter and haunts Windsor Forest. Herne is the Wild Huntsman, an archetypal image of a hunter who is doomed to hunt forever. Sightings of the specter in Windsor Forest were reported as recently as the twentieth century and he remains a popular figure in art, books and TV series. Is it possible that Victoria's Coronation Oaks come from the same stock as Herne's oak?

CHAPTER 8
Following the Birds

"Follow the Birds to Victoria" was a popular slogan used to promote tourism in Victoria. It was introduced in 1918 by the Commissioner of the Publicity Bureau, George Warren. With its coast, meadows and urban forests, the habitats of Victoria support a wide diversity of birds—over 380 species.

In many myths, birds were considered to be links between heaven and earth as heavenly messengers. Some birds may be linked to the creation of the world whereas others are linked to death.

Gulls

Gulls are everywhere in Victoria. The most common local gull is the Glaucous-winged Gull, with "glaucous" referring to the blue-gray colour of their wings. Other gulls include the mew gull, Bonaparte's gull and western gulls. As opportunistic feeders, these birds pose problems for humans during their 15 years of life. They are increasing in numbers due to the abundance of food.

Seagulls often sit on the sills of windows in buildings in Victoria and peck at the window. Some believe that this is an omen of death. British folklore suggests that it is unlucky to kill a gull as they are the souls of mariners lost at sea. Could it be the soul of a lost sailor pecking at the window or is it an attempt to get food?

Seagulls are believed to have the ability to predict weather. British traditions say that when seagulls fly inland, expect a storm. Some Northwest Coast myth holds that the seagull has powers over storms and weather.

A Victoria Gull

A Chinook story, the "Raven and Gull Myth," recorded by anthropologist Franz Boas tells how the gull went to the beach every day to find food but the raven beat him to it. Angry, the gull killed the raven. When the raven's sister, the crow, was told about this, she called together all her people, the land birds, and attacked the gull's people, the sea birds. The sea birds won the battle and the gull was forced to agree to their terms which allowed the crow to forage for food at low tide early in the morning. Consistent with the story, the Northwestern Crow specializes in foraging at low tide along the sea shores around Victoria.

Crows

The crow is noisy, destructive, amusing and intelligent. We notice crows and they notice us. They are certainly birds with an attitude.

In myths, crows range from creators and divine messengers to tricksters and omens of death. Early hunter-gatherers held positive views of crows (or more likely ravens) because scavengers often indicated the presence of herds to hunt. With the advent of agriculture, crows became pests, eating crops in farmers' fields.

The crow proved to be very adaptable to living near people, especially compared to the more solitary raven. With urbanization, crows successfully exploited new feeding opportunities in our gardens and our garbage. Urban crow populations are exploding. According to Robert Alison, writing in the *Winnipeg Free Press* in 2008, Victoria is the "crow capital" of North America and its crow population has increased more than 500 per cent in the past 40 years. Greater Victoria hosts close to 10,000 crows.

The cawing of crows is loud, frequent and varied. Perhaps this is why several myths feature a gossiping crow that gets into trouble due to his indiscretion. In Greek mythology, a crow, white in those days, told the god, Apollo, that Apollo's lover, Coronis, was having an affair with a mortal. Apollo became enraged and cursed the crow, scorching its feathers and turning them from white to black. Coronis was flung into the sky to become the constellation, Corvus, or crow.

Many myths around the world include stories about birds that are black now but once were white. The Shawnee tell a story about how the pure white crow warned the buffalo when Shawnee hunters approached. One of the hunters captured the crow and took him back to camp. The enraged hunter threw the crow into the fire, singeing his white feathers and turning them black. The smallest hunter saved the crow and in gratitude, the crow agreed not to warn the buffalo about hunts if the Shawnee remember to thank the buffalo for his sacrifice.

A similar story about the white raven appears in Coast Salish mythology where ravens symbolize vanity. According to the tale, a proud white raven ate the sun in the hope of becoming brighter but instead, he turned black.

Since crows feed on carrion, they became associated with death, especially the death of warriors. The Irish goddess of war, Badb, took the form of a crow. Likewise, the Norse Valkyries who chose which soldiers would die on the battlefield could transform into crows or ravens. One of Vincent van Gogh's last paintings depicted a wheat field with crows filling the cloudy sky. Some believe this was an omen predicting van Gogh's death. In India, many believe that the crow is an avatar of dead relatives who revisit their loved ones on the fourteenth day after their death. Legend holds that the soul of King Arthur survives today as a crow.

The flights of crows led to crow augury and vestiges remain today in the nursery rhyme in which the number of crows you see predicts the future. "One for sorrow, two for mirth, three for a wedding, four for a birth," and so on.

Some cultures believe that crows forecast the birth of special babies. The Japanese saw crows as divine messengers that could predict the birth of a healthy child. The present Dalai Lama describes how a pair of crows roosted on the roof of his house for several days after he was born. He noted that similar incidents occurred at the birth of the First, Seventh, Eighth and Twelfth Dalai Lamas. After the birth of the First Dalai Lama, bandits broke into his home and his parents ran away, leaving the baby. When they returned, they found him protected by a crow.

Like us, crows are very social. Biologist John Marzluff believes that to know the crow is to know ourselves. With the increasing number of crows in our neighbourhoods, we will have many opportunities to get to know crows.

Raptors

One of the most impressive sights in Victoria is the outspread wings of bald eagles as they soar overhead on rising air currents. A variety of birds of prey make Victoria home, including golden eagles, rough-legged hawks, Cooper's hawks, peregrine falcons and red-tailed hawks. Birds of prey have excellent eyesight, strong talons and sharp beaks and these characteristics feature in myths involving raptors.

Eagles soar high into the heavens and can see to the horizon. Perhaps because of their ability to reach the sky gods, they have been a symbol of divine power for millennia. A myth from ancient Babylon relates how the legendary King Etana saved an eagle and then the eagle carried him to the heavens to get the plant of birth so that he could have a son. The mythology also included a sacred tree with an eagle perched at the top.

Zeus, the head of the Greek pantheon, assumed the form of an eagle to carry the beautiful shepherd boy, Ganymede, to Olympus to serve the gods and become immortal. According to an early myth, Zeus adopted the eagle as his symbol when it appeared to him as a good omen before the war with the Titans. In recognition of his victory, Zeus put the golden eagle on his war standards and in the sky as the constellation Aquila. In Hindu mythology, the constellation is associated with the Garuda, a half-human, half-eagle divinity who carried the elixir of immortality from the heavens.

The tradition of reading omens from the flights of birds goes back at least to the fourteenth century BCE, as referenced in the Amarna tablets from ancient Egypt which noted that the king of Alasia in Cyprus required an 'eagle diviner' to be sent from Egypt. In ancient Rome, augurs would read the flight patterns of the birds to interpret the will of the gods. The signs could be auspicious or inauspicious (the word "auspicious" is derived from the taking of auspices).

Jupiter, the Roman equivalent of Zeus, also had an eagle as his sacred animal. Jupiter was associated with kingship and sovereignty. A legend tells how a teenaged Gaius Marius found an eagle's nest with seven chicks, foretelling his future success and power. He was elected consul of Rome seven times. He decreed that the eagle would become the symbol of the Senate and People of Rome and he established the Aquila eagle as the sole symbol on the standards of the Roman legion in 102 BCE. It was this symbol that was carried into numerous battles.

The eagle has been commonly used as a symbol of governmental power. In 1782, the bald eagle was adopted as the emblem of the United States, symbolizing supreme power and authority. The eagle on the seal and coat of arms of the US holds thirteen arrows in its left talon (symbolizing the thirteen original states) and an olive branch in its right, denoting war and peace. Its head is turned towards the olive branch as it favours peace.

In Norse mythology, the god Odin often took the form of an eagle. The Tree of Life, Yggdrasil, was the center of the Norse cosmos. High on the branches of the world tree sat an eagle, and between the eyes of the eagle, sat a hawk.

The Iroquois Confederacy adopted the eagle as a symbol of peace. The eagle held six arrows, one for each of the six member nations, illustrating that six arrows together can not be broken like a single arrow. Similar to the Norse world view, Iroquois legends envision an eagle sitting at the top of the Tree of Peace, scanning the horizon for any sign of trouble and warning the people of the Confederacy of danger.

Many cultures place a high value on eagle feathers. Highland clan chiefs in Scotland are entitled to wear three eagle feathers on the crest badge on their bonnets to indicate their rank. Many Indigenous people of the Americas use eagle feathers in their spiritual practices, believing that the eagle is the symbolic link between the spiritual world and the physical world.

Owls

Owls have haunted the human imagination for millennia. The oldest known cave paintings in the world, 30,000 years ago, include the image of an owl. A 4,000-year-old Babylonian relief shows a winged woman with the talons of a bird flanked by two owls. Owls are often associated with women. Australian aborigines believe that an owl is the soul of women whereas a bat is the soul of men. In France, it is believed that if a pregnant woman hears an owl, she will give birth to a girl.

Owls are becoming more common in Victoria. In addition to the Western Screech-Owl, the Great Horned Owl and the Barn Owl, more owls are showing up. The Barred Owl has expanded its range to western Canada, first appearing on Vancouver Island in the late 1960s. Although Barred Owls have reputations as wilderness birds, they adapt well to the urban forest and tolerate living near to people. In late 2012, the appearance of Snowy Owls created excitement among the birders of the city.

The idea of the owl as a very wise bird is celebrated by poets. The sacred animal of Athena, the Greek goddess of wisdom and of war, was the Little Owl. For over three hundred years, Athens produced silver coins, known as "owls," with the head of Athena on one side and her owl on the reverse. Whether this symbolized the wisdom of establishing a stable currency or the aspect of raising funds for war is not known. The coins gave rise to the phrase "like taking owls to Athens," indicating pointless activity. Athena carried a shield with an owl on it, a talisman of good fortune in battle. The "owl-eyed" Athena could shape-shift into an owl. The ancient Greeks believed that if an owl flew over a battle, it was a sign of victory. The link to good fortune is also seen in the Indian goddess of wealth, Lakshmi, who rides a white owl, symbolizing her all-seeing wisdom. In modern times, MENSA, the high IQ society, has adopted the wise owl as its mascot.

However, in Greek mythology, a different species of owl was associated with Hades, the ruler of the underworld. The ancient Romans also associated the owl with death. The death of Julius Caesar was said to have been predicted by a hooting owl. As the owl is a predator and a creature of the night, its association to death can be found in many cultures. In England, it was believed that the hoot of an owl flying past a sick room indicated that the patient would die soon. First Nations mythology related owls to souls of the dead who live in the world of the dead by day and the world of living by night. Inland Salish people believed the Screech Owl announces death. The Chinese also saw the owl as a harbinger of death.

Some preservationists suggest that animals with strong cultural profiles, such as owls, have an advantage for conservation efforts regardless of whether that profile is negative or not. However, since many cultures view owls as evil, they often persecute them. The practice of nailing owls to barn doors to ward off evil was common. Even now, humans cause most owl fatalities through vehicle accidents, habitat loss or even shooting the birds. However, most people are delighted to see owls in their neighbourhoods, returning to the positive appreciation of the wise old owl.

Hummingbirds

Victorians can look forward to the early March when the Rufous Hummingbird returns from its winter habitat in Mexico. Anna's Hummingbird stays in the area all year round, extending its range northward over the years, helped by the amount of insects in their diet and abundance of backyard feeders.

As hummingbirds are only found in the Americas, most of the mythology surrounding them reflects the stories of Indigenous peoples of the western hemisphere.

The iridescence of hummingbird bird feathers reflecting beams of light may have led the Maya of Mexico and Central America to visualize the sun as a hummingbird. Their folklore includes a story about the sun, disguised as a hummingbird, courting the Moon Goddess. In some myths, the return of the hummingbird parallels the return of the sun.

Like the Maya, the Aztecs associated the hummingbird with the sun. They worshipped Huitzilopochtli as the god of war and a solar warrior. The name *Huitzilopochtli* means "hummingbird on the south" and the god was often depicted as a hummingbird. He was conceived when a ball of hummingbird feathers impregnated his mother. Born fully armed, he immediately killed his sister and 400 brothers who had plotted to kill him, throwing them into the sky to become the moon and stars. The action symbolized the sun destroying the moon and stars as it does every day when it rises. Huitzilopochtli was in a constant fight with darkness and required sacrifices to sustain him in this battle. The sacrificial victims served the sun for four years, and then returned to earth as hummingbirds. If you have seen a hummingbird at a feeder aggressively defending his food, it is not hard visualize this bird as a warrior.

A morality tale for modern times can be found in the Cochiti story about the hummingbird that had food. The Cochiti people are an Indigenous tribe who live in New Mexico. When the people lost faith in Mother Earth who sent the rains, she became angry and put the clouds away. It did not rain for four years and the people grew weak from thirst and hunger. Only the hummingbird remained strong, for Mother Earth had told the hummingbird to go to the place of the dead to feed from the nectar of the flowers there. Finally, the people learned that they had offended Mother Earth with their lack of faith. Hopi folklore had a complementary theme with the hummingbird convincing the god of fertility to bring rain during a drought. It was important to respect Mother Earth by showing respect for her creatures, such as the hummingbird.

Here on the west coast, traditions held that hummingbirds nested in the hair of the Wild Woman of the Woods, flying around her as she walked through her forest domain. The Wild Woman is both the protector of forest creatures and the bringer of wealth, as well as representing the dangerous aspect of nature. Haida stories describe high-ranking women tying live hummingbirds to their hair to symbolize their beauty, wealth and prestige. Hummingbirds were believed to transform sunlight into weightless jewels.

Modern West Coast native artists incorporate the hummingbird into their work as a messenger of good fortune and healing. It is good luck to see a hummingbird before a major event and if a hummingbird appears during a time of pain and sorrow, healing will follow. On the Saanich Peninsula, having the hummingbird as a guardian sprit was said to make a man a good warrior who was very fast on his feet.

Hummingbirds do give the feeling of joyful delight as they dash from flower to flower. As symbols of the returning sun, prosperity and the fragility of nature, hummingbirds in our gardens can indeed bring good luck.

Peacocks

Visitors to Greater Victoria are often surprised by the variety of flora and fauna of Victoria. They certainly do not expect see the flamboyant peacock in residential neighbourhoods. Yet the peacocks from Beacon Hill Park do wander around James Bay and Fairfield. Peacocks have lived in Beacon Hill Park since the first peacock was purchased in 1891. At Hatley Park, Blue Indian peafowl have lived free on the college grounds since the 1960s.

The peacock sheds every year, renewing its bright feathers. Like the phoenix, it symbolized the resurrection in early Christian art. The Chinese equate the peacock with dignity, beauty, luck and fame, seeing the peacock as 'the heavenly phoenix on earth.'

When the peacock raises and spreads his tail like a fan, he displays the beautiful elongated tail coverts highlighted with "eyes." The story of the "eye" in a peacock's tail is found in a Greek myth. Argus was a giant with a hundred eyes all over his body. He served the goddess, Hera, by guarding Io, the lover of Zeus who had been changed into a heifer, since none of his eyes slept at the same time. He was lulled to sleep, and then killed by Hermes at Zeus's command. Out of respect for his service to her, Hera put his hundred eyes on the tail of the peacock, her sacred symbol. Argus was also known as Argus Panoptes, or "all-seeing," representing all-seeing knowledge. However, many cultures consider the eyes to be evil and peacock feathers to be unlucky.

Sarasvati, the Hindu goddess of knowledge, may be accompanied by a peacock, which represents arrogant pride in its beauty. Its association with Sarasvati suggests that devotees should not be concerned with appearance but value knowledge over worldly things.

Swans

Ever since 1889, swans have delighted bird lovers as they glided over Goodacre Lake in Beacon Hill Park. But swans no longer grace

Goodacre Lake. In the 1960's, the City of Victoria stopped clipping their wings and over time, the swans left the park. Fred, the last swan in the park, died in 1997 when his neck was broken by a dog.

The swans in Beacon Hill Park were Mute Swans, introduced from Great Britain. The introduction of Mute Swans as decorative waterfowl in North America became popular in the 1800s. Our native swans are Trumpeter Swans. The two species can be distinguished as the Trumpeter Swan has a black bill and holds its neck straight, whereas the Mute Swan has an orange bill and a curved neck.

Swans figure prominently in mythology and they symbolize a bevy of values, such as royalty, purity and love. A popular mythological reference is the swan song. The Mute Swan is not totally mute; it grunts, and when disturbed, it hisses. But the song of the swan is much celebrated in Greek mythology. Once, according to Greek myths, the swan had a beautiful song. When the sun god Apollo was born, swans circled his island birthplace seven times, uttering songs of joy. The ancient Greeks believed that swans were sacred to Apollo and, accordingly, they had the gift of prophecy. Plato wrote that one night in 407 BCE, Socrates dreamed that a cygnet grew out of his chest and "flew forth into the open sky uttering a song that charmed all hearers." The next date, Socrates met his student, Plato. Plato recorded the belief that when swans know that they are dying, they sing more than ever as they rejoice that they will be returning to the god Apollo.

Several Greek myths tell about the hero, Cycnus, whose name means "swan." In one of the myths, Cycnus was a friend of Phaëton. When Phaëton tried to drive the chariot of the sun, Zeus struck him down with a thunderbolt and he fell flaming into a river and died. Cycnus, who had a beautiful voice, grieved the death of his friend. To alleviate his grief, he was transformed into a swan.

Swans moult once a year for about four to six weeks in the summer and cannot fly during this time. Their habits of moulting and migration have led to tales of swan maidens, common in European folklore. In these stories, swans come to earth and take off their feathers, becoming beautiful maidens. A hunter may find the feather cloak of a swan, and if he hides it, the swan is forced to stay in her human form. The hunter often marries the swan maiden, who cannot take flight, like a swan in moult. But one day, when she finds her hidden cloak, she leaves him and takes flight, like a swan in migration. These tales suggest the mythologization of the molting and migration of swans.

When a pair of mute swans meets beak-to-beak, the curve of their long necks resembles a heart. Swans mate for life, and they have come to symbolize love. As such, they are a popular motif for weddings. The wedding march comes from Wagner's *Lohengrin*, an opera about the Swan Knight. The ballet, *Swan Lake*, is a tribute to eternal love.

It is surprising to discover that there are no swans on Goodacre Lake. The good news is that they are surviving on many shorelines in Greater Victoria. Even better, our native Trumpeter Swans are no longer near extinction and are fairly common in the winter on the waterways of Victoria, no longer trumpeting their swan song.

The bird populations of Victoria are constantly changing as the environment changes. Species, such as the Snowy Owl and Brown Pelican, not usually seen in the area, are appearing whereas other species are dwindling. However, bird-watchers and others continue to "follow the birds to Victoria."

CHAPTER 9
Favouring Fauna

Fauna, the animal life of an area, is named after Fauna, the Roman goddess of fertility and the female counterpart of the god, Faunus. These deities of the woods could predict the future and protect the land. The name *Fauna* may be derived the verb *favere*, "to favour," and Fauna was referred to as the "favourable goddess." Fauna and Faunus are accompanied by fauns, who are half-man and half-goat, and represent a fusion of humans with animal spirits and the untamed wilderness.

The unique climate and location of Greater Victoria influence the type and abundance of wildlife living in the area. Vancouver Island, as an island location, has fewer species than the mainland. Over 17,000 years ago, mammoths, mastodons and musk ox lived in the Victoria area. As the climate changed, these large animals died out. Bison appeared about 11,000 years ago, and they died out as the climate grew colder. Elk appeared about 11,700 years ago and became widespread, but hunting and habitat loss have virtually eliminated the population from the southern part of the island. Black-tailed deer remain very abundant. Wolves, cougar and black bear usually appear where their prey live, but they have been virtually eliminated from rural and urban areas. However, the occasional cougar does show up in Victoria. The meadows and forests support insects including butterflies. And with human occupation came domestic animals such as the dog and the rabbit.

The symbolic value of the animals provides people with a deep, personal connection to nature and the region. Myths recognize the inter-connectedness of people and non-human animals. Deities may become associated with specific animals because of symbolic associations. Other myths explain how certain features and traits of animals originated. Yet other myths tell about the transformations of humans into animals and vice versa. Ovid's *Metamorphoses* features a man who was turned into a donkey. Other myths talk about animals as ancestors of high profile families.

In First Nation narratives, supernatural beings may take the form of animals in the human world. The supernatural animals live in their own villages as humans. Many stories tell of the encounters between humans and the supernatural beings, and these stories are brought to life in masks and dance. On an individual level, First Nations peoples call up animal guardian spirits in vision quests or dreams.

Deer

In the past, Indigenous peoples and early European settlers hunted deer for food in the Victoria area. Today, the deer population has adapted to humans and is thriving. In the last thirty years, there has been a population explosion, with attending problems. City-dwellers have differing views on the deer. Some are thrilled to see the deer in their yards and feel their presence more than compensates for the loss of a few plants. Others see the deer as a nuisance and call for a cull.

What does the deer symbolize? It is a potent symbol that can evoke strong emotions. Human reactions to deer go back thousands of years when early people depended upon deer for survival. The hunter's need to anticipate the actions of the deer led to rituals focused on becoming one with the deer. This may have been the purpose of a composite human-deer figure in a cave painting from 13,000 BCE, known as the *Sorcerer of Les Trois Frères*. Greek and Celtic mythology have many stories of shape-shifting between deer and humans. The Greek goddess of the hunt, Artemis, could take the form of a deer. Depictions of the Celtic god, Cernunnos, show him as a man with the antlers of a stag. The Irish goddess, Sadb, took the form of a doe.

Myths about humans transforming into deer can be found in many cultures. What is remarkable is that deer dances are still performed today. The Yaqui people of the southern U.S. and Mexico believe that the world's existence depends on their annual performance of Easter rituals which include the deer dance. The dancers wear a stag's head as a headdress and imitate the deer in their dance, suggesting its life and death at the hands of the hunter. The dance is performed to honour and thank the deer.

In Staffordshire, England, the Abbots Bromley horn dance takes place every September. The dance is performed by twelve performers who include six men carrying the antlers of reindeer. First performed in 1226, the tradition has continued for nearly 800 years.

Deer in Victoria

Old Pierre told Diamond Jenness a story about his Katzie people of Pitt Lake who drove deer into a deep gulch, killing a large number of them. Their sister watched them butcher the animals and then taste the heart of the deer. She changed herself into a deer and became the queen deer, restricting the slaughter of deer to a few and allowing a hunter to take a deer only if he prayed to her.

Several Coast Salish stories tell about a man who heard that the Transformer was coming to earth to punish evil-doers. The man decided that he would kill the Transformer. One day, as he was sharpening shells to use as arrow tips to kill Hayls, he met a man he recognized as a neighbour but who was in fact the Transformer.

When he explained that he was planning to kill the god, Hayls made him hand over the shells and then stuck them in the man's forehead where they became antlers. Hayls transformed the man into a deer, saying that in the future, people would hunt him.

In Chinese symbolism, the deer represents wealth and long life. As a Buddhist symbol, the deer represents harmony and peace. In Tibetan myths, the shy animals try to resolve conflicts, make them easy prey for hunters.

The modern myth-maker, J.K. Rowling, conjures up a deer in her Harry Potter novels as Harry's Patronus, or protector. A Patronus represents all the positive feelings within oneself. Harry's Patronus took the form of a silver stag, like that of his father. Again, there is a blending of deer and human.

Harry Potter's mother had a Patronus in the form of a doe. You only have to look at a doe with her fawns butting into her to feed to see the image of a good mother showing unconditional love. Many mythical heroes were raised by a doe. Sigurd, the hero in Norse mythology, was abandoned in a glass bottle which floated downstream where he was found by a doe and nursed. Telephos, Heracles' son, was exposed in the wilderness, then saved and nursed by a doe. The Irish hero and poet, Oisin, whose name means "fawn," was the son of the doe goddess, Sadb.

Finally, who could forget the stag, the name we use for a bachelor party? The stag is associated with puberty rites in many cultures. With the long history of interactions between humans and deer, it's no wonder that the sight of a deer stirs our emotions so deeply and leads to our differing reactions to the sight of a deer in our gardens.

Wolves

A sub-species of gray wolf, the Vancouver Island wolf, is unique to the island. The medium-sized wolves are often gray but can be so light-coloured that they appear to be white. Their main food source is black-tailed deer and Roosevelt Elk. They tend to avoid human contact, living on the northern part of Vancouver Island. Their population is estimated to be less than 150 animals.

The wolf is a strong spirit for the Coast Salish people and they believe it has strong supernatural powers. The Coast Salish people revered the wolf because it was a good hunter. The wolf guardian spirit helps men to become excellent hunters and women to become good mat-makers and weavers. Songhees elder James Fraser said that he had a wolf spirit that helped him hunt deer. Grave monuments often included carvings of wolves, perhaps indicating that the deceased warrior had a wolf spirit. Whale hunters would paint the image of a Lightning Snake with the head of a wolf on their canoes to bring summon the hunting power of the wolf.

The Songhees and Esquimalt peoples belong to the wolf clan. As wolves mate for life, live in packs and teach their young to hunt, the wolf came to symbolize family values. The image of the wolf as a symbol of Coast Salish people can be seen in public art throughout Victoria. The Unity Wall on the Ogden Point Breakwater depicts a stylized wolf, representing both the Esquimalt and Songhees nations as a symbol of family unity. A Spirit Pole carved by Butch Dick in Victoria's Spirit Square within Centennial Square incorporates a wolf. In the description of his art, Dick says, "Our observation of wolves gives us a sense of awe about their power, beauty and sense of family. Wolves live within a matriarchal system. This teaches that the voices of women are strong within our families."

In 2012, a wolf made the news when it came to frequent several islands off Oak Bay. The wolf was observed on Chatham Island and on Discovery Island on Songhees reserve lands. The Songhees First Nation named the animal, *Staqeya*, which means "wolf" in Lekwungen. Trevor Absolon, the Songhees bylaw enforcement officer, noted that many of the band members found it interesting that Songhees Chief Robert Sam passed away about the same time that the wolf appeared. Some First Nations people believe that wolves are the reincarnation of hunters who have passed on.

In many regions of the world, the wolf is feared and despised. In Norse mythology, it is destined that the monstrous wolf Fenrir will kill the god Odin at Ragnorok, the end of the world. European fairy tales like "Little Red Riding Hood" and "The Three Little Pigs" portray wolves as ravenous and evil beasts. Other cultures claim ancestry from wolves. The Indigenous people of Japan, the Ainu, believe that they were born from the union of a wolflike creature and a goddess. Romulus and Remus, the founders of Rome, were nursed by a maternal wolf.

The werewolf is a popular legend and illustrates the transformation of a human into an animal. Several Greek myths recount the fate of Lycaon, a king of Arcadia. In order to test the god Zeus, Lycaon served him a dish consisting of parts of a child. The enraged god turned Lycaon into a wolf. The birthplace of werewolf legends is Mount Lykaion in Arcadia, Greece. A sanctuary of Zeus Lykaios, or Wolf Zeus, was located on this mountain and archaeological evidence indicates that the ash altar was in use as long as 5,000 years ago. Pausanias, writing in the second century CE, noted that King Lycaon sacrificed an infant on this altar to Zeus and was transformed into a wolf. Pausinias went on to say that local legends told how initiates of Zeus Lykaios would turn into wolves for a period of nine years. If they did not eat human flesh during that time, they would regain their human forms. The message is clear— wolves eat human flesh, humans do not. During the Middle Ages in Europe, people believed in the existence of werewolves, reflecting the anxiety of the times.

Dogs

Residents of Victoria are enthusiastic about their dogs and can be seen walking them on the streets and off-leash areas. Over 150 years ago, the Songhees people kept little white dogs and used their inner hair for weaving capes and blankets. The dog breed, now extinct, was shown in paintings done in 1847 by artist Paul Kane.

So what can mythology reveal about this strong relationship between us and our dogs? The relationship goes back thousands of years to that unknown time when dogs were first domesticated.

The Penobscot tribe of Maine explained the close connection between human and dog in a creation tale. Just before humans appeared in the world, the hero called all the animals in the forest together to ask them what they would do when humans appeared. Only the dog offered to live with humans and share their poverty. The hero declared that from that time forward, all the other animals would fear not only humans but the dog as well. Since then, humans and dogs have shared a hunting partnership.

Ancient Egyptians worshipped Anubis, a god with the head of a black dog or jackal, as the guardian of the dead. Greek mythology also featured a dog as the guardian of the underworld—the three-headed hound Cerberus guarded the gates of Hades.

The brightest star in the sky is the "Dog Star", Sirius, located in the constellation, Canis Major, which represents the larger of Orion's hunting dogs. The term "dog days of summer" reflects the time when Sirius rose at the start of the heat of summer. Sirius Black was the name used by mistress of mythology, J. K. Rowling, for the character who could turn into a dog. Phantom black dogs are a common omen in British folklore.

The earliest domestic dog may have arisen in China. The chow chow is among the most ancient breeds. The Chinese associated the dog, as seen in the traits of people born in the Year of the Dog, with loyalty and honesty.

One touching tale of the faithfulness of a dog is that of Ulysses' dog, Argos. Argos was the first to recognize Ulysses when he returned home from the Trojan War after twenty years. Homer recounts how Argos was lying on a pile of manure, despondent until he laid eyes on his master again, gave a feeble wag of his tail and then with a whimper, died. In modern times, Greyfriars Bobby, the Skye terrier who sat at the grave of his police constable partner for fourteen years, exemplifies this faithfulness. Tourists still flock to Bobby's statue, Edinburgh's most sentimental tourist attraction.

Irish myths link the dog to healing, hunting and death. The greatest Irish hero, Cuchulainn (*Cu* meaning "hound"), acquired his name when he served a king as a guard dog to atone for killing the king's actual guard dog. King Arthur had a hunting dog named Cabal. Cabal's paw print was imprinted in a stone placed at the top of a pile of stones. Whenever people removed the stone, it always returned mysteriously to the original pile. The Celts believed in fairy dogs that were shaggy and dark green. In the nineteenth century, Scots referred to Shelties as "peerie" or fairy dogs.

Whether hunter, guardian, or just plain friend, dogs are definitely stars. As Will Rogers said, "No man can be condemned for owning a dog. As long as he has a dog, he has a friend; and the poorer he gets, the better friend he has."

Rabbits

Another animal that evokes controversy in the Victoria area is the rabbit. Vancouver Island has no native rabbits or hares. In 1964, Eastern Cottontails were introduced to Sooke. The only other species of rabbit found on Vancouver Island is the introduced European rabbit, ancestor of 80 varieties of domestic rabbit.

The rabbit population became a problem in the Victoria area. In the mid-1980s, pet rabbits were abandoned at the University of Victoria and over time, the campus became overrun with feral European rabbits. By 2010, the estimated rabbit population was 1,600. Despite public dispute, the university arranged for the removal of more than 900 rabbits from the campus to sanctuaries and in 2011, declared the campus to be free of rabbits.

In mythology, rabbits are often found as fertility figures, tricksters or cultural heroes. Many ancient peoples looked up at the moon and saw in its markings the image of a rabbit. Cultures as diverse as ancient China, Japan, Korea and Mexico have stories about a rabbit in the moon.

The Chinese worship Ch'ang-O as the goddess of the moon. Once Ch'ang-O and her husband, Houyi the archer, lost their immortality. Houyi obtained the pill of immortality from the Queen Mother of the West but Ch'ang-O took more than her half of the pill and floated up to the moon. There, her companions were the Jade Rabbit who continually pounds out the elixir of life and the woodcutter, Wu Gang, who continually chops down the tree on the moon that always grows back. When Apollo 11 made its first moon landing in 1969, Houston asked astronaut Mike Collins to watch for the beautiful Chang-O and the large rabbit. Collins replied, "Okay, we'll keep a close eye for the bunny girl."

Similar to the Chinese legend, Japanese and Korean myths include the rabbit on the moon that makes rice cakes.

Several stories talk about the rabbit sacrificing itself. A Buddhist legend tells how Lord Buddha was a hare in an early incarnation, traveling in the company of an ape and a fox. The god Indra, disguised as a hungry beggar, decided to test their hospitality. Each animal went in search of food, but only the hare returned empty-handed. Determined to be hospitable, the hare built a fire and jumped into it, feeding Indra with his own flesh. The god rewarded this sacrifice by transforming him into the Hare in the Moon. There is a similar story about the Mayan god Quetzacoatl.

In Greek mythology, hares were associated with Artemis, goddess of wild places and the hunt. Newborn hares were not to be killed but left to her protection. The historian Philostratus said the most suitable sacrifice to Aphrodite was the hare as it has her gift of fertility to a superlative degree.

Ostara, the Teutonic goddess of spring, brought the dawn and the spring of the year. Her name reflects the east where the sun rises at dawn. She was celebrated on the first full moon after the vernal equinox. Today, Easter is celebrated on the first Sunday after the first full moon after the vernal equinox. The English and German words for "Easter" are derived from Ostara. Her sacred symbols were the hare and the egg. The hare symbolized both fertility and the moon, as worshippers of Ostara saw the image of a hare in the full moon. The egg was another symbol of fertility, symbolizing the cosmic egg from which the world was created.

One myth tells of how Ostara saved a bird with frozen wings by turning it into a hare better suited for the severe weather. However, the hare still could lay eggs, like the original bird. And this story may have given rise to the Easter tradition of rabbits and eggs

Butterflies

In the late nineteenth century, millions of butterflies filled the air over Victoria. Naturalist George Taylor commented in 1884 on Victoria's extreme abundance of butterflies, noting nearly 40 species. Butterflies were once so numerous that, according Dr. James Fletcher writing in 1901, "Towards the end of the season, in August, the dead butterflies may be seen in vast numbers floating on the sea around Vancouver Island or thrown up along the beach in windrows sometimes an inch or two in depth."

Garry oak meadows provided excellent habitat for butterflies, but as the host plants disappeared, so did the butterflies. Now there are fewer butterflies and at least ten species are in jeopardy or extinct.

Butterflies have specific traits that led to the myths about them. One of their most striking features is their life cycle where they change from caterpillar to pupa to butterfly, a literal metamorphosis. They appear to have died and become mummies, and then they emerge in a totally new form with wings, ready to take to the skies. As this process captures the idea of death and rebirth, butterflies came to symbolize the soul in many cultures. As Thomas Bulfinch wrote in the *Age of Fable*, "There is no illustration of the immortality of the soul so striking and beautiful as the butterfly, bursting on brilliant wings from the tomb in which it has lain, after a dull, grovelling, caterpillar existence, to flutter in the blaze of day and feed on the most fragrant and delicate productions of the spring."

In Greek mythology, Psyche was the goddess of the soul and was depicted with the wings of a butterfly. The ancient Greek word for soul and for butterfly was the same—psyche. Ancient Greeks believed that human souls become butterflies while they looked for new reincarnations. Thantos, the god of death, was depicted often in Roman reliefs with a butterfly companion.

In Aztec mythology, butterflies were believed to be the souls of fallen warriors. Two goddesses were associated with butterflies. Itzpapalotl or Obsidian Butterfly was a ferocious war goddess with butterfly wings and claws. Her counterpart was a goddess of creativity, Xochiquetzal or Precious Flower, representing female sexuality, love and beauty. She was followed by butterflies and birds. Like a butterfly frequenting flowers for their nectar, Xochiquetzal was associated with flowers. However, the warlike Aztecs equated blood gushing from a wound with a flower blooming, which brings the symbolism back to the souls of dead warriors. Much of the mythology was aimed at showing warriors that if they lost their lives on the battlefield, they would be rewarded with a carefree life as butterflies living close to the great sun.

Did the observation that butterflies fly around flowers lead to the practice of bringing flowers to a funeral to attract the souls of the departed?

George Taylor described the beauty of Victoria's butterflies, resplendent in colours such as azure, sulphur and copper. The beauty of butterflies is captured in versions of the old Irish myth, "The Wooing of Étaín." Étaín was a legendary beauty. It was said that "every lovely form must be tested by Étaín, every beauty by the standard of Étaín." In the myth, Midir, the fairy king, fell in love with Étaín. His jealous wife turned her into a butterfly and sent a wind to carry her away. Étaín spent a series of seven years as a butterfly and then, one day, she fell into a glass of wine where she was swallowed by the wife of a chieftain who became pregnant. Étaín was reborn and went on to marry the high king of Ireland.

The Desert People or Tohono O'odham Nation (previously known as the Papago) of the Sonoran Desert in the American Southwest have a legend about the origin of butterflies. Elder

Brother was enjoying the beauty of the day, the joy of the children and the loveliness of the women when he realized it would all end one day. So he collected blue from the sky, white from cornmeal, yellow from the sun, black from women's hair and other colours from flowers, and put them in a bag. He asked the children to open the bag, and when they did, hundreds of butterflies flew out. The butterflies continue to brighten the days of people and bring joy and happiness.

In China, butterflies are a symbol of love. The legend of Han Ping and his wife, dating from the fourth century, recounts the tale of faithful love. The couple was separated when the king took the wife as his concubine. Han Ping was made a convict and died. His wife committed suicide, by jumping from a high terrace. She took care to ensure that her clothes would tear easily to prevent the servants from grabbing her as she fell. The torn pieces of her clothes became butterflies. Later, the popular legend of the Butterfly Lovers presented the story of Liang Shanbo and the beautiful Zhu Yingtai. When Liang learned that Zhu was betrothed to another, he died heartbroken. On the day of her wedding, Zhu threw herself into Liang's grave and they emerged as a pair of butterflies, together for eternity. Two butterflies flying together became a symbol of devoted love. A jade butterfly pendant is a popular piece of jewelry to represent undying love.

Butterflies are seen as omens of both doom and good luck. In medieval times, swarms of butterflies were considered bad omens, predicting war and epidemics. In some areas, a white butterfly indicates death. In other areas, butterflies might predict a coming marriage or a return to good health. Some people believe that if the first butterfly of the season is white, good luck will follow.

Today, attracting butterflies is seen as bringing good luck because butterflies pollinate plants and control pests. Cities such as Victoria encourage citizens to plant butterfly gardens with nectar plants to support a variety of butterflies. A Native American legend suggests that if you whisper a wish to a butterfly, it will carry that wish upwards to the heavens where it will be granted. A whisper to a butterfly as a wish for more butterflies would bring good fortune.

Salmon

Many cultures believe that salmon are sacred. For centuries, the Coast Salish peoples depended upon salmon as a major food source. They revered the salmon, referring to the fish as "elder brother." They believed that salmon were immortal human beings who lived in houses in the ocean. Every year, the salmon king would order the people to put on fish skins and offer themselves as food to the humans. To honor this gift, the people treated the salmon with reverence. They held First Salmon Ceremonies to welcome the salmon as they returned to the streams. The ceremony required appropriate rituals to show respect for the sacrifice of the salmon. Singing the salmon was a related ceremony in which local Salish women would go to the mouths of streams in late summer and sing the salmon back to their spawning grounds.

On southern Vancouver Island, the Straits Salish people used a unique fishing method, the reefnet, to capture the salmon as they migrated along the coast to the larger rivers on the mainland. The method involved anchoring the reefnet to the ocean floor and suspending it between two canoes. The men from the old Lekwungen village at Cadboro Bay would paddle to San Juan Island to fish for salmon from July to September. Fishing was linked to the spiritual world. The salmon people taught the humans to make the fishing nets, including how to weave at hole in the net to allow the salmon who did not wish to sacrifice themselves to swim out. Ceremonies were performed before and after fishing, first to welcome the salmon and then to thank them. Ritual words were spoken during the actual netting operation.

A critical component of the respect shown to the salmon people was that salmon skeletons must be returned to the water so the salmon could reconstitute themselves and return to their ocean houses, continuing the cycle of life. Anyone who has seen the salmon fighting up Goldstream Creek to spawn in the fall can see how salmon became linked to sacrifice and renewal. The death of the salmon provides nutrients for the creek ecosystem which, in turn, supports the salmon fry when they emerge the gravel.

Historically, salmon were plentiful in the Greater Victoria area. Reports from over 150 years ago describe the abundance of salmon in Victoria harbour, the Gorge and local streams such as Colquitz and Bowker Creeks. But factors such as pollution, habitat loss and overfishing have contributed to drastic declines in salmon populations. First Nations legends attribute shortages of salmon to human disrespect and refusal to live by the wisdom of the elders. Several communities are again performing the First Salmon Ceremonies to show respect to the salmon people.

Some Indigenous myths tell about people who were kidnapped by salmon and taken to their underwater villages. Eventually, they returned home with the sacred knowledge that enabled them to become great shaman. The idea that salmon can impart wisdom is repeated in Celtic mythology. A tale about the hero Fionn related how a salmon ate nine hazelnuts that had fallen into the well of knowledge and so became wise. The salmon was caught and Fionn was given the job of cooking it. When a drop of oil from the fish burned his thumb, he put it in his mouth to cool it and acquired the wisdom of the salmon. He could access all the knowledge of the world whenever he bit his thumb.

Salmon are very important on the West Coast, representing the energy of transformation. Hopefully, this awareness will lead to a change in our actions towards the salmon people and an appeased salmon king will once again offer his people as a gift in abundance.

CHAPTER 10
Questing for the Beast

The waters off Victoria support a wide variety of marine life, including fish, invertebrates and sea mammals such as seals and whales. The sea is a mysterious element, deep and vast, and its denizens have been feared as monsters or respected as a type of ocean-dwelling human. Herman Melville captured the mystery of the sea in his classic 1851 novel, *Moby-Dick*, writing,

> *Consider the subtleness of the sea; how its most dreaded creatures glide under water, unapparent for the most part, and treacherously hidden beneath the loveliest tints of azure..... Consider all this; and then turn to this green, gentle, and most docile earth; consider them both, the sea and the land; and do you not find a strange analogy to something in yourself?*

In mythology, monsters symbolize our greatest fears. They are dangerous and destructive, representing a violation of the natural order. Some of the earliest myths, such as the Sumerian myth of Tiamat, describe heroic battles with sea monsters. A Greek myth, illustrated in pottery from the sixth century BCE and included in accounts by early writers, tells about the sea monster summoned by Poseidon. When the Trojans refused to pay Poseidon for building the walls of Troy, the god sent a sea monster to punish them. King Laomedon of Troy, following the advice in an oracle, offered his daughter, Hesione, as a sacrifice to get rid of the monster. Hesione was chained to the rocks. But as the monster approached, the hero Heracles appeared, killed the beast and rescued the maiden.

Whales

Whale watching is a very popular activity off Victoria. Residents and visitors alike are excited to see orcas, gray whales, humpback whales and Dall's porpoises.

Whales, dolphins and porpoises are classified as Cetaceans. The name is based on Cetus, a monster from Greek mythology that was defeated by the hero Perseus. In the myth, Perseus rescued the maiden, Andromeda, chained to a rock as a sacrifice to Cetus. In *Moby-Dick*, Melville referred to Perseus as the first whaleman, recalling the mythic theme of a noble hero defeating a monster to rescue a maiden. In Western civilization, whales were often seen as monsters of the deep. Therefore, battling the beasts was considered to be a noble occupation.

Orcas, or killer whales, are not actually whales, but the largest species of dolphin in the world. Killer whales often travel in maternal family groups or pods. Three pods of about 100 animals form the resident orca population in the waters off Victoria. As well, transient killer whales, animals that eat only marine mammals and birds, frequent the waters.

The genus name of the orca, *Orcinus*, means "belonging to Orcus," the Roman god of the underworld and the punisher of broken oaths. The association of Orcus with death and the underworld led to the name being used for demons and other underworld monsters. Pliny the Elder, writing in 70 CE, described orcas as "an enormous mass of flesh armed with savage teeth."

For Indigenous peoples of the west coast, the orca was a powerful mythological figure. They believed that orcas lived in villages under the ocean where they would remove their black and white skins and live like people. The orca is a popular design in Northwest art.

Many Aboriginal people consider orcas to be the reincarnations of great chiefs. When a great chief died, an orca would come close to shore to take the chief's spirit. The belief is carried through to the present day. When Luna, a young killer whale, became separated from his pod and moved to Nootka Sound, the Mowachaht/Muchalaht First Nations considered Luna to be a reincarnation of the tribe's late Chief, Ambrose Maquinna, who had died in July 2001. They said that because Maquinna had declared that after his death he wished to return as an orca or a wolf, the appearance of Luna a few days after his passing was symbolic and likely was his reincarnation.

Indigenous people observed that killer whales often hunted in pods similar to wolf packs and their myths characterize killer whales as sea wolves. The image of the killer whale on the Unity Wall mural on Victoria's breakwater shows the whale transforming into the sea wolf. It was said that a pod or pack of sea wolves travelled in many directions, establishing villages along their way.

The Thunderbird would hunt and eat orcas, killing them with the two lightning snakes he kept under his wings. Lightning snakes have the heads of wolves and are revered for their great hunting capability. These lightning snakes were often painted on the sides of canoes and then covered up by another coat of paint. The power emitted from these snakes would help the native whalers in their hunt.

Many Coast Salish stories illustrate the mythical enmity between the Thunderbird and the orca. A legend from the Cowichan tribes explains that the people depended upon salmon for food. One day, the orca swam into the bay, frightening the salmon away. Soon the people began to starve. They called upon the Thunderbird for help. The Thunderbird swooped down, grabbed the orca and carried him out to the sea. The salmon returned and the people were no longer hungry. Thus, the Thunderbird was known as a protector of the people and deeply revered.

Sea Monsters

There have been reports of sea monsters off the coast of Vancouver Island for hundreds of years. An even longer time period is suggested by the references to sea serpents in Indigenous myths and depictions in petroglyphs. For example, the mythic *sisiutl* is frequently depicted as a double-headed sea serpent with human head and hands in the middle of the body. The *Hiyitl'iik* was a sea serpent reported in native folklore in Clayquot Sound and described as wriggling from side to side.

Pauline Johnson included a story about a sea serpent in the legends told to her by Chief Joe Capilano of the Squamish Nation. It was a story with a moral. During the gold rush, a young man, Shak Shak or "hawk" by name and by nature, became consumed with greed and avarice. To punish him, the Sagalie Tyee turned him into a loathsome two-headed sea serpent, the Salt Chuk Oluk. The gigantic monster rested one head on a point of land and the other on a group of rocks by Mission, B.C., blocking entrances to the waters. A boy named Tenas Tyee or Little Chief jumped into the sea and hunted for the serpent for four years. He found the heart of the monster and stabbed it with his hunting knife. His generosity and cleanness proved strong enough to kill the disease of greed for all his people.

A local sea serpent achieved international fame in 1933. On October 1, 1933, Major and Mrs. Langley were sailing near Discovery Island when they saw a fast-moving, greenish-gray creature with a big coil in front. The *Victoria Daily Times* called the Langleys that very evening and published an article on October 5, 1933 with the headline "Yachtsmen Tell of Huge Sea Serpent off Victoria." In addition to the sighting by the Langleys, the article included a reference to Fred Kemp, who, with his wife and son, saw a similar creature near Chatham Island the previous year on August 10, 1932. The witnesses were credible. Major Langley was a barrister and clerk of the B.C. Legislative Assembly and Mr. Kemp was an employee of the Provincial Archives.

The news excited widespread interest and put Victoria in the public eye. Reports of Nessie, the Loch Ness Monster, had dominated headlines earlier in the year so it was known that such sightings were good media topics. The *Victoria Daily Times* received so many reports about sightings of the sea serpent that the editor of the paper, Archie Wills, called for suggestions for names. He selected the name Cadborosaurus in reference to a sighting in Cadboro Bay. According to the *Vancouver Sun* newspaper, the whole continent was intrigued by Caddy's capers. The coverage was a welcome diversion from the economic depression. Not to be outdone, the *Victoria Colonist* suggested the name Amy for the sea serpent, but Caddy it remained. Caddy even acquired a mate, Penda, first seen off Pender Island on December 3, 1933 by Cyril Andrews and Norman Georgeson. Penda swallowed a duck and then snapped at the sea gulls swooping at her. Because the animal lacked serrations on its back, it was suggested that it was a female.

The monster was also referred to as Hiaschuckaluck Cadborosaurus. A Pennsylvania newspaper reported in 1934 that Caddy and Amy Hiaschuckaluck Cadborosaurus had a youngster when eyewitnesses from Jordan River reported a twenty-five-foot long sea serpent they called Jorda.

Archie Wills recognized the publicity value of Caddy and featured him in the *Victoria Daily Times* often. He was frustrated with those who doubted the existence of Caddy, writing,

> *Your modern man would rather disbelieve something than believe it. He likes to think he is cynical and hard-boiled, whereas he is the most credulous creature ever made. When he can't understand a thing, like astronomy, or relativity, or finance, he believes anything you care to tell him, if you tell him with sufficient scientific or financial trimmings. But the trouble is he can understand a sea serpent. He can visualize it. Therefore, he disbelieves it. His disbelief flatters his vanity, makes him think he is a superior fellow. Well, it doesn't make him a superior fellow. Any fool can disbelieve in sea serpents...*

Caddy has been seen from Alaska to California, with the most sightings in the Juan de Fuca Strait and the Strait of Georgia during the colder months, October to April. Witnesses have reported seeing sea monsters off Cadboro Bay, Cordova Bay, Willows Beach, Trial Island, Oak Bay, Clover Point, Victoria, Ogden Point Breakwater, Saxe Point, Saanich Inlet and many other locations in the Salish Sea.

According to witnesses, the animal resembles an enormous serpent with a long neck, a horse-like head on an elongated neck, and often a pair of flippers. It is thirty or forty feet long and its coils or humps, possibly serrated, break the water as it swims and dives at speed.

In their book, *Cadborosaurus: Survivor from the Deep*, Drs. Paul H. Leblond and Edward L. Bousfield reported 182 sightings between 1881 and 1994. The scientists have gone as far as proposing that the sea serpent be identified as a reptile called *Cadborosaurus willsi* (in honour of Archie Wills) and classified as a new genus and a new species.

Is Caddy a myth or an actual animal? Only eye witness accounts suggest that Cadborosaurus truly exists. There are no existing specimens or carcasses to provide hard evidence of a sea serpent. One of the most promising was a carcass of an unusual creature which was found in July 1937 in the stomach of a sperm whale caught near the Naden Harbour whaling station in the Queen Charlotte Islands (now Haida Gwaii). Francis Kermode, director of the provincial museum, identified the carcass as a premature baleen whale but no specimens were preserved to allow for verification of this. Other carcasses have been identified a sharks, whales or seals, such as the carcass found on Kitsilano Beach in March 1941 named Sarah the Sea Hag which was identified as a shark.

There have been hoaxes using sea serpent models and contrived stories about sightings of Caddy over the years. It has been suggested that sightings of Caddy are actually lines of seals, floating logs, beds of kelp, a series of breaking waves, basking sharks or baleen whales.

A 100-foot long concrete Cadborosaurus can be seen in Cadboro Bay's Gyro Park. In the 1960s, concrete structures of Caddy, an octopus, a whale and a boat were built for children's play.

However, the desire to believe in sea monsters is enduring. Sea serpents suggest a world that is beyond the limits of our science, a world of imagination and dreams. An Editorial in the *Victoria Daily Times* in May 1963 stated, "There is a Caddy because there ought to be one—and that is proof enough for anyone."

Rather than being terrified, people are intrigued by Caddy. When Mrs. Langley was interviewed by the CBC in 1956, she said, "I wasn't afraid, just interested. It took my fancy that it wasn't anything we'd seen before. Absolutely it was real, something neither of us had ever seen before."

In 1933, the *Daily Colonist* offered a $20 prize for a photograph of Caddy and in 1951, the *Victoria Daily Times* offered $200. And rewards for proof of the existence of the Cadborosaurus continue to be offered. In 2003, Oak Bay Tourism offered $10,000 and launched Oak Bay's first annual Cadborosaurus sighting season between May and September.

In *The Log from the Sea of Cortez*, John Steinbeck mused about a sea serpent known as the Old Man of the Sea, noting, that the monster "might well be a myth except that too many people have seen him. There is some quality in man which makes him people the ocean with monsters and one wonders whether they are there or not. In one sense they are, for we continue to see them." One day, a decaying carcass washed up on a beach near Monterey, California and an expert advised that the carcass was a basking shark. According to Steinbeck, this identification was

> *a blow to the people of Monterey. They so wanted it to be sea-serpent....When sometimes a true sea-serpent, complete and undecayed, is found or caught, a shout of triumph will go through the world. "There you see," men will say, "I knew they were there all the time. I just had the feeling that they were there." Men really need sea-monsters in their personal oceans. And the Old Man of the Sea is one of these.... if the Old Man of the Sea should turn out to be some great malformed sea-lion, a lot of people would feel a sharp personal loss—a Santa Claus loss... An ocean without its unnamed monsters would be like a completely dreamless sleep.*

Steinbeck went on to suggest that we have a sea memory deep in the mind, buried in the unconscious and the sea serpent is a symbol of that unconscious.

Sightings of the Cadborosaurus continue. In 2011, the Discovery Channel aired a video taken by salmon fisherman Kelly Nash of a 20 to 30-foot long animal with humps, a possible *Cadborosaurus willsi* swimming in an Alaskan bay.

The Thetis Lake Monster

Another monster seen in the Victoria area was the Thetis Lake Monster. On August 19, 1972, two teenage boys were chased from the beach at Thetis Lake by a silver monster. Gordon Pike, age 16, and Robin Flewellyn, age 17, described the monster as triangular in shape, nearly five feet high and five feet across the base. The creature slashed Flewellyn's hand with the six sharp points on its head. The boys went to the Royal Canadian Mounted Police who launched a brief investigation. A few days later, Mike Gold, age 14, and Russell Van Nice, age 12, claimed to have seen the same creature, with a human body, a monster face and scales. The local paper noted in August of 1972 that the Thetis Lake Monster had poor timing in its challenge of the Cadborosaurus as it was during a provincial election when monsters were not news.

One theory was that the monster was an escaped lizard. The *Province* newspaper received a call on August 26, 1972 from a man claiming to have lost a pet Tegu lizard in the area the previous year. These lizards, indigenous to Latin America and mostly carnivorous, can grow up to four feet in length. But it is thought to have been unlikely that the tropical lizard could have survived the winter in the lake.

The Kwakwaka'wakw tribes of the central coast of British Columbia have a spirit that resembles the Thetis Lake monster. Masks of the *Pugwis*, or "Wild Man of the Undersea World", feature a fish-faced creature with two large teeth. Often he is shown with a loon or a sea urchin on his head. He is also referred to as an undersea serpent and a merman.

A similar monster found fame in the 1954 movie, *Creature from the Black Lagoon*. Another theory about the Thetis Lake Monster is that the reports were inspired by the 1965 film, *Beach Girls and the Monster*, featuring a slashing gill-man, which aired on the local TV station the week before the sighting.

In 2009, Van Nice admitted that the claim was a big lie for attention. However, people are still interested in tracking down the truth of the original sighting.

Seals and Sea Lions

Harbour seals and Steller and California sea lions are common sites on the Victoria waterfront. The heads of curious seals bobbing out of the water sometimes look like humans. In Scottish folklore, selkies are seals that shed their skins to become human. Many stories tell about a man hiding the skin of a female selkie so that she would be forced to remain on land and would marry him. But she would always yearn for the sea. If she found her seal skin, she would put it on, and slip back to her ocean home forever.

Coast Salish people envisioned seals as mermaids. A harbour seal is depicted on the Unity Wall on Victoria's breakwater with accompanying text noting that the harbour seal was also known as the mermaid due to its visible arms and legs. In one story, the seal was transformed from human to fish and Kaals the Creator tied the feet together to make a fish.

The Vancouver Island Mermaid

Active Pass, June, 1967: Passengers on the B.C. Ferry, the *Queen of Saanich*, see a long-haired blonde with the tail of a fish or porpoise, sitting on a rock and eating a silvery salmon. The *Daily Colonist* reported the sighting and noted that at least two pictures were taken of the "dimpled blonde," one by a tourist on the ferry and one by a local man who flew overhead in an airplane. It was observed that the mermaid was topless. The Underseas Garden offered a reward of $25,000 for the mermaid. The mermaid herself was offered a contract that included a special comb that mermaids use.

Southern British Columbia is one of the places in the world where mermaids have been reported. Why here and then? Well, it was 1967, the time of the summer of love and drugs. But mermaids reflect the fact that we live on an island, with water vistas in every direction. The sea plays a major role in our lives and our consciousness.

Tales of mermaids date back to Neolithic times when people were farmers or fishermen. For example, mermaid folklore was common in the oral traditions of the Orkney Islands, handed down through the common people since prehistoric times. In these stories, mermaids are lovely creatures who lure human men with their songs and beauty. They wish to marry humans because if they marry their own kind they become progressively uglier every seven years. One legend explains that the mermaid was changed from her perfect and naked human form to a creature with a tail because the queen and all the women in the land were jealous of the mermaid's beauty. However, the men of the land added a proviso that the mermaid could regain her original form if a human man fell in love with her. Orkney is another location where mermaid sightings have been reported. Hundreds of people saw the Deerness Mermaid over two or three summers in the 1890s.

One of the earliest mermaids was the Syrian goddess, Atargatis, known as Derketo to the Greeks. She was depicted on coins as a goddess with a fish tail. Fish were sacred to her, and her worshippers abstained from eating fish. In a Greek account from the fifth century BCE, she was said to have fallen in love with a shepherd and after having a baby, drowned herself. As a goddess, she could not die but took the form of a fish with a human head. Atargatis also had a role as protector of specific cities. Depicted with a headdress of two fish, she was associated with the constellation of Pisces which is also represented by two fish. As her worship spread to Greece, she became identified with Aphrodite, goddess of love born from the sea foam. With this connection, the mermaid gained the reputation for beauty and attractiveness. European fairy tales repeat the theme of how a mermaid would give up her soul for love. "The Little Mermaid" by Hans Christian Andersen is one of the many such tales of a mermaid seeking the love of a mortal man.

Pliny the Elder, a Roman author and naturalist in the first century CE, described Nereids or sea nymphs, noting that the part of their body that resembles humans is still rough all over with scales. He noted that reports from Gaul mentioned several Nereids found dead on the shore.

Many cultures viewed the mermaid as an omen of death. It was common for fishermen to be lost at sea, and mermaid myths provided an explanation of their fate. The men had gone to join beautiful and enchanting mermaids in fabulous underwater kingdoms. The myths also gave shape to the world beneath the sea as coastal dwellers gazed at its beautiful, but impenetrable, surface.

Just as the sea both feeds humans and kills them, mythology illustrates the dual nature of the mermaid that endures today. In Greek myth, she appears as both the fatal seductress who lures sailors to their doom and the benevolent protectress, the Nereid.

A June 27, 1863 article in the *New Westminster Columbian*, titled "A Mermaid in The Gulf," reported on a sighting by a Mr. Graham in the Gulf of Georgia. "It was about 6 o'clock p.m., when he saw it gradually rise above the surface of the water within about 30 yards of where he was, showing the entire bust, in which position it remained for the space of five minutes looking in the direction of the boat in which he and two Indians were sitting, when it slowly sank into its native element." The creature was described as a female with long yellow-brown hair drooping over its shoulders and dark olive skin. The natives with Mr. Graham were alarmed at the sight. According to native legend, if the creature was seen and not killed, those who saw it would pine and die.

In the early twentieth century, human female swimmers were often referred to as mermaids. Champion swimmer, Audrey Griffin, was called "B.C.'s Mermaid Marvel" in the *Victoria Daily Times*. Griffin won the "Annual Through-Victoria" swimming competition nine of the twelve times she entered between 1915 and 1929. The three-mile swim from the Empress Hotel up the Gorge Waterway to the Gorge Bridge attracted over 10,000 spectators. When Griffin attempted to swim across the Gorge while tethered to a rod and reel, the line broke before she finished, supporting the old myth that it is difficult to catch a mermaid. Later, Florence Chadwick was deemed a "world famous" mermaid. In 1954, she attempted to swim across the Juan Fuca de Strait. She was swept into an arc and ended up only seven miles from where she left from Beacon Hill Park. References to women swimmers as mermaids may have been popularized by the 1911 movie, *The Mermaid*, about the Australian champion swimmer, Annette Kellerman.

Mermaid sightings are good for tourism. Tourism Victoria's website reported the 1967 sighting of the mermaid on its myths and legends page. The mermaid theme is evident in marketing. For example, Sooke Harbour House has a mermaid-themed room. Nautical Nellie's, a restaurant on Wharf Street, derived its name from a mermaid. According to a delightful story by "Old Dan Ryan," a mermaid arrived in Victoria harbour on the back of a sea serpent in January of 1997. Nellie, the mermaid with "enticing beauty and dazzling charms," decided to call Victoria home. She gave the restaurateurs secret recipes from her travels on the seven seas. On moonlit nights, one might see Nellie and her sea serpent, Thor, frolicking in Cadboro Bay with the other sea serpents.

Many coastal areas feature mermaids. Up the B.C. coast in Saltery Bay Provincial Park, a popular attraction for divers is the *Emerald Princess*, a three-metre tall bronze mermaid who lures divers to the depths of Mermaid's Cove. The bronze statue was in sunk in twenty metres of water in 1989 to raise British Columbia's profile as a top diving location. Divers visit the mermaid in the emerald waters and follow the tradition of kissing the *Emerald Princess* before they return to the surface.

Even landlocked areas such as Alberta find tourism value in mermaid lore. The town of Sylvan Lake has long featured a mermaid theme with its annual "Mermaid Ball" to honour outstanding citizens. In 2000, the town received federal funding to create a bronze, eight-foot tall statue of a mermaid and child sitting on top of a fountain.

In 2009, the Israeli town of Kiryat Yam offered a prize of $1 million for a photograph of a mermaid that had been seen on its shores. The reward attracted a lot of interest worldwide, with several reports in the news media. The Mermaid Medical Association of Brooklyn, New York even threatened to sue the town because the offer "badly and outrageously damages the legendary mermaid legacy." The mayor of Kiryat Yam pointed out the tourism value of the mermaid would exceed the $1 million prize. Clearly, people want to believe in mermaids.

Starbucks features a mermaid on its logo, linking its coffee to the irresistible song of the siren. The original image of the twin-tailed siren, used from 1971 to 1987, was based on a sixteenth century woodcut. Over the years, the image was streamlined to hide the mermaid's bare breasts and navel. Starbucks is named for Captain Ahab's first mate in the novel, *Moby-Dick* and the logo continues the theme of sea.

Scientists seek explanations for the many sightings of mermaids. Some say mermaid sightings were actually sightings of manatees in the Caribbean and walruses in the north. Christopher Columbus saw three mermaids off the coast of Haiti in 1493. His comment that the mermaids were not as pretty as expected led to the suggestion that he had actually seen manatees. It is more difficult to believe that sailors with Henry Hudson saw marine mammals near Norway in 1608 as they described the creature as a white-skinned, black-haired woman with the tail of a porpoise.

Mermaids serve as a powerful source of inspiration for artists, poets and playwrights. One of the most famous paintings of a mermaid is by John William Waterhouse and shows a beautiful mermaid combing her long red hair. Edvard Munch painted a mermaid transforming into a human. In a *Midsummer's Night Dream*, Shakespeare described how the dulcet song of a mermaid calmed a rude sea, "and certain stars shot madly from their spheres to hear the sea-maid's music." William Butler Yeats' poem describes how a mermaid found a swimming lad and plunged down, drowning him. Author Anaïs Nin suggested that she must be a mermaid as she had "no fear of depths and a great fear of shallow living."

Today, mermaids represent more our fascination for the sea, rather than our fear. Mermaids, who can move between sea and land, represent the links between humans and the sea, expressing our feelings about the sea. This is why divers kiss the lips of the *Emerald Princess* before returning to land.

CHAPTER 11
Finding the Forbidden City

Movies often show Chinatowns as exotic and mysterious places. Victoria's Chinatown has an intriguing history, with gambling dens, opium factories and brothels. The historic area is rich with symbols, rituals and immortals from Chinese legends.

Victoria's Chinatown is the oldest in Canada and second oldest in North America after San Francisco. The first Chinese immigrants arrived in Victoria in the summer of 1858 from California, and then from China, after the discovery of gold in the Fraser Valley. They set up tents and shacks along a ravine where Johnson Street currently runs. By 1886, Chinatown had grown to over four city blocks, including the present day site of Centennial Square which had been purchased by wealthy Chinese merchants.

Old Chinatown has been referred as a "Forbidden City," exclusive for Chinese people and a reminder of the separation between them and the European settlers. Modelled after villages in China, Chinatown was a confusing labyrinth of courtyards, alleys and linking passages. Fan Tan Alley, in particular, was famous for gambling dens where games such as Fan Tan were played. The alley is the narrowest street in Canada. Although opium production was legal, gambling was not. Features such as locked gates helped to slow down police raids on the gambling dens.

Many of Victoria's Chinese businesses became prosperous in the 1880s not only by supplying labor and goods to gold miners, but by trading in opium as well. Opium sellers required a licence and brought revenues to the government. Between 1860 and 1908, Victoria was the largest opium refining center outside of Asia. By 1888, there were 13 opium factories producing nearly 90,000 lbs of opium a year. The opium trade was prohibited in 1908.

Opium is a mythical elixir in its medical use for pain relief, its ability to inspire creativity through the dreams it brings and its addictive effects. In ancient Sumeria, it was known as the "joy plant." Egyptian myths referred to Isis giving opium to the god Ra. A Minoan goddess wearing a crown of three opium poppies was discovered on Crete. The poem, "Kubla Khan," is believed to have been composed by Samuel Taylor Coleridge under the influence of opium and the poem reflects that experience.

The Chinese immigrants brought the legends, religions and rituals from their homeland in China. But there was often no harmony in the various beliefs. In 1909, a fight broke out between the merchants of Chinatown and the labourers over the four Daoist temples called "joss houses" in the town. The merchants wanted to close down the temples as they were relics of the old superstition, out of keeping with the new China. The labourers countered that the temples represented the religion of their fathers. The merchants proposed a vote on the abolition of the temples and set up ballot boxes in the new Chinese school. But before the vote could be taken, an angry mob of 300 labourers stormed the school and smashed the ballot boxes, saying that they had paid for the upkeep of the temples and they would never consent to the gods being cast out. The gods stayed.

The oldest Chinese temple in Canada is located in Victoria, the Tam Kung Temple. Tam Kung was believed to have been a historical figure born in Guangdong Province during the Yuan dynasty (1206–1368). When he was only 12 years of age, he had the ability to cure patients. He was executed in 1279 by the Mongols after he had helped the Emperor escape from the invaders. Later, he was deified.

In Victoria, the statue of Tam Kung was first set up in a roadside shrine in the Johnson Street ravine. One day, a man named Ngai Tse had a dream in which Tam Kung asked him to build a temple. Accordingly, a shrine to Tam Kung was built at Government and Fisgard Street in 1877. When the Hakka people in Victoria formed the Yen Wo Society in 1911, the Society built the Tam Kung temple on the top floor of their brick building at 1713 Government Street.

Today, visitors may climb the 52 stairs to the temple. It is an astounding place, with rich red silk banners on the walls, gold calligraphy, antique censers and other altar pieces and offerings of fruit and flowers, all under a translucent dome. A red bell stand contains a cast iron bell, dated 1887, with a drum on its top. The bell and drum are struck twice a day to seek the attention of Tam Kung. Worshippers light incense or joss sticks and divine their fortunes by choosing one of many numbered yarrow sticks. Each number corresponds to a fortune in the multi-drawer cabinet in the temple. Tam Kung is invoked for safety at sea and for his powers of divination. Devotees present offerings and gifts in gratitude to Tam Kung. His statue has a youthful face, suggesting the legend that the god had joined at the immortals at the young age of twelve. He discovered the secret of youth and is viewed as an 80-year-old man with the face of a 12-year-old boy. The window of the temple's enclosed balcony looks out over the Gate of Harmonious Interest.

Tam Kung Statue

Palace of the Sages

Inside the Chinese Public School on Fisgard Street is the shrine of the Palace of Sages (Lid Shing Kung). The temple housed images of five deities: Tian Hou, the Queen of Heaven; Guan Yu, the God of Righteousness; Hua Tuo, the God of Medicine; and Zhao

Gongming, the Martial God of Wealth. The great Chinese philosopher, Confucius (551–479 BCE), is represented by a modern statuette. Most of the Chinese gods were once human. They were martyred and then deified as examples of righteous living.

Tian Hou, the Queen of Heaven, is a sea goddess. Commonly known as Mazu, she was born as Lin Moniang on March 23, 960 in Fujian. According to legend, she went into a trance and saved the lives of her brothers who were drowning off at sea. In one version of her death, it was said that she drowned at the age of 16 after swimming far into the ocean trying to find her father who had been lost at sea. After her death, the families of many fishermen and sailors began to pray to Mazu in honour of her acts of courage in trying to save those at sea. In some stories, she wears red clothes while standing on the shore to guide fishing boats home, even in storms.

Guan Yu was a historical general at the time of the Three Kingdoms in the third century CE. A historical novel, *Romance of the Three Kingdoms*, written by Luo Guanzhong in the fourteenth century, popularized the legends of the people and events from this period, and stories based on the novel remain popular to this day. The historical Guan Yu was executed about 219, and it was reported when his severed head was sent to warlord, Cao Cao, it spoke. He was deified in the Sui dynasty (581–618), and is still worshipped today. Epitomizing loyalty and righteousness, Emperor Guan is portrayed as a red-faced warrior with a long beard.

Hua Tuo was a Chinese physician during the Three Kingdoms. He was famous for his abilities in surgery, anesthesia, acupuncture and herbal remedies. He was executed by warlord Cao Cao about 208.

Zhao Gongming is a Daoist spirit of wealth. Like Guan Yu, he is portrayed as a warrior with a thick, black beard. Marshal Zhao is believed to have died in battle and subsequently, was deified. He carries an iron rod for a weapon and often rides a black tiger. He is the Martial God of Wealth and commands four other gods of wealth, suggesting that there are five ways to seek wealth.

The altar and shrine in the Palace of the Sages were created in South China and brought to Victoria in 1885. Pewter censers on the altar are dated 1885 and stamped with the name *leishenggong* or "Multi-Deity Temple." Originally, the shrine was located in the Chinese Consolidated Benevolent Association (CCBA) building at 554–562 Fisgard Street. Richly furnished with costly carvings, the temple was wealthy. The CCBA erected the temple as a source of income and the management of the temple brought in an annual income of over $1,000. In 1996, the shrine was moved to the Chinese Public School and re-dedicated. The shrine is no longer an object of worship but represents local heritage.

On January 23, 1876, the *Daily British Colonist* described the dedication of a Chinese temple on Government Street. According to the paper, two gods and a goddess were set up in the new establishment. The central figure wore a crown, had a black beard and his face was covered in red ochre. Possibly he was Guan Yu, the military general. The crowned figure on the left represented a pretty woman and might have been Tian Hou, the Queen of Heaven. It is not clear who the figure on the right, a man with a grey beard and moustache, represented.

The Gate of Harmonious Interest

The entrance to Victoria's Chinatown is marked by the Gate of Harmonious Interest, constructed in 1981 to symbolize the cooperation between the Chinese and non-Chinese people of Victoria in building the city. In ancient China, such gates were not merely decorative but had symbolic features to offer protection and confuse evil spirits.

The Gate of Harmonious Interest

The Gate of Harmonious Interest displays many symbols illustrating the concept of "unity in duality." Harmony is important in Chinese thought and is conceptualized by the principle of yin and yang, the opposite and complementary extremes of nature. Yin represents the masculine, day, sun and fire whereas yin represents the feminine, night, moon and water.

The Yin-Yang principle is captured on the Gate by the male symbol of blue dragons, depicted on long panels, balanced by similar panels illustrating the female symbol of green phoenixes. The colour blue recalls the sky and green, the earth. The dragon is a symbol of power, strength and good luck, and the phoenix indicates virtue and peace.

The Yin-Yang duality is also illustrated in the guardian stone lions placed at the foot of the gate. A gift from Victoria's sister city of Suzhou, the lion is seen as the protector of dharma in Buddhism. The male lion on the north holds a ball in his forepaws while the female lion to the south nurses her cub, symbolizing the cycle of life. The placement of the lions is important to achieve their beneficial aspects, with the male on the left when looking out of the structure and the female on the right.

The dragon is a powerful symbol in many cultures, including China. Chinese people consider themselves descendants of the dragon. The Chinese dragon rules the waters. They can make it rain and can control floods.

Chinese legends tell about a powerful dragon that had nine sons (the number and names of the sons varies in different stories). Each son had his own character and function. Images of the sons were often used to decorate buildings. The Gate of Harmonious Interest includes images of several of the dragon's sons. The first son, *Bixi*, looks like a turtle and likes to carry large loads. He can be found on the base of the arch. Another son, *Chiwen*, loves to gaze into the distance, so is displayed on opposite sides of the roof ridge as a sentinel. As he likes to swallow evil, he is called the "Ridge-Biter". He resembles a lizard without a tail. He also controls rain, serving to protect the structure from fire. The adventurous *Chaofeng* is put on roof tops to frighten evil spirits. He likes precipices and is displayed on every roof of the buildings in Beijing's Forbidden City to prevent disasters.

Each corner ridge on the main roof displays a series of three figures, the lion, phoenix and *Chaofeng*, from top to bottom. The roar of the lion frightens evil spirits, the phoenix brings blessings and *Chaofeng* gives protection. Metal bells hang at the corners of the gate, and when the winds blow, their sounds ward off evil spirits.

In the top center of the gate is a gourd-shaped pagoda to symbolize the gourd carried by Li Tieguai, one of the Eight Immortals of Daoism. It is placed there to ward off evil spirits. Although often ill-tempered, Iron-Crutch Li is kind to the poor and treats those who are sick with special medicine from his gourd.

Chinese New Year

Chinese New Year is the most important Chinese festival and it is celebrated in mid-January to mid-February, reflecting the lunar cycle. It usually falls on the second new moon after winter solstice and spans fifteen days. It is an important time for family gatherings and public celebrations.

In Victoria, the Lunar New Year is celebrated with great feasts at Chinese restaurants. Most of the food served has symbolic value. For example, noodles provide long life and chicken is eaten for prosperity.

Performances take place in Chinatown and include fan dances, dragon dances and lion dances. A dragon dance is performed by many dancers who hold the dragon on poles, whereas only two people wear the lion costume, one for its head and one for its rear.

Lion dances are joyous performances, held to not only Lunar New Year but openings of businesses, temples, weddings and other festivities. Performed to bring good fortune and ward off evil spirits, the dance begins with the traditional dotting of the eye of the lion to bring it to life.

In Victoria, the Chinese Consolidated Benevolent Association sponsors the Lion Dance at Chinese New Year, with members of local kung fu clubs performing the dance. Shop owners hang greens, usually lettuce, and paper money on strings in the entrances of their stores. The lion dances up to the "green," which is associated with good fortune, plucks it and rips it into pieces, spreading the prosperity. The cash is retained by the dance troupe. The lion has an extensive retinue, including musicians, replacement performers, a fire cracker master and a man holding a three-pronged fork. The dance is accompanied by the beat of a drum, the crash of cymbals and the sound of a gong. After the lion accepts the offering, firecrackers are let off. With the large number of stores in and around Chinatown, the dance can take up to two hours. The ritual brings good fortune to the shops and the noise produced scares off evil spirits.

The legendary origin of the lion dance centers around a monster called the Nian who has the head of a lion and body of the dragon. It lived either in the depth of the ocean or the tops of the mountains. At sunset before the New Year, the Nian would come to villages and eat the villagers' food, livestock and even the villagers, especially the children. The villagers would offer food to the Nian so it would eat the offerings, rather than the people. One day, an old man told the villagers that three things frightened the Nian: loud noises, light and the colour red. So the villagers would make loud noises, light firecrackers and hang red lanterns on the eve of New Year to frighten the Nian. With all these preparations, the Nian never bothered them again. However, the rituals continue to be performed in case the Nian is lurking. The word Nian means "year" and has come to be associated with celebrating the New Year.

Many traditions are followed for good luck in the New Year. People wear red, the colour of joy. They give money in red envelopes. And they do not sweep their houses to avoid sweeping away their luck.

CHAPTER 12
Hearing from Hestia – Architecture

Architect Frank Gehry once said, "In the end, the character of a civilization is encased in its structures." The character of Victoria is made solid in its buildings. They reflect the spirit of the time of their construction and the sense of place. In Greek mythology, the divinity related to architecture was Hestia, the goddess of the home and the fire in the hearth in both private and public buildings. She was said to have discovered how to build houses, and accordingly, her shrine appeared in the center of every home.

Samuel Maclure was one of Victoria's iconic architects. Many of his residential designs included impressive two-storey entrance halls with large fireplaces in the central area, giving a warm heart to the home. In this sense, Maclure served Hestia of the hearth. Maclure himself had mythic elements in his life. His birth was special. He made history as the first baby born of white settlers in the capital of New Westminster. His marriage suggests the many tales in the Arthurian cycle and Celtic myths about the marriage of a handsome young man to a loathsome old hag. After the wedding, the hag becomes a beautiful young woman. This myth was relived in part by the Maclures. One night in August, 1889, Maclure left Victoria on the boat with a hobbling old crone and the next day, he married her in New Westminster. However, his bride was not an old crone but the young and beautiful Daisy Simpson, the stepdaughter of the rector of St. Andrew's Presbyterian Church in Victoria. Her family did not support marriage with Maclure as he was not seen as having good prospects, so Daisy disguised herself as an old woman, carrying a cane and wearing a shawl to avoid being recognized by her stepfather as she boarded the boat. Reportedly, the couple was very happy together.

Victoria is rich in heritage buildings, with about 65% of the designated heritage sites in B.C. As many as 240 heritage buildings can be found downtown. Most of these buildings were designed in the Victorian era and represent the values and fashion of that era. The Victorian era, based on the reign of Queen Victoria from 1837 to 1901, was one of change. Industrialization led to increased urbanization and supported a growing middle class. It also provoked a reaction against a machine-based society, resulting in a return to human-made, organic forms.

The use of symbols was popular to convey cultural meaning. During Victoria's reign, the British Empire doubled in size. As a colony of Britain, the City of Victoria saw the use of symbols to demonstrate the splendour of the empire. These symbols included the crown, the rose, and the lion, representing royalty. Architecture in the Victorian era combined functional requirements with an expression of symbolic values related to the building.

Neoclassical architecture was popular at the beginning of the Victorian era. It celebrated the values of reason and order, taking inspiration from the Classical world of ancient Greece and Rome and incorporating elements such as the columns and pediments of Greek temples. The temples had been built to honour the gods and goddesses who became the subject of myths. The interest in myths resurged during this era with the popularity of literature such as Bulfinch's *The Age of Fable*, first published in 1855, and Alfred, Lord Tennyson's *Idylls of the King*, published in various combinations between 1856 and 1885.

But Neoclassical architecture faced a new contender in the Victorian era—Gothic Revival. Influential writers such as John Ruskin and A.W.N. Pugin saw the Middle Ages as a time when religion was purer. Pugin suggested that the Gothic style reflected true Christian architecture and argued for a return to the faith and social structures of the Middle Ages. Ruskin proposed that Gothic buildings excelled over other architecture because of the "sacrifice" of the stone-carvers in intricately decorating every stone. He believed that the Gothic Revival style celebrated individual creativity, compared to the standardized approach of the Neoclassical.

Cathedrals and churches took on the air of medieval cathedrals. In Victoria, Christ Church Cathedral, designed in 1896 in the Gothic Revival style, looks like a thirteenth century cathedral. Its central entrance with a large arch flanked by two square towers, and its interior with ribbed vaulting, resembles the early Gothic Durham Cathedral in northern England. It also has flying buttresses such as those found in Notre Dame Cathedral in Paris. St. Andrew's Roman Catholic Cathedral, which opened in 1892, was another significant building in Victoria designed in the Gothic Revival style. These cathedrals, and many other churches in Victoria, have beautiful circular rose windows. Rose windows may have their origins in Roman occuli, suggestive of an eye from the heavens.

The Roman writer, Vitruvius, advised that the temples of the gods who protect the city and temples of the main gods should be built on a prominence with a view of the city. The practice of siting sacred buildings on prominent sites continued in early Victoria. Christ Church Cathedral was built on Church Hill, overlooking the city. The spire of St. Andrew's Cathedral was the highest point in the city when the cathedral was built. This siting served to remind people symbolically that churches were close to heaven, just as the ancient ziggurats of Babylon rose up to the skies.

As a contrast to Gothic Revival churches, the First Church of Christ Scientist, 1205 Pandora Avenue, built in 1919, is a Neoclassical building, complete with Ionic columns and a dome. It resembles the Pantheon, the Roman temple to all gods, with columns and central dome. Its Neoclassical style reflects the American origins of this faith.

Of particular influence on the choice of architectural styles in the Victorian era was the rebuilding of the Palace of Westminster, or the Houses of Parliament, in London, England in the Gothic Revival style. Charles Barry won a competition in 1836 to design the Palace of Westminster, and his design was in the Gothic Revival style. A.W.N. Pugin assisted with the design. The Gothic Revival style was believed to embody conservative values. In contrast, the Neoclassical style featured in the design of major buildings in the United States, such as the federal Capitol building and the White House. The use of the Neoclassical style served to create an American identity by linking the new republic to ancient Greece and Rome. The classical references implied the political ideals of ancient Rome as well as values of harmony and simplicity. To the British, it suggested revolution and republicanism, whereas the Gothic Revival style was in harmony with monarchism and a parliamentary democracy.

The Gothic Revival style came to symbolize Canada's identity. In 1859, a competition was held to select architects to design the Parliament Buildings in Ottawa. The judges chose the Gothic Revival style over Neoclassical, consistent with the ideal of parliamentary democracy and following the lead set by Britain.

Rattenbury, B.C.'s Most Celebrated Architect

Victoria's triumvirate of iconic buildings surrounds the Inner Harbour. The Parliament Buildings opened officially in 1898, the Empress Hotel opened in 1908; and the present CPR Steamship Terminal opened in 1924. All three buildings were designed by Francis Mawson Rattenbury, B.C.'s most celebrated architect.

Rattenbury himself led a life of mythic dimensions. He was a controversial figure, often exaggerating his experience and underestimating the costs of his work. Like a young King Arthur pulling a sword from a stone, Rattenbury competed against sixty-two experienced architects to win the 1892 competition to design the Parliament Buildings in Victoria. At the time, he was only 25 years old and had no experience in Canada. Many myths feature contests or trials to determine birthright or destiny, such as Arthur proving that he was the true king by removing the sword from the stone. Like the Greek architect Daedalus who built a tower on Sicily to store the king's treasures, Rattenbury designed buildings that store the heritage treasures of the province and topped his work off by ensuring these treasures would be safe from fire. Like a modern Merlin, he conjured up a Crystal Palace, together with architect, P.L. James. Rattenbury's designs include a marble palace, a Sleeping Beauty château, a crystal pleasure palace, temples of finance, and a temple to the Greek god Neptune.

Rattenbury designed a large number of celebrated buildings throughout British Columbia, despite, as he wrote in a letter in 1894, finding that the land induced lotus-eating. The lotus-eaters, in Greek mythology, were a race of people living on an island who enjoyed the fruits and flowers of the lotus. The food was narcotic and therefore, the people lived a sleepy, peaceful life. Alfred, Lord Tennyson, captured this idea in his 1832 poem, the "Lotos-Eaters", writing, "Surely, surely, slumber is more sweet than toil." Even Kipling referred to this idea of Victoria as a sleepy town for retired people, writing in *From Sea to Sea and Other Sketches*, "I found in that quiet English town of beautiful streets quite a colony of old men doing nothing but talking, fishing, and loafing at the Club. That means that the retired go to Victoria."

Rattenbury's own home on the Oak Bay waterfront was built on a site with a rich mythical heritage. He named his house, *Iechinihl*, "place where a good thing happened." He told the story about the origin of this name in a letter he wrote in 1900, noting that there were many clam shells in his garden and that it had a fresh water spring. An old timer told him that the area had been used for centuries by First Nations people. According to a legend, men were originally dumb and looked at each other like owls. But one day, the Great Spirit conferred on them the gift of speech—at the place where Rattenbury's garden was located.

However, Rattenbury's life did not remain favoured by the gods. He lost money in various business ventures and overindulged in alcohol. Like an old king seeking renewal in a younger wife, he left his first wife, Florence, and married Alma in 1925, thirty years his junior. In the vein of the courtly love of troubadours, he described Alma as a fragile Madonna and declared that butterflies would eat from her hand. Rattenbury had treated Florence very badly, and as result, Rattenbury and his new wife were shunned in Victoria. They decided to leave in 1929 and settled in Bournemouth. Like the cuckold King Arthur, Rattenbury was betrayed by his beautiful young wife and killed by a boy who, it could be said, he treated like a son. Rattenbury had hired seventeen-year old George Stoner as a chauffeur-handyman in 1934 and they had enjoyed evenings playing cards and chatting. Alma's musical career kept her busy, composing ballads under the name of Lozanne, and performing. But she became bored with her depressed husband and entered into an affair with the young, virile Stoner. Over time, Stoner became increasingly jealous and one night, he hit Rattenbury three times with a mallet; Rattenbury died a few days later. Both Stoner and Alma confessed to the murder, and the couple was tried for the crime at the Old Bailey in a sensational trial in 1935. Alma was acquitted but Stoner was convicted and sentenced to death. After the trial, Alma committed suicide, stabbing herself in the heart then falling into the River Avon to float away. It is easy to picture the musical Alma as Tennyson's "Lady of Shallot" who fell in love with a knight and was cursed to die in a river singing her final song. Public pressure after Alma's suicide resulted in the reduction of Stoner's sentence to life imprisonment. Stoner was released from prison after seven years and lived to the age of 83.

Rattenbury is the flawed hero of his story and has been the subject of the radio and stage play and movie, *Cause Célèbre*, books, and lately, an opera. His story is popular with tourists, especially the tales about his ghost haunting the Parliament Buildings and the Empress Hotel.

The Parliament Buildings, 501 Belleville Street

Rattenbury won the 1892 competition to design the Parliament Buildings with his design which incorporated Romanesque, Classic and Gothic influences, capturing the spirit of the place and time. His design incorporated symbolism of Britain's imperial age together with symbols celebrating the province. He used local materials in the building—pearly gray stone from Haddington Island off northern Vancouver Island for the façade, granite from Nelson Island in the Strait of Georgia for the front stairs and foundation, slate from Jervis Inlet for the roof, and local timber for the wood-panelled interior rooms. It was critical that the Parliament Buildings, the home of the Legislative Assembly, epitomized the spirit of British Columbia.

The silhouette of the thirty-three domes and turrets of the Parliament Buildings outlined in the setting sun resembles the imperial architecture of India. Are the buildings fit for a maharajah? It was rumoured that Rattenbury copied the design from a blueprint for a maharajah's palace in India created by his uncles' firm in England, but the rumours have never been substantiated.

The imperial link was further indicated by Rattenbury's plan for the gilded figure at the pinnacle of the building to be that of Britannia, the female personification of Great Britain. Britannia was shown on coins of the Roman Empire as a woman warrior with a spear and shield. During the Victorian era, with the rise of British naval power, the image of Britannia grew in popularity. A key illustration of the importance of Brittania was an 1847 fresco painting by artist William Dyce, entitled *Neptune Resigning to Britannia the Empire of the Sea*. The painting shows Neptune in his horse-drawn chariot surrendering his trident to Britannia. A royal lion hides behind her robes. The painting includes other marine themes, such as mermaids and tritons, as well as Mercury as messenger of the gods. The painting was commissioned by Queen Victoria and Prince Albert for their home in the Isle of Wight. During Queen Victoria's reign, Britannia acquired attributes such as Neptune's trident and the British lion, and in portrayals, Britannia was always fully clothed.

Rather than Britannia, it was a gilded statue of explorer Captain George Vancouver that was ultimately placed on the apex of the Parliament Buildings. The image of Britannia, with helmet and trident, and wearing a lion's head as a belt bucket, can be seen on the former Bank of Toronto building on the corner of Yates and Broad Street (now the Legacy Art Gallery and Cafe, 630 Yates Street).

The Parliament Buildings were officially opened on February 10, 1898. Their construction cost nearly double the initial budget of $500,000. Symbolism was used throughout the building and the grounds to display the power of government and express the cultural values of the day.

The Parliament Buildings

The size and setting of the Parliament Buildings overlooking the harbour make it significant, and its stone walls, Ionic columns, turrets, cupolas and domes make it the stuff of legends, calling upon the symbols of past great civilizations to provide a meaningful context. The *Victoria Daily Times* bestowed the title the "Marble Palace" on the Buildings at their opening. Since then, layers of symbols have been added to suggest the values of each succeeding generation. Architect Alan Hodgson who supervised the renovations of the Buildings beginning in 1973 commented on Rattenbury's design, "In appearance it is a design full of emotional resonance."

One of the most striking features of the Parliament Buildings is its central dome. Alan Hodgson noted, "The Domical hall, located on the axis of the cross shaped central block, is positioned to represent the crossroads of power which flows out of the Legislative chamber." The octagonal dome resembles the Renaissance dome of the fifteenth century Florence Cathedral, designed by Filippo Brunelleschi. The symbolism of the dome calls to mind the very heavens themselves. Brunelleschi was inspired by the classical architecture of Rome, especially the dome of the Pantheon. In his 1892 book *Architecture, Mysticism and Myth*, W.R. Lethaby suggested that the mythology of architecture is a direct imitation of nature, noting that the dome represents the canopy of heaven. Temples represent the concept of the sphere of the earth, and according to Lethaby, the Pantheon was the most superb example of this.

The new settlers to Vancouver Island brought the mythological heritage of their homelands with them. Rattenbury came from England and the craftsmen who worked on the Parliament Buildings included Carlos Marega who had trained in Italy, Albert Franz Cizek, trained in Austria, and George Gibson who had learned ecclesiastical decoration in Edinburgh. Many of the motifs from these areas were incorporated in the decoration of the buildings. As well, Victorian era architects were trained in the perspectives of Greek and Roman buildings, incorporating these elements into their work.

The classical influence can be seen in the leaded and stained glass windows that line the halls of the Parliament Buildings. One series of windows celebrates classical statesmen and lawgivers, such as Socrates, Aristides, Plato, Solon, and Zaleucus. Minos, the legendary king of Crete, is named in one of the windows, a clear reference to classical mythology.

Another set of windows illustrates the Latin art and sciences. The window dedicated to industry calls upon the symbols of the bee and hive, and the spinning wheel and loom, to represent hard work. One stained glass window is dedicated to Hygeia, referring to public health, and it displays a double-snake caduceus. Hygeia was the Greek goddess of health and a daughter of Asclepius, the god of healing. The word "hygiene" is derived from her name. She was often associated with the staff of her father, Asclepius, which has a single large serpent coiled around it. A myth explains the origin of the snake-entwined rod. One day, Asclepius was tending to a patient when a snake coiled around his staff. Alarmed, he killed the snake. Another snake appeared with a leaf in its mouth and revived the dead serpent. Because it sheds its skin, the snake is often associated with regeneration and healing. Asclepius kept the leaf and used it to become an even more successful healer.

Hygeia on Stained Glass Window

An excellent example of the rod of Asclepius, with a single snake, in its association with medicine can be seen on the Fort Royal building at 1900 Richmond. The large silver sculpture of a snake-entwined rod includes maple leafs, symbolizing Canada, to bring the iconography to represent both the medical function of the building and its place.

A series of interior stained glass windows on the second floor of the Parliament Buildings displays the coats of arms of the provinces of Nova Scotia, New Brunswick, Quebec and Manitoba, incorporating the salmon, galley ship, maple leaves, and buffalo symbols which represent these provinces, respectively.

A comparison of the Diamond Jubilee Window celebrating the sixtieth year of Queen Victoria's reign in 1897 with the Golden Jubilee Window for Queen Elizabeth in 2002 illustrates the changing approach to the use of symbolism. The Diamond Jubilee Window includes the symbols of the monarch, such as the crown and the crowned lion. The provincial coat of arms in this window is interesting because it places the setting sun of the western most province above the Union Jack, suggesting that the sun does set on the British Empire. In contrast, the 2002 window features symbols of British Columbia. Eight medallions show provincial wildlife, such as the provincial bird, the Stellar's Jay, the moose, the cougar, the orca, and other provincial animals. Stylized ocean, trees and mountains celebrate B.C.'s natural features. One notable difference is that the provincial coat of arms in the 2002 window shows the Union Jack above the setting sun, as was approved in 1906.

Orca on Golden Jubilee Window

The Memorial Rotunda displays commemorative plaques to people who gave their lives for Canada. Its decoration includes references to the monarchy with the royal lion appearing as a carved face above the ceremonial entrance to the Buildings and in the trim as gold carvings.

Nods to classical mythology can be seen on the roofline where Romanesque statues of women stand. One of the figures carries a law book, another wears armour and carries a sword, another holds a globe and a fourth holds a bowl. Likely inspired by the idea of the Greek muses, they symbolize values such as the rule of law, military strength, a global perspective and abundance.

A common decorative element found throughout the Parliament Buildings is the face, either of men, animals, or mythical creatures. Many incorporate the flowing designs suggestive of the Celtic Revival style. Stained glass windows outside a second floor office feature ten medieval-looking faces of men with stylized yellow leaves and berries. One of these faces has leaves obscuring his mouth. Two other faces, framed in serpents, appeared frightened.

Faces peer out of foliate ornamentation throughout the building. In the Legislative Chamber, plaster faces of men stare out from under the main ceiling moulding. No one knows who the heads represent, but some of theories suggest they are ancient philosophers, or craftsmen who worked on the building, or members of the public keeping an eye on the elected officials, reminding them who they are representing.

Pairs of bare-breasted women wearing skirts of leaves frame the upper round windows in the Legislative Chamber. They are the Nereids of Greek mythology, water nymphs often associated with Neptune. They lived in a silvery cave in the sea. Over fifty Nereids were identified in Greek mythology, each representing a different aspect of the sea, such as sea currents, sea foam, calm seas and the raging sea. Some of the Nereids had the power to still the winds and calm the seas, a trait often needed in the politics. The Nereids in the Legislative Assembly were another imperial symbol of Britain's sea power.

Rattenbury gave his personal attention to the design of many of the decorative elements of the Parliament Buildings. However, as his drawings were lost in a fire that destroyed his office in the Five Sisters building on Government Street in 1910, many of the details of his work are not known.

On the exterior of the building, faces gaze from the casements of many of the windows and from the ornamentation about the entrance. They refer back to the carvings that medieval stone masons placed in cathedrals and other buildings in Great Britain and Europe.

Other grotesques on the building recall powerful mythical creatures such as gargoyles and griffins. The portrayal of faces continues in the office wings and Legislative Library designed by Rattenbury in 1914. Above the door to the library, an enigmatic and particularly handsome Green Man gazes down.

Green Man on the Legislative Library

The Legislative Library is impressive. Its rotunda is three storeys high, ringed with eight large Ionic columns. Eight heraldic beasts poise ready to jump down from the dome. It has been said that the library with its marble walls and impressive rotunda was more like drowning in a Roman bathhouse than being a place to study.

Niches on the top of the library exterior display twenty-six statues—fourteen men of historical significance and twelve mythical females in classical dress. The figures were chosen by the Legislative Librarian, Ethelbert O.S. Scholefield himself. The females, recalling Greek goddesses or muses, were placed in groups of threes around each of the four domes and represent the arts of painting, music, sculpture and architecture. They were created by the assistant carver, Bernard Carrier. The historical statues were sculpted by master carver, Charles Marega, and include legendary figures of the province such as Chief Maquinna, Captain George Vancouver, Captain James Cook, Sir Francis Drake, Sir Alexander Mackenzie and Simon Fraser. The nine-foot tall statutes were thought to have been inspired by the figures of English kings on the Bradford Town Hall in England, designed by the architectural firm owned by Rattenbury's uncles. The town hall featured 35 statues of past monarchs in chronological order on the façade, with Queen Victoria and Queen Elizabeth I in canopied niches on either side of the main entrance. In a similar fashion, statues also stand on either side of the main entrance of the Parliament Buildings, those of Governor Sir James Douglas and Judge Matthew Baillie Begbie.

In addition to the statues, six medallions of literary figures appear on the exterior walls of the library wing. They include Homer, the father of Greek mythology and author of the *Iliad* and the *Odyssey*, Sophocles, Socrates, Dante, Shakespeare and Milton—all well versed in the use of mythological themes. Other sculptures include books and crowns, obvious symbols of the function of the library and the monarchy. A portico with a row of columns on the south of the building lends weight to the idea of the library as a temple to learning.

Symbolic references also can be found in the precinct grounds. An obelisk was erected in 1881 by the people of British Columbia in memory of Sir James Douglas. The obelisk originated in ancient Egypt where it symbolized the Egyptian sun god, Ra. It was viewed as a petrified ray of the sun disc and the locus of the god. It also had phallic associations of the god uniting with the goddess of the sky. In the nineteenth century, the Egyptian Revival led to adoption of the obelisk as a memorial. Its simple structure was less expensive than many elaborate memorials and it was considered to be uplifting and elegant in its verticality. There are many obelisks in the Victoria area where they may commemorate heroes or honour the deceased as grave markers. In cemeteries, the obelisk was often associated with freemasons. Within its 4,000-year history, the obelisk has transformed from the sacred place of the sun god to memorializing leaders as well as ordinary people.

A statue of the young Queen Victoria, unveiled in 1921, gazes out over the Inner Harbour. Queen Victoria became associated with the ancient queen of the Iceni, Boudica, as the names of both British queens mean "victory." Boudica was seen in the Victorian era as a British heroine who had died defending her land from invaders. A bronze statue of Boudica in a regal chariot was commissioned by Prince Albert and worked on by Thomas Thornycroft from 1856 to 1871. It was placed by Westminster Bridge in 1902. Queen Victoria's poet laureate, Alfred, Lord Tennyson, wrote a poem about Boudica, comparing her to a lion in the lines, "So the queen Boadicea, standing loftily charioted, brandishing in her hand a dart and rolling glances lioness-like." Boudica was portrayed with strong symbolic links to royalty of the Victoria era, such as wearing a crown, standing on a throne-like chariot, and being like a lion. The statue of Boudica suggested protection of the British Houses of Parliament from invaders, whereas the position of Queen Victoria in front of the Parliament Buildings in Victoria gazing out on the harbour suggests her taking a calm overview of her realm and establishes her central position.

Not far from the statue of Queen Victoria, a seven-foot tall bronze statue of a medieval queen stands by Confederation Square off Menzies Street. The statue, called the *Spirit of the Republic*, commemorates the British Columbians and Canadians who offered their lives in defence of democracy in the Spanish Civil War. Of the over 1,500 Canadians who fought in Spain, 721 died. The queen holds her arms high and carries a dove in her left hand and a wreath in her right, symbolizing peace. The statue was created by Jack Harmon, who designed the statue of Themis, Goddess of Justice, at the Vancouver Law Courts and illustrated Harlequin Romance covers in the 1950s. Visitors love to pose with the statue, perhaps inspired by the symbolism of her message of peace.

Spirit of the Republic by Jack Harmon

A western red cedar tree planted in 1988 on the precinct grounds commemorates its adoption as the official tree of the province of British Columbia. The western red cedar was a sacred tree in Indigenous culture and totem poles were usually carved from cedar.

The Knowledge Totem on the west part of the grounds was erected in 1990 at the closing of the Commonwealth Games in New Zealand to begin Victoria's role as host of the 1994 Games. Master Carver Cicero August of the Cowichan Tribes carved the pole with his sons Darrell and Doug August, releasing stories from the wood. The pole presents symbols from oral traditions of the Aboriginal peoples. According to Cicero August, the frog at the bottom of the pole is from an old myth and symbolizes a tear; the bone player refers to a non-verbal game that can be played by people who do not share the same language; next, the fisherman represents the traditional Aboriginal way of life; and the loon at the top is "the teacher of the speakers" and an interpreter of Aboriginal languages. The symbols represent lessons of the past and hope for the future. In Coast Salish myths, the frog often symbolizes new beginnings at the end of winter. Living in both water and on land, the frog is seen as adaptable and a link between the natural and supernatural.

The use of animal symbols prevails at the Centennial Fountain on the south side of the Parliament Buildings. The fountain, designed by Robert Savery and activated in 1962, commemorates the union of four territories that were amalgamated in 1862 into the colony of British Columbia. The four territories were Vancouver Island, the Queen Charlotte Islands (now Haida Gwaii), British Columbia and the Stikine Territory. The fountain features five bronze animals that symbolize the geography and history of the province. The central gulls and otter on the central rock indicate the approach from the sea. The eagle represents the Aboriginal peoples of Vancouver Island and the Colony of Vancouver Island; the raven is the symbol of the Haida of Haida Gwaii; the bear represents the interior Aboriginal peoples and the mainland colony of British Columbia and the wolf represents the Stikine territory.

At night, the Parliament Buildings are lit by over 3,000 lights. Their first use in 1897 celebrated Queen Victoria's Diamond Jubilee. The image of the lit Parliament Buildings is iconic and contributes to the fairyland image of Victoria.

The Empress Hotel, 721 Government Street

In 1903, the Canadian Pacific Railway decided to build its most westerly hotel in Victoria. The City of Victoria offered the company a newly created site on the harbour. The site was located on the reclaimed James Bay mud flats that had been created by the construction of a dam in 1901 to hold back the tidal waters. The hotel was built on nearly 3,000 wooden pilings to provide a stable foundation for the building that emerged from the mud and sea.

Emily Carr wrote in *The Book of Small*, "The CPR watched the West grow. ... The CPR pillowed their heads upon the mud flats and dreamed a dream. First they tore down the old wooden bridge and built in its place a wide concrete causeway... The dream took shape in reality." And there stood the beautiful Empress Hotel.

The Empress Hotel

Again, Rattenbury was called upon to design the building. He chose a picturesque castle effect, combining elements of the French Château style similar to other CPR hotels, with Tudor features and references to the nearby Parliament Buildings. He blended symbols of the English and French heritage of Canada and maximized use of the reclaimed site. However, support for the use of local materials waned in the face of budget considerations and the plans changed from using local stone to bricks to save money.

The Empress Hotel officially opened on January 20, 1908. At the opening, poet Captain Clive Phillips-Wooley identified the City of Victoria as Sleeping Beauty in his address in which he compared the hotel to "Prince Charming" as "Victoria waited for the kiss of love and now comes into her own."

French châteaux were the country houses of French nobility, similar to palaces. The châteaux of the Loire Valley provided the inspiration for the Empress. It was a Loire Valley château, the Château d'Ussé, that served as the image for Sleeping Beauty's castle in the 1697 fairy tale by author Charles Perrault. So the appearance of the Empress Hotel suggests the tale of Sleeping Beauty, especially in its dilapidated state before the 1965 renovations.

The Empress Hotel evokes comparisons to castles and fairy land. Named for Queen Victoria in her role as Empress of the British Empire, the hotel has taken on the persona of the Grande Dame of Victoria. She has entertained kings and queens, princes and princesses. A ball held in 1919 to honour the Prince of Wales was described as entering fairy glamour, with music, soft lights, beautifully dressed women and men in uniform. The first visit from a reigning monarch took place in 1939 when King George VI and Queen Elizabeth attended a luncheon. Queen Elizabeth and Prince Phillip have visited several times, the last time in 2002. The Empress also hosted the Emperor and Empress of Japan in 2010.

Advertisements promoting the Empress Hotel drew on the castle imagery as the home of the aristocracy and Victoria's image as a bit of old England. An ad in *Canadian Homes and Gardens* in December 1930 enthused, "Nestling at the harbour's edge like a castle of antiquity, this stately hostelry is the scene of an Old English Yuletide—the mighty Yule-log roars on the hearth, gay Christmas carols await Christmas morn—join the happy throng of Canada's elite who gather here for this Yuletide celebration."

As well as royalty, celebrities have lent their allure to the hotel, including Rudyard Kipling, President Roosevelt, Charles and Ann Lindberg and Haile Selassie. When child star Shirley Temple fled from California under threats of kidnapping, she found safety in the arms of the Empress.

Rumours hold that the Empress is haunted. The ghosts include a little girl and an early twentieth century maid who shows up now and again on the sixth floor to help with the cleaning. The ghost of Rattenbury is also said to frequent the hotel he designed.

CPR Terminal Building, 468–470 Belleville

Rattenbury designed the original terminal for the steamship service in 1904 as a Neo-Tudor wooden building. The old terminal became obsolete and was demolished in 1923. Rattenbury, together with Percy L. James, designed a new terminal in the Neoclassical temple style, completed in 1924. The decoration—bearded heads of the sea god Poseidon over crossed tridents—carved by George Gibson, made it clear that this building was designed as a symbolic tribute to the sea on which Victoria's economy depended.

Poseidon on the CPR Building

The Crystal Garden, 921 Douglas Street

After his visit to Coney Island in 1905, Rattenbury wanted to create a fairyland for Victorians. He described Coney Island in an interview on August 1905 with the *Daily Colonist* as "a permanent place of amusement and fairyland of light and beauty," noting that the buildings were practically palaces.

In 1921, at the request of the Chamber of Commerce, Rattenbury designed an extravagant pleasure palace for Victoria. His design envisioned a huge conservatory over 100,000 square feet in size, with three heated sea-water swimming pools, ballrooms, shops and flowers under a glass and steel roof. At night, coloured lights at the bottom of the pools would produce a rainbow effect and the forty-foot fountain would be lit to create a living stream of fire.

Welsh mythology tells about Arianrhod or "Silver Wheel", who lives in a glass castle where she spins the web of life. The fate of each person is determined in the glass castle which is also associated with the movement of the stars. In Taliesin's poem "The Chair of Cerridwen," Arianrhod throws out a stream of rainbow to scare violence away from the earth, just as Rattenbury's rainbow-creating lights banished darkness.

In Celtic mythology, glass castles are enchanted places. Merlin fell in love with the beautiful Nimue and taught her about magic. But she grew tired of the old man, an age-old theme that resembles Rattenbury's life story. Nimue banished Merlin to a glass castle. He brought the Thirteen Treasures of Britain with him, and attended by nine bards, Merlin still lies in an enchanted sleep awaiting the return of Arthur. The Thirteen Treasures of Britain include a hamper that would feed a hundred, a drinking horn that produced whatever drink was wished for, and a cloak of invisibility. Several of the treasures served to separate brave men from cowards and the well-born from the others.

The Crystal Garden was inspired by the Crystal Palace which had been showcased at the Great Exhibition of 1851 in England. Queen Victoria noted that the Crystal Palace had the effect of fairyland. People in the Victorian era were obsessed with fairies and sought to create fairylands, those idyllic places where time stands still, in a variety of places.

The financial arrangements for the Crystal Garden were approved by referendum and the building opened in 1925, but with a downscaled design. It had only one pool but that pool was the largest salt water swimming pool in the British Empire. This temple of amusement drew inspiration from the Parthenon in Greece, with its white band of ornamental moulding. One of its earliest visitors was swimmer Johnny Weismuller, who later became famous for his role as the legendary Tarzan. Author Pierre Berton learned to swim at the

Crystal Garden and observed that the Crystal Garden has always been fairyland to him.

Carnegie Library, 794 Yates Street

In 1902, Andrew Carnegie gave $50,000 to Victoria for a library. Rattenbury had envisioned an impressive collection of public buildings framing the harbour, with a public library facing the harbour north of the Empress. However, the Carnegie Library was built inland on Yates Street, opening in 1906.

Architect Thomas Hooper designed the building in a blend of Neoclassical and Romanesque Revival styles. Eight-foot-high columns cut from single blocks, rustic stonework and medieval carvings carried associations to classical and medieval cultures. On either side of its entrance are the carved faces of 'grotesques', inspired by European medieval architecture. No one really knows why 'grotesques', images of demons or monsters, were carved on buildings. Some say that they were carved on churches and cathedrals to remind the worshippers of the fate that awaited them without salvation. Others say they were the remnants of pagan beliefs, or a joke of the stone masons. For the Carnegie Library, it could be said that the faces, somewhat comical in appearance, serve to frighten the demons of ignorance.

Thomas Hooper has the dubious distinction of being known as the Haunted Architect. It is said that all his buildings are haunted. He designed an impressive number of buildings in British Columbia. In 1903, he designed Rogers Chocolate Shop at 913 Government Street with John Teague. The Rogers family has a tragic story due to the suicide of their only son. The founders, Charles and Leah Rogers, managed their grief by working long hours in their chocolate shop. Their ghosts are said to still frequent the store. Hooper also designed a building for the Royal Bank of Canada at 1108 Government Street (present day Munro's Books). The bank had constructed a shooting gallery in the basement for employees to practise shooting in case of a robbery. Allegedly, ghosts of former employees haunt its basement. An employee died suddenly at the E.A. Morris, Tobacconist store on 1116 Government Street, also designed by Hooper, and haunts the building by opening and closing cupboard doors. It has been suggested that Hooper chose Mexican onyx for the entrance arch of the tobacco store because of its ability to attract spirits. The shop includes an electrolier carved out of Mexican onyx with two gas jets to light cigars. In 1912, Hooper designed the Hibben-Bone Block on Government Street. It became the Churchill Hotel and was the site of a stabbing. The ghost of the victim, Brady, was first reported in 1980, and he and his friend, Lady Churchill, reportedly haunt the site of the present day Bedford Regency Hotel. In Vancouver, sightings of seven ghosts have been reported at Hycroft Manor, a mansion designed by Hooper for General Alexander Duncan McRae in 1909-1911.

Royal Theater, 805 Broughton Street

The Royal Theater suggests its dramatic function with symbolic images. Carvings on its exterior wall include bearded satyrs with horns and pine cones, likely representing Dionysus, the Greek god of drama. Decorating a theatre with the image of the god of drama recalls the advice given by Roman writer, Vitruvius, about 15 BCE, advising that the temples of Apollo, as the god of music, and Father Bacchus, the Roman god of drama, should be located near the theatre. Other images on the Royal Theater include fruit, flowers and leaves, cherubs, angels and a bearded man wearing a crown, possibly Father Bacchus. Inside, a pair of Greek Muses lounges on either side of the stage, looking down on the audience. The pair may have represented Thalia, the Muse of comedy and Melpomene, the Muse of tragedy.

Satyr on the Royal Theater

135

Designed in the Rococo/Renaissance Revival style by architects William D'Oyly Rochfort and Eben W. Sankey, the theater was built in 1912-13. Famous Players acquired the building in 1930 and operated it as a movie theatre until 1972 when it was restored as a live theatre where the modern myths and dramas are played out for modern audiences.

Mosaic Building, 1061 Fort Street

A huge Thunderbird dominates the twin murals on the Mosaic Building. The building was designed by local architect, John DiCastri, and built in 1963. Two sets of murals, created by Mexican artist Andres Salgo, decorate each of the north and south sides of the building. The murals incorporate mythic, symbolic and historical elements. On the north side murals, a central Thunderbird figure is shown with Sir James Douglas, scenes of building Fort Victoria, and a seagull. On the south side murals, a maple leaf wreathed by dogwoods is surrounded by scenes of B.C. industries. The murals cover 7,000 square feet and consist of 16 million tiles in 50 colors.

Thunderbird Mural on the Mosaic Building

At the time of its creation, this work generated a lot of controversy about the nature of art. Building owner, Dr. Jack

Patterson had asked Salgo to create something new even if it caused a volcanic eruption. And the mosaics did cause an eruption in the local art world. The art was labelled by various critics as a dog, a turkey, a monstrosity and a travesty. The *Ottawa Citizen* newspaper captured the mood in 1963 with its headline, "It's Big But Is It Art?"

The cultural significance of the murals was important to Dr. Patterson. When the Thunderbird was criticized for being more Aztec than British Columbian, Patterson took out an ad defending the use of the Thunderbird as the most famous of the west coast totems and asserting that "Mr. Salgo has adapted with ingenuity one art symbol to unify and give meaning to the old Indian culture and our own historic past." Salgo himself commented on the symbolism of the maple leaf, noting that the maple leaf "beautifully represents the character of the Canadian people with its severity, serenity and sense of the good life."

The story of the Mosaic Building shows the importance of the use of mythic elements and symbols in defining a community and how this use can lead to controversy. The story of the Thunderbird murals on the Mosaic Building is forged in the flame of controversy.

The Mosaic Building got a new life when it was converted from an office building to a condominium and now it is considered a landmark in its district. In 2010, the shopping district was re-branded as Mosaic Village, recognizing the significance of this building.

CHAPTER 13
Calling on Mercury

The image of Mercury, the Roman god of commerce, was popular at the turn of the twentieth century on commercial buildings such as banks. In myths, Mercury travelled from place to place and arranged treaties, becoming associated with trade, travel and negotiation. He was the protector of merchants, shepherds, gamblers, liars and thieves. As a messenger of the gods, he carried a caduceus, a herald's staff around which coiled two snakes. Snakes were associated with wisdom and prosperity. His caduceus could turn into gold whatever it touched.

The source of Mercury's symbols can be seen in the myths about his Greek counterpart, Hermes. When Hermes stole cattle from his brother, Apollo, god of the sun, he was forced to give Apollo the first lyre in exchange for the cattle. As he was a thief, Hermes protected thieves. Later, he created the Pan pipes and gave them to Apollo, receiving Apollo's golden rod in exchange. As it was the rod of the sun god, it could turn anything into gold. The caduceus acquired its entwined serpents, in one myth, when Hermes separated two serpents that then crawled up his rod. The wings above the caduceus represented the idea that the god travelled so quickly it was like he flew.

The caduceus with its two snakes surmounted by a pair of wings is often confused with the rod of Asclepius which is associated with healing and has a single snake around the staff and no wings. The U.S. Army Medical Corps adopted the use of the caduceus for medicine in 1902 but mistakenly used the double-serpent caduceus of Mercury, the god of commerce, as their symbol instead of the single-serpent rod of Asclepius, the Greek god of healing.

Banks

The architecture of banks in the Victorian and Edwardian periods was designed to give the impression of tradition and conservatism, reassuring clients of the safety of their money in times when bank failures occurred. Symbolic elements served to provide an aura of stability and security. Stone and brick were chosen over wood as they indicated permanence. Classical architecture, based on ancient Greek and Roman buildings, suggested traditions going back in time to antiquity. The use of stone columns and over-sized mouldings around windows and entrances suggested architecture that had stood the test of time. Ornamentation related to Greek and Roman mythology harmonized with the Victorian era love of decoration. Bank architecture often carried references to the Renaissance style, recalling the great palazzos of the mercantile families of Florence who made their fortunes in banking.

Many stately bank buildings feature the use of Roman columns. In his multi-volume work *De Architectura* published about 15 BCE, Vitruvius wrote about the origins of structural columns and their use in the temples to the various gods. Doric, the oldest order of columns, was based on the proportions of a man and was unornamented. Ionic columns were based on the female figure. Volutes were added to their capitals and resembled a woman's graceful curling hair draped on each side. The channels sunk in the shafts of the columns resembled the folds in a matron's garment. Vitruvius indicated which order should be adopted for specific uses. Temples to Minerva, Mars and Hercules should be erected in the Doric order. The Corinthian order was more appropriate to Venus, Flora, Prosperine and Nymphs of Fountains. A medium between the two should be chosen for temples dedicated to Juno, Diana and Bacchus. The Ionic order balanced the severity of the Doric order with the delicacy of the Corinthian order.

The caduceus of Mercury was featured as a symbolic decoration by architect John Soane in his redesign of the Bank of England from 1788 until 1833. Soane's work had great influence on architecture in

North America. When the Bank of England was rebuilt starting in 1921, its great bronze doors incorporated a variety of symbols, including the heads of lions above caducei. On one door, two lions stand guarding a mound of gold, possibly inspired by the Lion Gate at Mycenae from the thirteenth century BCE.

The lion is a popular device in heraldry. As the lion was said to be the "king of the jungle" in ancient texts, it came to symbolize royalty. Lions were kept in the Tower of London and were named after the reigning monarchs. It was believed that the fate of the sovereign was tied up to that of the lion. When George II was ill two years before his death in 1760, people thought that his death was eminent because the oldest lion in the tower had died a fortnight before. Other traits associated the lion with bravery, valour and strength. The royal symbolism became more popular in the Middles Ages and the lion came to be seen as a symbol of the British people.

The protective function of lions was illustrated in the architecture of the art deco Williamsburgh Savings Bank Tower in Brooklyn, built in 1929 as a cathedral to thrift and prosperity. The bank decoration includes seated lions guarding the lock box. Mercury is also featured in the decorative elements, as well as squirrels guarding nuts to suggest thrift.

With the rise of Modernism and the dislike of ornamentation, the use of symbols to indicate the functions of buildings and cultural values fell into disfavour. Today, bank buildings take the form of anonymous high-rises, reaching towards the sky with lofty goals of ascending profits, but with little reference to values. The reputations they have established since 1945 may have eliminated the need to reassure clients with impressive, symbolic architecture. One wonders if the banking crisis in the United States in recent years will lead to the banks reconsidering their architecture.

The heritage bank buildings in Victoria display the recurring themes of stability and security in their architecture. References to Greek and Roman architecture and the use of the caduceus, the head of Mercury and lions as decorative elements are common.

Bank of British Columbia, 1022 Government Street

The former Bank of British Columbia building on the corner of Government and Fort Streets integrates Greek and Roman structures with decorations relating to Roman mythology within a Renaissance Italianate style, recalling sixteenth century Florentine banking palazzos. Sculptures of a youthful Mercury wearing a winged helmet appear over several windows and Mercury's winged caduceus can be found above the corner entrance. Heads of roaring lions defend the bank's assets.

Mercury on the former Bank of B.C. Building

The building was designed for the Bank of British Columbia by architect Warren H. Williams of Portland, Oregon and opened in 1886. Although the Bank of British Columbia was only formed in May, 1862, its stability and permanence were indicated by references to antiquity. Williams mounted a Greek gable above the corner entrance which is flanked by columns like a Roman temple. About the time he designed the palazzo-looking bank, Williams was hired by Robert Dunsmuir to design his dream castle, Craigdarroch Castle.

In 1901, the Bank of British Columbia merged with the Canadian Bank of Commerce. The symbolic motifs on the building worked well for the Bank of Commerce. It had opened in 1867 and its first logo was the caduceus, with the rod representing power, the serpents, wisdom, and the two wings representing diligence and activity. In 1908, the bank introduced a new seal which showed a stylized sailing ship in the lower part of the shield and three wheat sheaves in the upper part, combining symbols of transportation and agriculture. With its merger with the Imperial Bank of Canada in 1961, the new bank combined the Imperial Bank's crowned lion standing on a crown with the sailing ship of the Bank of Commerce to produce a new seal in which the lion replaced the wheat sheaves above the sailing ship. In 1966, the logo changed to an abstract chevron to convey the concepts of strength and progress. This logo became even more abstract in 1994, and even more stylized in 2003. According to the bank, the yellow and white arcs on its logo communicate forward thinking and convey renewed energy in shaping the future. These concepts are hard to identify from just two arcs and demonstrate the change in building styles from more overt symbolism to anonymity.

The Canadian Bank of Commerce employed poet Robert Service, also known as the "Canadian Kipling," as a bank clerk. From 1903 to 1904, Service lived above the bank in Victoria. It has been said that Service "cultivated the muses nine." Did he find that inspiration sleeping in a bank vault in Victoria? A few of his poems refer to living in an attic. He moved to Victoria after falling in love with Connie Maclean, an experience that may have awakened his muse. One never knows—but his short stay in Victoria has entered into the mythology of the City. There have been reports of his ghost still frequenting the bank building; indeed, the site is on the Victoria Ghost Walk Tours itinerary.

The building is now occupied by the Bard & Banker public house, named in recognition of Robert Service, the Bard of the Yukon. His ghost may have been pleased by the brews created in his honour, such as the Service 1904 Scottish Stone Fired Ale by Phillips Brewing Company.

Bank of Montreal, 1200 Government Street

An iconic Green Man can be seen above the entrance of the former Bank of Montreal building on Government Street by Bastion Square. Leafy tendrils enter the mouth of the Green Man, suggesting a blending with nature. F.M. Rattenbury designed the building in 1896 in the Château style. The style was commonly adopted by the Canadian Pacific Railway for its buildings and as the Bank of Montreal was a major financial backer of the railway, it was appropriate for this style to be adopted for the bank building.

The reference to the château palaces of France is furthered by the use of gargoyles on the building. Gargoyles are often used as water spouts. The inspiration for this practice can be found in a French myth which tells about a gargoyle that was a fire-breathing dragon. The dragon was killed by a hero and taken to the nearby town and burned. But its head and neck, tempered by the fire of its breath, would not burn, so were affixed to the cathedral to frighten evil spirits.

Green Man on the former Bank of Montreal Building

Royal Bank of Canada, 1108 Government Street

The main branch of the Royal Bank of Canada in Victoria was designed by Thomas Hooper in 1909 in the Neoclassical Revival style, suggesting a Roman temple with an entrance arch framed by Tuscan columns. Inside, a stained glass dome with the coats-of-arms of the province brought a local focus to the building. In 1984, the building was purchased by Jim Munro and remains as Munro's Books of Victoria.

The power of the lion as a symbol of royalty as well as protection can be seen in the adoption of the Royal Bank logo. When the Merchants' Bank of Canada expanded in 1901 to become the Royal Bank of Canada, its new emblem incorporated a close facsimile of Britain's Royal Coat of Arms, using the royal symbolism to suggest the ideals of tradition, strength and stability. In 1962, Royal Bank adopted a new emblem, retaining from the 1901 lion as a symbol of dominance, strength and authority, and the crown to suggest the royal connection. A globe demonstrated the international aspect of the bank's operations.

Merchants Bank, 1225 Douglas Street

The former Merchant's Bank of Canada (now the Bank of Montreal) on the corner of Douglas and Yates Street was built in the temple bank style. Its groupings of Ionic columns had their origin in ancient Greek and Roman temples and the triangular pediment framing the corner entrance encouraged clients to feel like they were entering an ancient temple, perhaps a mini-Pantheon. The thick stone cladding of the bank indicated permanence, as did the focus on fire-proofing the bank. Lions' heads and garlands decorated the building, with the lions suggesting that clients' money in the bank will be fiercely protected.

F.M. Rattenbury designed the building in the Beaux-Arts style and it was built in 1907. Many temple banks across Canada were designed in the Neoclassical Beaux-Arts style during this period, such as the Merchant's Bank built in Vancouver at 1 West Hastings Street in 1913. In 1922, the Merchants Bank of Canada merged with the Bank of Montreal.

The siting of the bank on a prominent city corner and its architecture were aimed at displaying financial dominance. In a display of prosperity, this bank was the most expensive building in the city for its size.

The British American Trust Company Building, 737 Fort Street

Another temple bank designed in the Beaux-Arts tradition was built on Fort Street for the British American Trust Company. The building was designed by architect Alfred Arthur Cox in 1912. The stone-cladding and two large Corinthian columns speak to the symbolism of the bank as a temple of finance, and on its pediment is the face of a man wearing a helmet, probably representing the god of commerce, Mercury.

Vitruvius related a story about the origin of the Corinthian column. He wrote that when a young woman of Corinth died, her nurse collected some of her favourite things in a basket and put the basket on top of her tomb, placing it under a heavy tile to protect it from the weather. An acanthus plant grew through the basket and around the tile. One day, Callimachus, a Greek architect, saw the tomb and it gave him the idea for the ornate Corinthian column. The

Corinthian column came to be identified with the figure of a young woman. From this story came the idea that the acanthus plant represented life emerging from the grave of death, rebirth and regeneration. The acanthus leaves became a popular ornamentation, especially in the Victorian era. Representations of the thorny plant were widely used in funerary art, suggesting the painful journey of life to death, and then regeneration.

Mercury on the former British American Trust Company Building

Merchant Buildings

Mercury was also a popular symbol on merchant buildings as the god of commerce. Other motifs may have referred to the birthplace of the buildings' owners or the use of the building.

Temple Building, 525 Fort Street

A striking two-storey red brick building located at the corner of Fort and Langley Streets features a series of human faces with leaves bursting from them. The Temple Building was designed in 1893 by Samuel Maclure as a commercial building for merchant Robert Ward. Ward was a Scottish immigrant with interests in real estate, insurance, import and export, salmon and sealing industries. His Scottish heritage was referenced in the thistle motif used throughout the building.

The work by Samuel Maclure represents the "organic design" movement initiated by Chicago architect Louis Sullivan who designed buildings to reconcile nature with technology. Sullivan incorporated

Celtic Revival ornamentation in his buildings, reflecting his Irish heritage and drawing on the tradition of Celtic mythology.

The foliate heads are images of a key Celtic figure, the Green Man. Traditionally, these images show a man's face merging with leaves, branches and vines. Thousands of images of the Green Man are found in medieval churches throughout the United Kingdom, France and Germany. The image, often found in hidden places, was commonly incorporated in cathedrals from the thirteenth to fifteenth centuries.

Green Man on the Temple Building

That the Green Man is a symbol of deep meaning is evident from the sheer number of images. However, there are no records to indicate what it symbolized to the medieval mind. The images vary; some appear regal, others malevolent, yet others mysterious. The disgorging types often appear frightened, suggesting a fear of the natural world. Indeed, medieval people had cause to fear the dark forest, and the face of a Green Man being taken over by vegetation may have reflected this fear.

One of the most famous examples of Green Man images is found in Rosslyn Chapel, a fifteenth century church in Scotland. Over seventy images of the Green Man show him aging from a child to a leafy skull. The aging of the Green Man may have been intended to parallel the cycles of nature. Rosslyn Chapel became popular when it was featured in the climax of the best selling novel, *The Da Vinci Code*. Author Dan Brown referred to the church as the "Cathedral of Codes" and "symbology heaven."

The image had a previous surge in popularity during the Victorian era, often reflecting the Victorian focus on mourning, with vegetation streaming down the Green Man's face from his tear ducts. During this time, the image became popular in secular buildings.

The term, the "Green Man," is of recent origin. It was first used in 1939 when folklorist Lady Raglan applied the term to a carving of a man's face encircled by oak leaves, with leaves springing from his mouth and nose. To Lady Raglan, the Green Man was an image of spring renewal and fertility. To others, the Green Man was an enduring image of nature suggested by a number of mythical figures, such as Robin Hood, the Green Knight and Peter Pan.

The Green Man is once again experiencing a revival in popularity, linked to the environmental movement and being at one with nature. As a popular ornament in gardens, the Green Man expresses gardeners' love of plants and nature. In this vein, the images tend to be of the foliate face type, rather than the more terrifying disgorging form.

The hunt for the Green Man proceeds. Websites are devoted to tracking sightings of the Green Man in specific areas, such as East Anglia in the United Kingdom. The adventure continues with new discoveries of Green Man images. Victoria can be added to the list of Green Man sightings, with the faces on the Temple Building, the Parliament Buildings, the former Bank of Montreal and many more buildings.

Pemberton Building, 1000 Government Street

Another place in Victoria to see foliate heads is the Pemberton Building, designed by Thomas Hooper in 1899. This brick building features rounded window arches and faces on the capitals of its piers. The Celtic faces work well with its present ground floor retail tenant, Out of Ireland.

Rithet Building, 1117–1125 Wharf Street

The caduceus symbol appears on each of the cast-iron columns on the Rithet Building located at the southern entrance to Bastion Square. The columns nearest to the square were made in San Francisco in 1861, reflecting Victoria's links to this city. The building was purchased by R.P. Rithet in 1888 and used for his mercantile and insurance company until 1948. The snake-entwined caducei likely symbolize Mercury as the god of commerce.

Caduceus on the Rithet Building

The buildings in Victoria have many stories to tell, catalysing interest in the past. In the Victorian era, the English architect William Lethaby wrote, "Old architecture lived because it had a purpose. Modern architecture, to be real, must not be a mere envelope without contents." Lethaby advised that the symbolism must be understood by the majority of spectators and suggested that the architecture of the future should aid life and train it, "so that beauty may flow into the soul like a breeze." Victoria's soul flows through its architecture, in the past, present and, we hope, the future.

CHAPTER 14
Aspiring to a Castle

On any list of the most beautiful castles in Canada, several mansions in Victoria will figure prominently. In the last 150 years, over half a dozen castles have been built as homes for prominent citizens, including Cary Castle, Craigdarroch Castle and Hatley Park. They were built by settlers from England and Scotland who struck it rich in the colony.

Castles were first built in England after the Norman Conquest as defensive sites. Castle-building went into a decline in the sixteenth century but in the nineteenth century, castles became fashionable as residences. Although not castles in the defensive sense, these homes incorporated castle-like features, such as towers, turrets, crenellations and thick stone walls.

The Gothic Revival style grew in popularity in the nineteenth century as an architectural movement with its root in medievalism. The style was particularly popular in Canada where it became forged with the essence of Canada. As interest in medieval castles took hold, nineteenth century taste-makers commissioned the construction of castles for their own homes. The famous Scottish novelist, Sir Walter Scott, built a fantasy castle, Abbotsford House, which was completed in 1824. It was the first Baronial Revival house to incorporate authentic elements of a Scottish castle in its design, not to mention actual pieces from ruined castles. Queen Victoria and Prince Albert had Balmoral Castle in the Scottish Highlands re-built in 1856. Following the Scottish Baronial style, it incorporated features of medieval castles, tower houses and the castle-like French châteaux. Balmoral Castle remains a home of the Royal Family to this day.

Complementing the growing interest in the medieval castles, *Idylls of the King* by Alfred, Lord Tennyson was published, retelling the legends of King Arthur in the form of twelve narrative poems. The poems featured Arthur as the embodiment of Victorian ideals and renewed interest in the purity of romantic love, inspired by the troubadours of the twelfth century France. As they captured the culture of the Victorian era, Arthurian themes became very popular.

Influenced by the Gothic Revival and romanticism, many people in the Victorian era dreamed of living in a fairy tale castle. Not only did such homes represent the current fashion, but they were a display of the wealth and power of the owners. Castles project power and authority. As the residences of kings and nobles, they indicate the high status of their owners. King Arthur had his Camelot, a castle that has come to symbolize a place of ideal beauty and happiness.

Castles evoke powerful symbolism. Castles are places where stories about kings and queens, heroic knights and beautiful princesses take place. They evoke feelings of safety from the attacks of enemies as well as indicating high status. But always, inner ghosts hide in their dungeons.

Castles figure prominently in mythology. Welsh poems tell about an otherwordly castle, Caer Sidi, where no one is ill or grows old. The actual location of Caer Sidi is unknown, yet it appears to be on an island, surrounded by ocean streams. Like most mythic castles, it is located nowhere and yet, it is everywhere. Heroes travelled to the castle in search of a magical cauldron, a vessel of inspiration which may have been the precursor of the Holy Grail legends.

One of the most well-known castles in mythology is the Grail Castle. Several medieval sources tell the story of the knight, Perceval. One day, Perceval encounters a fisherman who directs him to a castle described as square and flanked by turrets. He enters and is welcomed warmly by the wounded Fisher King. Then a procession enters the hall, led by a boy carrying a blood-tipped lance, followed by a maiden carrying a golden jewel-encrusted grail. Trained in chivalry, Perceval does not ask the meaning of the items. He falls asleep and when he awakes the next day, the castle is deserted. He leaves the castle and comes to regret that he did not ask why the lance bleeds and whom the Grail serves. Perceval spends five years searching for the castle. Finally, he finds it and asks the questions, with the result that the king is healed and the land rejuvenated. The Grail Castle is enchanted, disappearing and reappearing at any moment. It represents the ideal, which proves elusive and can only appear to those who are ready to find it. No wonder people aspire to live in castles, the attainment of the ideal, where illness and old age are unknown.

Cary Castle

The earliest castle in Victoria was the home of George Hunter Cary, the first Attorney General of British Columbia and Vancouver Island. Built in 1860, the castle featured a three-storey round tower topped with crenellations resembling the battlements on a castle. In the castle tradition, Cary's Castle was situated on a prominent site, located on twenty-five acres on the Rockland escarpment. It featured stunning views over the Juan de Fuca Strait to the snow-capped Olympic Mountains.

Why did Cary want to live in a castle? Trained as a barrister in London, England, Cary came to Victoria in 1859 to take the position of Attorney General of British Columbia. Familiar with English castles, he may have wanted a grand home to demonstrate his new status. The *British Colonist* newspaper described Cary in 1861 as "almost devoid of correct governing principles yet ambitious enough to aspire to rule a Colony." And what better status symbol than a castle from which to rule.

Cary had a reputation for impulsiveness. He made the news when he raced a horse over the James Bay Bridge and when he used a horsewhip on a man. He had hoped to make his fortune in the Cariboo gold rush but his resulting financial losses meant that he had to sell the castle unfinished, with only the tower and a few rooms completed. In 1865, Cary was declared insane and returned to England where he died the following year at the young age of 34 years. Maybe the stone castle spoke to his desire for stability, protection and longevity.

There is something inspiring about living in a stone castle beyond mere prestige. Psychologist Carl Jung built a stone tower in 1923 on the shores of Lake Zurich in the village of Bollingen, Switzerland. Initially, he planned to build a primitive hut with a central fire but he felt compelled instead to build a stone tower. There he retreated for solitude and inspiration, writing in his diary, carving mythical inscriptions in stone and painting wall murals. The tower was a maternal womb to him, making him feel that he was reborn in stone. His comments in his book, *Memories, Dreams, Reflections,* provide insight into the meaningfullness of living in a stone tower. He wrote, "In the Tower at Bollingen it is as if one lived in many centuries simultaneously. The place will outlive me, and in its location and style it points backward to things of long ago." Maybe Cary felt similar connections to his ancestral traditions in his stone tower.

Like Cary, many owners of castles in the Victorian era came to face financial ruin. Sir Walter Scott himself was close to bankruptcy in 1826 when a banking crisis occurred and his publishers failed. The expense of building Conundrum Castle, as he referred to his home, had overstretched his finances.

Cary Castle went on to become the official residence of the Governor of Vancouver Island. In 1865, Arthur Kennedy succeeded Sir James Douglas as Governor of Vancouver Island. Kennedy persuaded the legislature to approve $50,000 for the governor's residence and Cary Castle was Kennedy's choice for his residence. Although the site was criticized for being wind-swept, the magnificent views across the Juan de Fuca Strait may have influenced Kennedy's choice. Born in Ireland, Kennedy was described as autocratic, an ideal candidate for castle life.

Kennedy's successor, Frederick Seymour, became the first Governor of Vancouver Island and British Columbia in 1866 and moved into Cary Castle in 1869, but he was a practical man and living in a damp castle on a bleak site was not appealing to him.

When British Columbia entered Confederation on July 20, 1871, Cary Castle became Government House, the official residence of the Lieutenant Governor of B.C. As such, Government House also became the official residence of the sovereign and other members of the Royal Family. Like medieval castles which served as the home of kings, queens and nobles, Government House has hosted a procession of Royal and Vice-Regal visitors.

In 1882, a princess became enchanted by Cary Castle and stayed there for eleven weeks. Princess Louise, daughter of Queen Victoria and wife of the Marquess of Lorne, the Governor General of Canada, described Cary Castle as "halfway between heaven and

Balmoral." The view inspired her to paint a watercolour of the scenic sweep to the Strait from the castle.

In 1939, Victoria had its first visit from a reigning monarch. King George VI and Queen Elizabeth stayed at Government House. More Royal visits followed. In 2002, Her Majesty Queen Elizabeth and Prince Philip stayed at Government House, with their entourage filling its 105 rooms.

In Arthurian myths, knights of the Round Table would ride out of castles to protect the realm. Historically, knights were mounted warriors who performed military service for the king. By medieval times, they came to be identified with chivalry and the ideal virtues of nobility. Since the sixth century, honourary knighthood has been conferred for service unrelated to military service. The knights who lived or stayed at Cary Castle fell in the latter group with honourary titles. They include Sir Joseph William Trutch and Sir Francis Stillman Barnard.

Coats of arms were originally used to identify warriors on the battlefield. Knights have the right to bear coats of arms. In the Middle Ages, knights would hang their coats of arms on the walls of their dining halls. This tradition has continued at Cary Castle since 1876 with the display of the coats of arms of members of the Royal Family and Governors General, and recognize the date of each honouree's first overnight visit to Government House.

Castles were attacked in history and myth, and Government House was no exception. When a German submarine sank the Lusitania in May 1915, an angry mob marched on Government House and threatened the chatelaine. Martha Loewen was the wife of Lieutenant Governor Francis Barnard and the daughter of Joseph Loewen, the German-born owner of the Victoria Phoenix Brewing Company. Anti-German sentiment during the Great War led to the attacks on German families. Like the knights of old, troops were called out to protect the family, dispersing the mob. Later, in 1919, Francis Barnard was knighted and his wife became Lady Barnard.

Rather than fulfilling the symbolic promise of permanence, Cary Castle was destroyed by fire in 1899. Like the phoenix, a new building on the Rockland escarpment emerged from the ashes, and this happened not once, but three times. The site was located on a windy bluff, and wind and fire worked together in their destructive force. Cary Castle was the second building on the site. The original structure was built in 1852 and burned to the ground after only three months. Cary Castle was the second structure. The third building was designed by Victoria's two foremost architects, Francis Rattenbury and Samuel Maclure and constructed from 1901 to 1903. It featured an elegant ballroom with scenes from native legends decorating its ceiling. That building burned to the ground on April 15, 1957 as winds up to 60 kilometres an hour fanned the flames. Only the features most resembling a castle, its stone porte-cochère and tower survived the fire.

The fourth building and present Government House was opened in 1959 with a princess, Princess Margaret, in residence. The 5,800 square metre Tudor Revival mansion retains the porte-cochère designed by Samuel Maclure in 1909. The entrance from the porte-cochère still displays the sculpted heads of the monarchs of its day, King Edward VII and Queen Alexandra.

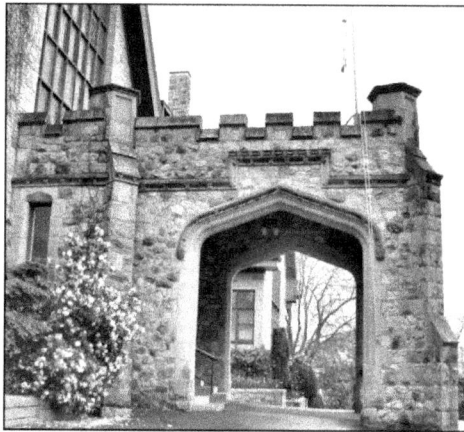

Government House Porte-Cochère

Roses were another symbol of royalty. A Victorian Rose Garden was created at Government House in 1994 by Lieutenant Governor Dr. David Lam. It was based on a rose garden at Warwick Castle in England. Warwick Castle, like Cary Castle, has a history of visits from royalty and damage by fires, albeit its history spans over 1,000 years.

Not a place of paranormal sightings, there is a strange story about the present Government House. Portraits of the Lieutenant Governors of British Columbia line the foyer and used to be lit constantly until one night in November in 1982 when the light over the portrait of former Lieutenant Governor Clarence Wallace went out. It turned out that Wallace had died that night.

Government House remains the official residence of the Lieutenant Governor of B.C. Located at 1401 Rockland Avenue, it is open to the public and many events are held in the house and grounds. It is a favourite site for visitors who enjoy the estate and the same stunning vistas that royalty and madmen saw from Cary's Castle.

Armadale

The next castle-like mansion to be built in Victoria was Armadale, designed by architect Thomas Trounce in 1877 for Senator William John Macdonald. Macdonald came from the Isle of Skye in Scotland where the original Armadale Castle served as the seat of the Macdonald clan.

Armadale Castle in Scotland was a Scottish Baronial castle built in 1815 as a show home, rather than for defence. Armadale village was the home of the stepfather of the legendary Scottish heroine, Flora MacDonald. Flora was famous for helping Bonnie Prince Charlie to escape to the Isle of Skye disguised as her maid, Betty Burke, after the Jacobites' defeat at Culloden in 1746. Since 1925, Armadale Castle, abandoned by the Macdonald family, has fallen into ruin. A tourist who visited the castle in 1974 said the gardens were like Sleeping Beauty's, with brambles growing into the windows.

William J. Macdonald came to Victoria in 1851 as an employee of the Hudson's Bay Company. His Armadale was a large two-story stone and brick residence with 22 rooms, situated on 28 acres of land in James Bay. It incorporated castle-like elements, such as a square gatehouse and round tower. And it was visited by royalty, specifically Queen Victoria's daughter, Princess Louise. It was destroyed in 1944 and part of its grounds became Macdonald Park.

Craigdarroch Castle, 1050 Joan Crescent

Like a romantic hilltop castle, Craigdarroch Castle dominates a small hill overlooking Victoria. Designed in the Scottish Baronial style like Balmoral Castle, the building has 39 rooms, 17 fireplaces and seven chimneys. Its steep roofline resembles that of a French château, its Italianate veranda recalls an Italian palazzo, and its stone walls and towers suggest a Scottish castle. Eighty-seven stairs lead up to a circular room in a tower with vistas to the sea, a perfect setting for the fairy tales of Rapunzel and princesses confined to towers. A dance hall on the fourth floor evokes images of princesses in a fairy land dancing through the night.

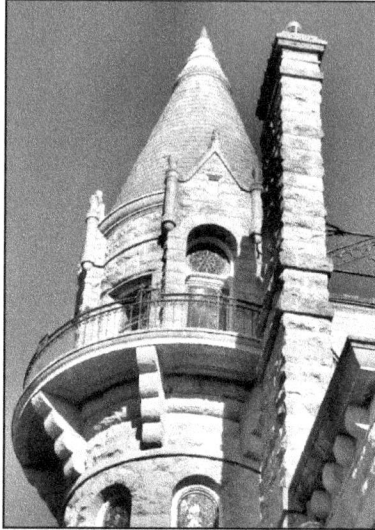

Craigdarroch Castle Tower

Craigdarroch Castle was the dream castle of Scottish coal baron, Robert Dunsmuir. Dunsmuir was born in Ayrshire, Scotland in 1825. His story could be considered a fairy tale, from orphan to millionaire. He became an orphan at age 7 and was raised by his grandfather who worked in the coal industry, leasing coal properties. His grandfather died only three years later and Robert became the ward of his aunt and uncle. At the age of 22, he married a very pregnant Joan Oliver White who gave birth to their first child eight days after the wedding—a scandal in those days. The family left Scotland for the coal fields of northern Vancouver Island in 1850. According to legend, Dunsmuir promised to build Joan a castle if she went with him to the colony—a trade-off for a better life. It was a humble start to married life in the small cabins they lived in for the next several years.

The lure of gold brought many fortune hunters to Vancouver Island. But it was "black diamond"—coal—that made Dunsmuir's fortune. He managed and developed coal seams for the Hudson's Bay Company and other mining companies. Then one day in October 1869, his life took a marvellous turn. He discovered a rich coal seam, the start of his fortune. He formed a company, obtained capital and became a successful colliery owner. The account of his discovery of the richest part of the Wellington coal seam in 1871 has a strong element of serendipity. It was said that he tripped over the root of a fallen tree and when he rose, he found his hands blackened with coal. Eventually, Dunsmuir became the wealthiest man in the province, going from $5 a week as a HBC miner to a worth of $15 million when he died.

His wealth increased substantially when he signed a contract with the government of British Columbia in 1883 to build a railway between Esquimalt and Nanaimo. He received a large land grant, a cash grant of $750,000 and mineral rights along the railway.

With his profits from building the Esquimalt & Nanaimo Railway, he was able to start planning his dream castle. It is said that castles are made of stone and bones, and Craigdarroch Castle is no exception. Robert Dunsmuir had the reputation of being a ruthless employer. Many believed that he had exploited his workers to make his fortune. Explosions in his mines took many lives. He hired Chinese labourers because they would work for low wages. He was anti-union, locking out and evicting his workers from company houses when they threatened to strike. When they returned to work, he made them take a cut in pay.

In 1882, Dunsmuir and his wife, Joan, travelled in Scotland and Europe where they would have seen many castles. In the same year, Dunsmuir began to accumulate property, taking five years to acquire the land that would eventually make up his 28-acre estate.

Dunsmuir hired architect, Warren Heywood Williams of Portland, Oregon in 1885 to design his mansion. Both Dunsmuir and Williams died before the castle was finished in 1890. Williams' associate, Arthur L. Smith, finished the job. In a strange twist, Dunsmuir had a premonition of his early demise and went to a spiritualist in 1889 who told him he would die in April. And he died on April 12 of that year.

Dunsmuir was proud of his Scottish heritage and the castle has many references to Scotland. *Craigdarroch* was the name of the home of Annie Laurie, the real-life heroine in a poem about estranged lovers. The famous poem was originally written about 1700 by William Douglas who was in love with Annie Laurie. Her father would not allow them to marry, likely because Douglas was a Jacobite. Douglas poured out his heartache in the poem, "And for bonnie Annie Laurie, I'd lay doun my head and die." Both lovers went on to marry other people. Annie Laurie married Alexander Fergusson, 14th Laird of Craigdarroch, and directed the building of Craigdarroch House in Scotland in 1729.

As mentioned before, castles are the natural habitat of royalty and nobles. The Provincial cabinet made a recommendation to Queen Victoria that Robert Dunsmuir receive a knighthood to celebrate the Queen's Golden Jubilee. But in December 1887, the *Portland News* published an interview with Dunsmuir stating that he regretted that Vancouver Island was not a part of the United States. The statement was considered to be treasonous and the proposal for his knighthood was dropped. However, he did receive the dubious title of King Grab. In 1888, a week after the first train steamed into Victoria along the E & N Railway, the *Times* newspaper published a 'Provincial Anthem' that went "I am King Grab, you see, I own this country; I am King Grab, Now my bridge is complete, Mayor, Councillors en fete, Come grovel at my feet, I am King Grab."

Dunsmuir was described as brusque, practical, shrewd and capable. He seems like the last man to want to live in a castle. So why would he build a castle? Terry Reksten wrote in *The Dunsmuir Saga*, "he was nostalgic not for the Scotland of sooty colliery towns but the land that lived in the works of Sir Walter Scott, a romantic medieval paradise of stags and crags, of gothic castles and noble knights, or pageantry and chivalry."

Some say Dunsmuir built his castle to fulfill his promise to Joan. Others say it was to find appropriate husbands for his daughters. More likely, it was to demonstrate his power and stature—the orphan boy who made good. Known for conspicuous spending and criticized as greedy, the Dunsmuirs were not accepted by Victoria's elite. The castle may have been Dunsmuir's attempt to display a noble character.

The castle home may have helped at least one of the Dunsmuir daughters to marry into the aristocracy. In 1891, Jessie married Sir Richard Musgrave, Baronet, of Waterford, Ireland. The lavish wedding in Victoria would have suited royalty. The bridal party included twenty attendants, all dressed in white, like the bride. After the ceremony, the couple received 200 to 300 of their friends at Craigdarroch Castle.

With the Irish connection in place, another Dunsmuir daughter followed family tradition and lived in a castle. Emily was widowed, and then subsequently married Harry Burroughes. After he lost their fortune, the couple rented rooms from Lord Charles and Lady Cavendish in Lismore Castle in Ireland. Lady Cavendish was the former Adele Astaire, the sister of Fred Astaire.

Craigdarroch Castle has exquisite stained and leaded glass windows, most of which have floral themes. The central stained glass window in the library displays a beautiful image of Scottish thistles, the national symbol of Scotland. Bluebells of Scotland are illustrated in one of the side panels, representing Robert's side of the family, and English holly in the other side panel indicated the English origins of Joan's mother, Agnes.

The Drawing Room features an intriguing stained glass window which shows a pensive woman with a peacock feather fan leaning on a wall while a white swan gazes up at her. The restored window is based on an 1862 painting by Sir Frederic Leighton, *Odalisque*. An odalisque was a female slave in a harem and became a popular subject in the Orientalism art movement in the nineteenth century. The Victorian era symbolism of the painting suggests purity with the white swan, vanity by the peacock feathers and the soul by the butterflies in the picture. The image of the maiden and the swan was popular in Victorian England. It suggests the Greek myth of Leda and the swan in which Zeus took the form of a swan to seduce Leda. Dunsmuir's Scottish roots may be reflected in this choice of image. A Scottish folk song, *Clout the Cauldron*, says, "Love, Jupiter into a swan, Turn'd for his lovely Leda." The poem "Annie Laurie" states that Annie's neck was like a swan.

Odalisque in Stained Glass

The theme of the swan and the Turkish harem was played out at a fancy dress party in December 1885. Dunsmuir's daughter, Emily, wore a costume of swan down and frosted moss, described as 'Winter'. A man dressed as Turkish pasha became interested in her, and six months later, Emily married the man in the pasha costume, Captain Northing Pinkney Snowden, her first husband.

Themes from classical mythology were popular in the Victorian era. Craigdarroch Castle's main hall has a large fireplace with a beautiful quotation, "Welcome ever smiles and farewell goes out sighing." The quote is from a speech made by Ulysses in Shakespeare's *Troilus and Cressida*, a play about star-crossed lovers in the Trojan War. The play draws upon Greek mythology and medieval romances.

As for ghosts, Joan Dunsmuir has been seen in her bedroom on the second floor. Other visitors report the smell of candle smoke. One can picture Joan Dunsmuir sitting in her tower room looking out over the town, like a fairy tale maiden, waiting to be rescued. One wonders if she was the queen of the castle or a prisoner.

Unlike the multi-generational nature of royal castles, the castle dynasties of the nouveau riche are short-lived. The Dunsmuir family lived in Craigdarroch Castle for only one generation. Nine months after the death of Joan Dunsmuir in 1908, the entire contents of Craigdarroch Castle were sold in an auction. The grounds were subdivided into 144 lots and a lottery was held in 1910 for the lots and the castle. Solomon Cameron won the castle in the lottery and promptly took out a mortgage to finance other investments. When he couldn't make the mortgage payments, the bank foreclosed in 1919. Like Sleeping Beauty's castle, the castle fell into disrepair.

Enchanted castles in fairy tales like Sleeping Beauty are under a spell. A good fairy puts everyone in the castle to sleep and surrounds the castle with a forest of trees, brambles and thorns, shielding it from the outside world and preventing anyone from disturbing the princess. Only a prince can awaken the princess and bring the castle back to life.

And the prince did come to the castle. On September 25, 1919, Edward, Prince of Wales, opened a military hospital at Craigdarroch Castle. For the next sixty years, the Castle housed various public institutions, including a military hospital, a teachers' college, a school board and a conservatory of music. It is now owned by the Craigdarroch Castle Historical Museum Society and the legendary landmark is operated as a museum. Over 150,000 visitors a year have the thrill of visiting the reawakened castle built by a coal baron.

Hatley Castle, 2005 Sooke Road

Like his father, Robert, James Dunsmuir chose to live in a dream castle. James managed his father's businesses and brought even greater fortune to the family. Active in politics, he served as the Premier of British Columbia from 1900 to 1902 and the Lieutenant Governor from 1906 to 1909. As Lieutenant Governor, he lived at the second Cary Castle and, together with his wife, Laura, hosted many parties.

James Dunsmuir was not a man who enjoyed politics and parties but he did like hunting, fishing, sailing and golf. In 1908, James Dunsmuir and his family travelled to Scotland to pick up his new yacht, the *Dolaura*. While in Scotland, Dunsmuir would have seen the castles and manor houses in the land of his father's birth. When he returned from Scotland, he returned with plans to build a home more in keeping with his wealth and position.

When an opportunity arose in 1908 to purchase 250 acres of waterfront property on Esquimalt Lagoon, Dunsmuir bought Hatley Park. Hatley Park had been owned by Roland Stuart who had built a Tudor-style house on the property in 1892. The house had burned down in 1905. The setting was beautiful, overlooking the Juan de Fuca Strait and the Olympic Mountains.

James Dunsmuir did not want to repeat the Scottish Baronial style of his father's castle. When his son, Robin, suggested that the family home reflect an English manor house, James Dunsmuir commissioned architect Samuel Maclure to build a home in that style.

Maclure was 48 years old at the time. His young assistant, 20-year-old Douglas James, had studied architecture in England. One of James' jobs in England had been to survey the details of Compton Wynyates, a fifteenth century Tudor mansion located in Warwickshire. Compton Wynyates featured crenellations and turrets, four foot thick walls and a moat. One of its early owners was Sir Edmond Compton, a close friend of King Henry VIII. The king stayed many times at Compton Wynyates and a bedroom window still retains the king's coat of arms in stained glass. The visits from the monarch greatly enhanced the status of the family. In addition to Henry VIII, Compton Wynyates hosted an impressive list of monarchs, including Elizabeth I, James I, and Charles I. Douglas James incorporated some of the elements in Compton Wynyates into Hatley Park Castle, such as the 3 ½ foot thicknesses of the walls in the tower.

Hatley Castle is a Tudor Revival-style manor house. The elements that give Hatley Castle its castle-like appearance include the crenellated rooftop and tower, combined with granite walls and massive size. The house is four-storeys tall and has 40 rooms. The estate included a dairy, stables, a slaughter house, and a smoke house; as well as a Chinatown to accommodate a virtual village of 120 gardeners. It took on the dimensions of a feudal estate, with James and Laura Dunsmuir as lord and lady of the manor. When Dunsmuir erected a wall around the property in 1913, the image of a walled feudal estate was complete. Or it anticipated the modern day equivalent, the walled community.

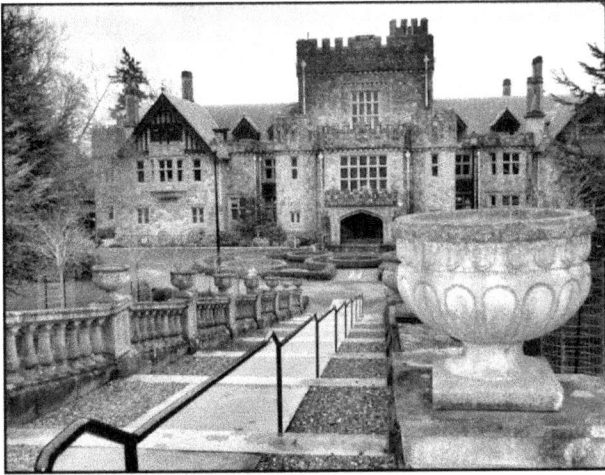

Hatley Castle

In medieval England, a licence to crenellate, or fortify a building, was required from the king. Originally, it restricted nobles from fortifying their castles but it came to represent the high status of the owner, indicating that the owner had royal support. For the Dunsmuirs, their crenellated home was a status symbol.

As was popular in the era, themes from classical mythology were featured in the house and grounds. The stained glass windows displayed the names of the goddesses of the four seasons: Flora, Hebe, Pomona, and Ceres. The windows were designed and produced by William Morris of England. Masonic symbols were inscribed in the library, reflecting James Dunsmuir's affiliation with freemasonry. George Gibson, the same architectural sculptor who had worked on the Parliament Buildings and the CPR Terminal, created the vine and foliated wood and plaster detailing at his Shawnigan Lake studio.

The grounds had a fairy tale dimension with forest glades and waterfalls, the likes of which are frequented in myths by nymphs and fairies. The *Victoria Colonist* newspaper described Hatley Park and its view on May 8, 1910, "Truly this was a magic casement opening on the foam of perilous seas in fairy lands."

The landscape firm, Brett and Hall of Boston, designed the garden and included paths which led to statues of Greco-Roman goddesses representing the four seasons. The Greek god of the Sea, Neptune, appears as a statue at the top of a series of cascading steps leading down the embankment to the front door. Originally intended to be a waterfall, they became known as "Neptune's Steps."

Like Craigdarroch Castle, ownership of the castle died with the first generation. It was too expensive for the family to maintain after the death of James' widow, Laura. The Dunsmuir family sold Hatley Park to the federal government for $75,000 in 1940.

As always, beautiful castles attract royalty. In May, 1939, King George VI and Queen Elizabeth visited Hatley Park while in Victoria. At the outbreak of World War II, Hatley Castle was considered for a residence, the New Windsor Castle, for the Royal Family if there was a German invasion of Great Britain. However, it was decided that if the Royal Family left England during the war, it would lower morale, and so the family remained in the Great Britain for the duration of the war. Prime Minister Mackenzie King visited the King and Queen at Balmoral Castle in August 1941. King wrote in his diary that they asked about the Dunsmuir estate. He suggested that it would make a fine Canadian residence for the King and Queen and he would welcome the opportunity of arranging it to that purpose. However, the King and Queen may have been thinking that Hatley Castle would have been a better residence for the Duke and Duchess of Windsor, the former Edward VIII and his wife, Wallis Simpson.

The military function of castles was suggested during the years that the estate served as a military college. The Nixon Block, built in 1954–56, included symbolic defensive features such as crenellated parapets and decorative shields.

Reports from Hatley Park suggest that it is haunted by several spectres. The "Lady in White," thought to be Annabelle, a servant who had committed suicide in 1911, first appeared in 1941 to cadets when the castle was a military college. Annabelle had jumped from a third floor window on learning that her fiancée, a sailor from Port Angeles, was already married.

James Dunsmuir's son, Jimmie or Boy, was killed on May 7, 1915 when a German submarine torpedoed the Lusitania. His youngest sister, Dola, claimed that she often saw his ghost on warm summer nights in the Japanese Garden. Laura Dunsmuir who died in 1937 never got over her son's death. In 1941, a cadet in the military college woke up screaming that a woman had tried to pull him out of bed. Laura's daughter, Dola, explained that the woman had been her mother, who was looking for her son, Boy. The paranormal at Hatley Park made the news in May 2012 when a visitor took a picture of a ghostly image of a mother holding a baby at the top of the stairs.

Today Hatley Park is the location of Royal Roads University. Modern myth-making continues at Hatley Castle. It has been the location site for over 33 major motion pictures. The earliest movie filmed at Hatley Park was *The Crimson Paradise*, made in 1933 with the financial backing of Dunsmuir daughter, Kathleen Humphreys. The *Crimson Paradise* was billed as "Canada's First All Talking Motion Picture." The castle has appeared as the mansion of Lex Luther in the television series, *Smallville*, as Professor Xavier's School for Gifted Youngsters in the X-Men movies, and the Queen mansion in the 2012 television series, *Arrow*.

Myths have arisen around the Dunsmuir family. One such myth centered about James Dunsmuir when he was a baby in Fort Rupert. It was recorded that the natives were so charmed by the flaxen-haired child that they offered to purchase him and make him their chief. One day, he was kidnapped and found in an Indian village. The story seems more myth than fact in that it resembles a common set of pioneer legends known as "Goldilocks on the Oregon Trail".

The castles of Victoria evoke the romance of medieval knights and a golden age of chivalry. A mythic atmosphere envelops them, raising visions of Sleeping Beauty and dancing princesses. Their construction points to the importance of image. Like the castles of yore, the castles of Victoria attracted royalty, drawing in kings, queens, princesses and knights.

Not only did the robber barons of the Victorian age crave dream castles, but many modern folk want to live in castles too. A Scottish-style tower house, looking like a medieval castle, was built recently on Saltspring Island on a cliff overlook the Salish Sea. Unlike the frightening gargoyles of medieval castles, this castle features gargoyles that take the form of First Nations art in the form of a salmon, orca, eagle, bear, seal, raven and raven mask.

Over time, unique residences such as castles take on a persona that makes them valued members of the community. Those that survive acquire new functions in keeping with the times. Cary's Castle and Hatley Castle are examples of "build it and they will come," attracting the attention of royalty and suggesting the modern reality that only government institutions can support the castles of the noble and the formerly rich. Visitors flock to castles today for a glimpse of a fairy tale life.

CHAPTER 15
Seeking the Holy Grail

The legends of King Arthur, "the once and future king," are some of the most enduring myths. Arthur was the legendary British leader who defended Britain from Saxon invaders in the sixth century. He was killed by his son, Mordred, and was taken to the Isle of Avalon by the Ladies of the Lake where he rests to this day until he is called upon to return to save England. Other stories in the cycle focus on the quest for the Holy Grail by the Knights of the Round Table, the stories of the magician Merlin, and the love between Arthur's queen, Guinevere, and Sir Lancelot.

References to a warrior named Arthur were first found in 830 CE in the *Historia Brittonum* written by the Welsh monk Nennius. The various legends were woven together by Sir Thomas Malory in *Le Morte d'Arthur*, first published in 1485. In the seventeenth and eighteenth centuries, there was little interest in the Arthurian legends. But during the Victorian era, they surged in popularity with the rise in medievalism in reaction to the evils of industrialization. The myths recalled a golden age in Britain, which was compared to the Imperial Age of the day. Alfred, Lord Tennyson's collection of poems, *Idylls of the King*, published in 1859, sold 10,000 copies within the first week. After the death of Prince Albert in 1861, Tennyson dedicated the work to Prince Albert; comparisons were made between the death of King Albert and the death of King Arthur. A group of artists, the Pre-Raphaelite Brotherhood, formed in 1848 and found inspiration in medieval art. They added to the popularity of the Arthurian legends with their creation of colourful, romantic images of symbolic realism, often illustrating scenes from Arthurian legends. Artists such as Dante Gabriel Rossetti and Edward Burne-Jones were fascinated by medievalism and created beautiful images of the Arthurian legends.

The City of Victoria was not immune from Arthurian fever. A new settler in Victoria wrote to the *Manchester Examiner* on April 5, 1885, quoting from *Idylls of the King* and suggesting that Avalon could be seen from Victoria. He wrote that among the Olympic Mountains, seen from Victoria, must be "...the island valley of Avalon, where falls not hail, or rain, or snow, nor ever wind blows loudly." Avalon is the place where the King Arthur was said to dwell, and indeed waits, to become king again.

In Victoria, the popularity of the Arthurian legends was evidenced in interior design. Gyppeswick, a mansion on Moss Street, was built in 1889 for Alexander Alfred Green, a local banker. The mansion had twelve fireplaces. The fireplace in the main hall was decorated with Minton tiles illustrating the Arthurian legends, including images of King Arthur receiving the sword Excalibur, of Guinevere and of the death of Arthur. In 1951, the mansion was donated to the Art Gallery of Greater Victoria and remains a gallery dedicated to the celebration of art to this day. Another house in the area, designed by Samuel Maclure in 1912 for Richard Hall on Linden Avenue, featured a large wall mural depicting a scene from the Arthurian legends.

Excalibur on Minton Tile

There may have been an actual British warrior named Arthur but most of the legends around King Arthur are myths. However, over the ages, many people have tried to identify the actual locations mentioned in the legends. Many medieval authors suggested that Avalon was located in Glastonbury in Somerset. Glastonbury has a long history of human habitation with artifacts dating as far back as 10,000 years ago. Glastonbury Tor, a tear-shaped hill, has served as a sacred site since prehistoric times.

Medieval historian Gerald of Wales wrote that sometime before Henry II's death in 1189, the king was told by a British soothsayer that the burial place of King Arthur was located near Glastonbury Abbey. In 1191, the monks at Glastonbury Abbey found a coffin containing two bodies and a stone that was interpreted as "Here lies King Arthur buried in Avalon." Thus, Glastonbury was linked to the otherworldly place of Avalon. After the Dissolution of the Monasteries instigated by Henry VIII in 1539, the abbey was vandalized and the bones disappeared. So little information is available about the Arthurian legends, it is said, because a powerful spirit in the form of a knight in black armour with glowing red eyes haunts the ruins of the Abbey to keep its secrets hidden.

Glastonbury on the Pacific

Victoria has a strong connection to Glastonbury. In 1925, an artist named Katharine Maltwood was commissioned to produce a map to accompany the Dent edition of *The High History of the Holy Grail*. The Maltwoods lived in Chilton Priory, a Gothic folly situated a few miles from Glastonbury. Katharine had read the adventures of King Arthur and she tried to locate the events in the landscape. During this process, she had a revelation. She saw the image of a lion outlined by the features of the landscape. It dawned on her that the other creatures that King Arthur had fought—the dragon, the griffon and the giants—were actually outlined by features of the landscape. And the whole area formed a zodiac, a Temple of the Stars, about 16 kilometres (10 miles) in diameter around Glastonbury Tor. The Glastonbury Zodiac consisted of thirteen giant effigies (the twelve sun signs plus the Girt Dog of Langport representing the constellation Canis Major), whose features are defined by natural contours, waterways and hills, as well as man-made roads and other structures. Maltwood suggested that the Zodiac was constructed about 2700 BCE. She theorized that the Knights of the Round Table were actually hunting nature gods, with Sir Lancelot representing the Lion, King Arthur the sun god Hercules and Sir Gawain the Ram. She believed that the seasonal passage of the sun in the pre-Christian era was captured in stories which were then interwoven with the legends of King Arthur. Her theories are controversial. Some critics have suggested that Maltwood erred by including modern features in the landscape and that she based the corresponding elements on conjecture. However, many believe that the images she identified retain the archetypal power to link the landscape with the skies in a meaningful way.

In 1938, the Maltwoods moved to Victoria. Katharine believed that Canada was wild, natural and unspoiled, and on the upward path of spiritual evolution. She was concerned that her art and the work she had done on the Glastonbury Zodiac would not be appreciated in Great Britain. By moving to British Columbia, her work could be preserved for future generations. Just as the ancient people had brought the sacred knowledge of the Grail west to Avalon, she hoped to bring the wisdom to a new "earthly paradise in the Western seas."

Katharine and John Maltwood lived on Beach Drive in Oak Bay until 1940, when they bought the Royal Oak Inn, a Tudor Revival house. They named their new home "The Thatch" and added a two story studio on the north side. A wood carving of the Glastonbury Zodiac hung above the fireplace in the great hall. Below the wood carving was Maltwood's sculpture, *The Holy Grail*. Maltwood carved the piece from alabaster in 1922, depicting a large figure holding a bowl. Maltwood believed that the bowl represented the knowledge that people must rediscover to find spiritual salvation. In early legends of the Holy Grail, the vessel provided a never-ending supply of food and drink to the knights. Over time, the grail became associated with spiritual salvation, which was how Maltwood saw it.

The *Holy Grail* by Katharine Maltwood

Maltwood died in Victoria in 1961 and her husband, John, donated Maltwood's art, their museum of collected treasures, and an endowment to the University of Victoria in 1964. Maltwood was cremated and her ashes spread over the grounds of the Thatch. The Thatch is now the Fireside Grill located at 4509 West Saanich Road. Seekers still visit the area to communicate with the spirit of Katharine Maltwood who is said to frequent the site as a shimmering white figure.

Other legends related to Glastonbury suggest that it was the place to which Joseph of Arimathea travelled from the Holy Land. The Bible identified Joseph of Arimathea as a rich man who took the body of Jesus to his own tomb after the crucifixion. When Joseph arrived in Glastonbury, he rested at the foot of a hill, now called Wearyall. He planted his staff in the ground and the next day, he found that it had turned into a living tree, a hawthorn, recalling the crown of thorns worn by Jesus on the cross. The tree became known as the Glastonbury Thorn. It was remarkable because it flowered twice a year, at the usual time in May as well as at Christmas. Experts trace the origin of the tree to the Middle East. In a tradition that goes back centuries, a Christmas blossom from the tree is sent to the reigning monarch to decorate her or his dining table. Legend also holds that Joseph brought the Holy Grail with him to Glastonbury and buried it for safe keeping just below the Tor.

Maltwood brought with her to Victoria a scion from the Glastonbury Thorn and planted it in the garden of her new home. When the museum was moved to the University of Victoria, the tree was moved to a site by the University Center where it continues to flourish. The sign at its base reads, "The Holy Thorn of Glastonbury, a graft from Joseph of Arimatheas staff that budded 60 A.D." Maltwood's statue, the *Holy Grail* (or *Samadhi* as it was later known) was displayed in the University Centre until 2012.

And Victoria's connection to the Holy Grail does not stop with Katharine Maltwood. Dr. Israel Wood Powell, a doctor, politician and freemason, is buried in Ross Bay Cemetery. The ancestral estate of the Powell family was located at Nanteos in Wales. The family safeguarded the Nanteos cup which was said to be the Holy Grail brought to Wales when the monks fled from Glastonbury during the 1539 Dissolution of the Monasteries. Research has revealed that the Nanteos cup is actually a medieval drinking bowl from the fourteenth century. However, the interest in the bowl as the Holy Grail persists to this day.

Landscape zodiacs are a part of the New Age movement, focusing on reconnecting with the earth as a spiritual site. The zodiac is used as a tool to align energies. Many landscape zodiacs have been identified since Maltwood's discovery. One was discovered in Victoria in 2010. Gatherings are held at the various sites in Greater Victoria corresponding to the zodiac at the appropriate time of year, with the first event held in Aries on April 17, 2011 on the anniversary of Maltwood's birth.

Labyrinths

A well-known Greek myth tells about the Minotaur, a bull-headed monster who dwelled in a labyrinth on the island of Crete. The myth begins with a prayer to the god of the sea, Poseidon. King Minos of Crete petitioned Poseidon for a bull as a sign of support for his sovereignty, and a snow-white bull appeared from the depths of the sea. However, Minos failed to sacrifice the bull to the god, so Poseidon induced Minos' wife, Queen Pasiphae, to fall in love with the bull. She consequently gave birth to a bull-headed son. The monster was confined in a gigantic labyrinth built by the architect Daedalus. A person could enter the labyrinth but could not find the way out.

Every nine years, seven young men and seven young women of Athens were sacrificed to the monster as a blood tribute to King Minos in compensation for the Athenians' murder of the son of Minos. One day, the hero Theseus, a son of Poseidon, arrived to kill the Minotaur. The King's daughter, Ariadne, fell in love with Theseus and told him how to find the way out of the labyrinth. Following her advice, Theseus unwound a ball of thread as he entered the labyrinth and encountering the Minotaur, killed him and followed the thread out.

The myth is referenced on Cretan coins dating from 500-400 BCE that depict the Minotaur on one side of the coin and a labyrinth on the other side. Some coins included a star in the center of the labyrinth. The Minotaur was named Asterion or "the starry one" and it is likely the star represented him. It may also have been a reference to the constellation of the bull, Taurus.

Over the centuries, the Minotaur was a common symbol in the center of some labyrinths, such as those on Roman mosaic floors. Sometimes the Minotaur was depicted fighting Theseus. Some scholars believe that the Minotaur of Crete was a representation of the sun god, not a monster as defined by their rival Athenians. The figure in the center of the labyrinth recalls the traditions of Indigenous people of Southwest North America in which the creator god, I'itoi, resides in the center of a maze which symbolizes the life journey.

The labyrinth design predates the myth of the labyrinth at Crete. Labyrinths have a long history, dating back over 4,000 years. They are found in India, Indonesia, Europe, North Africa, the American Southwest and South America. One of the earliest examples is a labyrinth-shaped petroglyph found in Goa, India which may be 4,500 years old. In Europe, the labyrinth first appeared in the late Neolithic and early Bronze Age, around 2000 BCE. At first, labyrinths appeared as petroglyphs on rock art panels and later, they were reproduced on artifacts, found from Spain to Syria. A clay tablet from the Mycenaean palace of Pylos in Greece illustrates the seven-circuit labyrinth. It is known that the tablet predates 1200 BCE as the palace was destroyed by fire at that time.

Labyrinths are often described by their number of circuits. The earliest labyrinth, the seven-circuit labyrinth found in ancient Greece, is known as the Classical labyrinth. The medieval labyrinth with eleven circuits was developed during the ninth and tenth centuries CE and used in manuscripts and on cathedral floors. The labyrinth constructed at Chartres Cathedral in France in the early 1200s was an eleven-circuit type and depicted the fight between Theseus and the Minotaur in its center. Medieval labyrinths were also built at Reims and Amiens Cathedrals in the same century. Mazes were created in the late Middle Ages based on medieval labyrinths but they incorporated choices in the paths which often led to dead ends.

In recent years, there has been a resurgence of interest in the labyrinth. Author Lauren Artiss founded Veriditas, the World-Wide Labyrinth Project, in 1996 by to "pepper the planet with labyrinths." Presently, Veriditas' Worldwide Labyrinth Locator database contains over 4,000 labyrinths in 70 or more countries.

Labyrinths have been built in churches, hospitals, parks and other community centers. They may take the form of a spiral walking path that inspires a walking meditation. They may be used as places for quiet contemplation, as an escape from stress, or as pilgrimages to a spiritual center. Labyrinths allow the right-brain to engage in creative thought as the logical left-brain is focused on following the path. People have reported that they feel more relaxed, clear, peaceful, centered and reflective after walking labyrinths.

Award-winning author Carol Shields lived in Victoria for several years until her death in 2003. A labyrinth was constructed in her memory in Winnipeg, Manitoba and opened in 2009. The Carol Shields Memorial Labyrinth is an outdoor garden labyrinth located in King's Park close to the University of Manitoba where Shields taught. Shields used the labyrinth symbolism in her book, *Larry's Party*. Two Quote Walls displaying quotes from Shields' works stand at the entrance to the labyrinth. Anyone entering the labyrinth passes through her words, physically signifying "the escape from daily life and the entrance into story, myth and imagination through sight, touch and experience."

Labyrinths do allow an entry into the world of myth. The mythology of the labyrinth suggests a quest to the center to fight monsters or meet god and restore the psyche, represented as the maiden. The Minotaur was composed of two different natures, man and nature, reconciled at the center of the labyrinth.

Victoria has an abundance of labyrinths. Its first labyrinth is believed to have been the eleven-circuit Chartres labyrinth painted in 1995 on the parking lot of the Garden City United Church, 4054 Carey Road. A seven-circuit labyrinth was opened in 1999 in Irving Park on the corner of Menzies and Michigan Streets in James Bay. An avenue of White Goddess (Shirofugen) cherry trees leads up to the circle of stones on the grass. The seven-circuit labyrinth in the yard of Christ Church Cathedral, 951 Quadra Street, is a restful place to take a break from the busyness of downtown. It was built in 2000 as a Millennium project funded by the federal government. Men from William Head prison laid the brick pavers to complete the labyrinth as a restorative justice project.

Labyrinth at Christ Church Cathedral

Since 2001, students dealing with the stresses of Christmas exams have been able to seek relaxation by walking the canvas labyrinth placed on the floor of the Interfaith Chapel on the campus of the University of Victoria. The labyrinth was modelled after the Chartres design. In early December of each year, members of the public are invited to walk the circuits of the labyrinth in contemplation in order to deal with the stresses of the season.

Other labyrinths can be found in the Victoria area in churches, parks and private gardens. A unique seven-circuit labyrinth featuring three cranes in its center is located at the First Unitarian Church of Victoria at 5575 West Saanich Road. The Cadboro Bay United Church, 2625 Arbutus Road, offers a full-sized, eleven-circuit Chartres labyrinth on its floor. A 40-foot seven-circuit Classical labyrinth made of recessed red brick on grass is located at Queenswood Centre, 2494 Arbutus Road. Residents often design labyrinths in their own gardens, and ephemeral labyrinths are carved in the sand of local beaches until the tide washes them away.

It has been suggested that in the fifteenth and sixteenth centuries, dances and ball games were held on some pavement labyrinths on Easter Sunday. The modern spiral dance which is performed by the Morris Dancers at Clover Point on the first of May recalls the practice of dancing and chanting along a spiral.

Labyrinths can help to build community. Many places hold open labyrinth walks on a regular basis. World Labyrinth Day is celebrated on the first Saturday in May to bring people from all over the planet together in celebration of the labyrinth as a symbol, a tool, a passion or a practice.

CHAPTER 16
Visiting Hades

The gravestone that marks the grave of artist and author Emily Carr at Ross Bay cemetery includes a quote from Carr:

Dear Mother Earth!
I think I have always specially belonged to you.
I have loved from babyhood to roll upon you, to lie with my face pressed right down on to you in my sorrows.
I love the look of you and the smell of you and the feel of you.
When I die I should like to be in you uncoffined, unshrouded, the petals of flowers against my flesh and you covering me up.
—Emily Carr, from her gravestone at Ross Bay Cemetery.

Cemeteries

The embrace of Mother Earth taking back her children is nowhere as obvious as at a cemetery. Death and the afterlife are major mysteries that have engaged people for millennia. The oldest burials date back over 100,000 years ago. Most prehistoric people were buried in simple pits and returned to the earth. However, many prehistoric burials, usually of high status individuals, included grave goods for the deceased to use in the afterlife. Rocks may have been placed on early burials to protect the remains from animals and to prevent the deceased from rising from the dead, a precursor to headstones.

People around the world and over time have practised ancestor worship. They presented offerings to their deceased ancestors as they believed that if they did not show respect, the ancestors would not watch over them or would return as ghosts and haunt them. In many cultures, it was critical to perform the correct rituals to ensure that the soul of the deceased would enter the afterlife.

Grave architecture and symbolism reflect the beliefs of the culture that produced them. The ancient Egyptians believed that the body had to be preserved to ensure its immortality. Mummies would be prepared and placed in coffins decorated with images of gods, such as Osiris, god of the underworld, and goddesses, such as the sky goddess, Nut. The markers for the remains of pharaohs were the pyramids.

The ancient Greeks and Romans believed that it was essential to perform the correct rituals for the dead to assure their successful passage into the afterlife. The winged god of death, Thanatos, was a relatively minor figure compared to Hades, ruler of the underworld. The Greeks were too afraid to speak the name, Hades, "the Invisible," and referred to the god as Pluton, "the Rich," referring to the hidden wealth of the earth in terms of agriculture and mining. They believed that the underworld was surrounded by water, either the ocean or rivers. The newly dead had to pay the ferryman, Charon, to carry them across the river to the abode of the dead. This belief was incorporated into burial practices with the placement of coins in the mouth of the deceased to pay Charon. Honey cakes had to be provided to appease Cerberus, the three-headed hound of hell. Much of the mythology refers to the Queen of the Underworld, Persephone, who was picking flowers in a meadow when she was abducted by Hades to serve as his Queen. While Persephone was in the underworld, her mother, Demeter, grieved and winter fell on the world. When she returned to earth, summer followed. Sacrifices were offered to Demeter for a safe passage. Rituals related to Demeter's mysteries involved sacrifices of sows in underground chambers. Demeter's Roman counterpart was Ceres, the goddess of grain, and it was common for wealthy Roman families to sacrifice a sow to Ceres.

In Victoria, the earliest burial sites were those of Indigenous peoples. Burial cairns consisting of large boulders were located on the slope of Beacon Hill and on the land that sloped towards Cadboro Bay. An 1854 sketch by William B. McMurtie shows a wooden structure with four carved figures surrounded by arbutus trees on the present day Laurel Point. The figures represented the warriors who were buried there. In 1850, the Island of the Dead, now Halkett Island in the Selkirk Waters, was a site where the Lekwungen people placed their dead in wooden boxes and canoes. They would come to the island at twilight to provide food for their dead ancestors. The use of canoes to hold the deceased suggest the concept of the spirits of the deceased sailing to an afterworld surrounded by water. In 1867, boys set the island on fire and the practices were discontinued. The Songhees people may have believed that ghosts haunted Craigflower Creek where it entered Portage Inlet as it was known in Lekwungen as *Pulkwutsang*, "the place of ghosts." It was referred to as Deadman River on an 1855 map.

The first cemetery in Victoria was the Fort Victoria graveyard, located in 1843 on the banks of the Johnson Street ravine. That site is now the southwest corner of Douglas and Johnson Streets. Hudson's Bay Company employees and their families were buried there. The cemetery fell into disrepair and pigs started to root in the graves, digging up the corpses, to the horror of residents. The association of pigs and graveyards recalls the practices in ancient Rome when a sow was sacrificed to the Roman goddess, Ceres, to ensure a safe passage to the afterworld.

In 1855, the Old Burying Ground was opened on Quadra Street and it provided space for about 1,300 interments between 1855 and 1873. The gravesites were often waterlogged, making it difficult to bury the coffins and keep them buried. Wandering cattle and pigs disrupted the graves. Burials at the Old Burying Ground were discontinued in 1873, and in 1908, the burying ground became a park called Pioneer Square.

The prominent architects of Victoria designed not only buildings, but grave memorials as houses of the dead. At the Quadra Street Burying Ground, Victoria City Hall architect John Teague designed a sandstone obelisk in 1866 as a memorial for the officers and men of the *HMS Sutlej* who died while stationed at Esquimalt. Thomas Trounce designed the 1872 Pritchard monument, topped by a pineapple ornament, for Captain Thomas Pritchard and his wife, Margaret. Ross Bay Cemetery hosts memorials designed by F. M. Rattenbury and Samuel Maclure. In 1915, Maclure designed an addition to the porte-cochère for William Agnew's Rockland Avenue home, then two years later he designed Agnew's tomb. Rattenbury designed a monument for the family of Henry Pering Pellew Crease who was born in Ince Castle, a manor house in Cornwall. Monuments featured styles favoured by the architects of the day. For example, the Gothic Revival Style was used in a white marble tablet in 1889 for Cecilia Tyrwhitt-Drake.

Many cultures believe that the spirits of the dead, or parts of them, remain on earth after their death. Superstition and legends are commonly attached to cemeteries and cemeteries are often seen as the sites of haunting. It has been said that Victoria is British Columbia's most haunted place. The *Ghosts of Victoria Festival* is held annually, indicating the popularity of Victoria's ghosts.

Several ghosts have been seen in Pioneer Square. Adelaide Griffin, the proprietor of the Boomerang Inn, was Victoria's first reported ghost. She had died in 1861 of typhoid and was buried in the Old Burying Grounds. Her husband, Ben Griffin, was a spiritualist who conducted séances with Victoria Mayor James Fell. In 1863, the *British Colonist* newspaper reported the sighting of a lady in white who glided over Langley Alley. She has also been seen at Pioneer Square. Less frequently seen is the ghost of Robert Johnson who slit his throat in a house across the street in the 1870s.

British Columbia's first Jewish Cemetery opened in 1860, with its first burial in 1861—that of Morris Price, a Freemason who was murdered at Cayoosh near the present town of Lillooet. It is B.C.'s oldest operating cemetery still in use today. Visitors often leave small pebbles on the gravestones rather than flowers. There are a number of explanations for this practice, including the idea that stones represent permanence relating to eternal life or that the presence of a pebble shows that someone visited the grave.

Ross Bay Cemetery, 1516 Fairfield Road

In the Victorian era, population growth resulted in the replacement of crowded churchyards by cemeteries for burials. The idea of beautiful landscaped cemeteries emerged from Europe with examples such as Paris's 1804 Père Lachaise Cemetery. Landscape designer, J.C. Loudon, suggested in his 1843 book, *On the Laying Out, Planting, and Managing of Cemeteries*, that cemeteries should be like gardens for the enjoyment of the living as much as repose for the dead. His book was widely influential and led to a new movement in cemetery design.

As the Quadra Street Burying Ground became crowded, the city began to look for a new site. Several acres near Ogden Point in James Bay were acquired but this plan was abandoned due to local opposition. In 1872, the City purchased 12 acres of land outside of town at Ross Bay for a new cemetery. Ross Bay Cemetery was opened in 1873 and it has been in continuous use since then.

Ross Bay Cemetery is a magnificent Victorian era cemetery. The Victorians, following the lead of their widow queen, were obsessed with grieving and overt expressions of death. Their burials are rich in symbolism and maudlin sentiment. But the symbols they adopted still speak to our collective unconscious. The stump of a tree symbolizes the tree of life cut down. The willow tree weeps in grief. An inverted torch indicates the life light extinguished. The checkerboard motif at the foot of some graves displays the duality of life, light and dark, heaven and earth. Particularly poignant are children's graves. The grave of D.B. Campbell, "A Little Hero" who died at the age of 17 months, has a small chair, empty but for a pair of baby shoes on the seat. It is the power of the symbols that mark the graves, coupled with the beautiful site, that form the essence of the sacred nature of Ross Bay cemetery.

Many of the symbols of death used in the Victorian era originated in ancient Egypt, Greece and Rome, suggesting the return to antiquity as the mark of civilization. During a time of rapid change, the symbols of the Victorian era were more inspiring than the macabre *memento mori* such as winged skulls of the eighteenth century.

The Egyptian revival is evident in the use of the obelisks as monuments. The obelisk symbolizes the Sun God, Ra, and eternal life. The tallest obelisk in the cemetery marks the graves of the Spencer family who founded Spencer's Department Stores. The family tomb of Sir Francis Barnard displays a striking red granite obelisk.

In ancient Greece and early Rome, cremation was common, with the remains placed in urns. In the Victorian era, a draped urn became a popular symbol on grave monuments with the urn symbolizing immortality and the drapery representing mourning. An example is the family gravesite of coal baron Robert Dunsmuir which consists of a gray granite pedestal topped with a draped urn. The dark gray granite monument for former B.C. Premier, the Honourable John Robson and family, suggests mourning with the use of a draped urn on a pedestal.

After the second century, cremation in ancient Roman was replaced by inhumation and urns by sarcophagi, above ground stone coffins. The word *sarcophagus* comes from the Greek and means "flesh-eating stone," referring to a type of limestone that was believed to decompose flesh. Sarcophagi were often decorated with reliefs of images from mythology. Nereids (sea nymphs) were carved on many sarcophagi, perhaps alluding to the Isles of the Blessed, a paradise in the western ocean. Seashells also became associated with funerary art. In contrast, the sarcophagi at Ross Bay Cemetery are quite plain. The Wilson family is interred in a gray granite sarcophagus. A daughter of the family, Victoria Jane Wilson, became famous for leaving the family house and fortune to her pet macaw, Louis. A double sepulchral sarcophagus was created for the Anscomb family in 1956.

The classic influence in the cemetery continues with the use of Greek and Roman columns on the monuments. Gateway monuments have two columns supporting an arch and represent a gateway or "portal to eternity." The Robertson memorial, made of red granite, features twin columns topped by an arch holding an urn. Bi-columnar monuments are often used when a couple is buried side by side, and this is true for the Robertson memorial. Under one column is the inscription for the husband, William Archibald Robertson, a veteran of the American Civil War. The other column references the wife, Martha Matilda Mayne Robertson. Portals to the underworld are common in mythology and many became associated with physical locations. The cleft in the earth through which Hades took Persephone to the underworld has been identified at various sites, including Enna on the Island of Sicily. Another portal to the underworld of Hades was believed to be located in a cave at Cape Matapan, the southern most point of the Greek mainland. In medieval times, a portal to purgatory, known as St. Patrick's Purgatory, was referenced as being located in a cave on Station Island in Loch Derg in Ireland and it remains a site of pilgrimages to this day.

The Gothic Revival style can be seen in Ross Bay Cemetery in monuments with four columns supporting a canopy topped with a draped urn, such as those for the Heathorn and Winters families. Three lobes in the arches signify the Trinity. Such monuments were modelled after the much larger Albert Memorial which was completed in 1876 to commemorate the death of Prince Albert, the consort of Queen Victoria.

Another Roman influence is the use of mausoleums. The wealthy Romans built mausoleums and the structures often contained kitchens and bedrooms for use by the living family on visits. About ten mausoleums can be found at Ross Bay Cemetery and they house the remains of prominent Victoria families. Inspired by classical forms, the Rithet family mausoleum was designed in a Romanesque style for former mayor, Robert Patterson Rithet. The Helmcken Mausoleum, built for lawyer Harry Helmcken and family, features an Egyptian-revival style.

Helmcken Family Mausoleum

Originally, the cemetery was divided into sections based on the religious domination of the deceased, such as Presbyterian, Anglican, Roman Catholic and "heathen." Many of the symbols on the gravestones referenced religious affiliations. The cross is the most common symbol in the cemetery as most of the interments were Christian. The cross symbol takes a variety of forms with different meanings. The Roman cross illustrates sacrifice. The Celtic cross

THE KEY TO MYTHIC VICTORIA

shows the union of the feminine circle of eternity with the masculine cross. A Celtic cross can be seen on the red granite tombstone of B.C.'s first governor, Sir James Douglas. The equal-sided Greek cross speaks of the four directions and the need for balance in life. A three-tiered base supporting a cross, as seen on the grave of Sir Matthew Baillie Begbie, symbolizes the Trinity or the three values of hope, faith and love. Some gravestones carry the initials IHS, a monogram for the name of Jesus, often thought to stand for *Iesus Hominum Salvator*, or Jesus, the Saviour of men. Doves as symbols of the Holy Spirit are found on many gravestones, such as the dove descending from heaven on the grave of Thomas Mills Bowden. In the Roman Catholic section, a beautifully carved statue of Saint Clare of Assisi marks the graves of the Sisters of Saint Clare. Saint Clare was a thirteenth century Italian saint who led a religious life of poverty. In 1958, she was designated as the patron saint of television because of the time when Saint Clare was too sick to attend Mass, she had the mystical experience of seeing and hearing it on the walls of her room.

Anchors are used to represent faith and are commonly found on the graves of seafarers. For example, the grave of Captain George E. Rudlin, a captain for the Canadian Pacific Navigation Company, features an anchor carved into a globe.

As on the prows of ships and hoods of early cars, female figures were commonly used on graves as a symbol of protection. Stone angels guard the graves of Christians and prepare to carry the souls to heaven. In ancient Egypt, the image of Nut, the sky goddess, was painted on the lids of coffins to protect the deceased.

The Blue Angel is a local legend. She marks the grave of Charles Edward Pooley (1845–1912), MLA and President of the Executive Council. According to his gravestone, he was "A Just Man Made Perfect." The Blue Angel received that name when she was sprayed with blue paint by vandals. She has come to be an oracle of young love. Lovers visit her for a sign, such as a smile, to indicate that their relationship will be good, or a tear, suggesting their affair is doomed. Sometimes they leave offerings for her, and coins or fir cones may be seen as her feet. On nights with a full moon, it is said that she will cry.

The Blue Angel on C.E. Pooley's Grave

The monument to the Wood family features a young woman in mourning. She wears the classically inspired Roman tunic. She looks downward and holds a wreath in her right hand over an urn. The circular wreath, with no beginning and no end, represents eternal life, a symbol of victory over death. The mourning maiden recalls the Greek myth of Niobe. When she boasted that she was a better mother than Leto because she had more children, she offended the goddess. As a result, all her children but two were killed. The gods turned her into stone and grief stricken, she continued to weep for her slain children as a spring flowing from a rock.

The mourning maiden on the Wood family monument is demure compared to figure on the Deans memorial which suggests the glory of a crowned goddess. The white marble statue of a young woman in a draped Roman tunic wears a wreath with a central star on her head. She raises her right hand and her finger points to heaven (the finger is now broken). Her left hand rests on a scroll over a large anchor, with the scroll symbolizing law or scripture and the anchor symbolizing faith. The image of the goddess in the cemetery recalls the Greek myth of Persephone, the spirit of nature who was forcibly taken by Hades to be his Queen. Like Persephone, the cemetery illustrates the cycle of life, with trees and bushes growing out of the graves, life renewed but transformed.

The concept of the maiden in the cemetery continues to the modern day. A 2001 document *Proposals for the Southwest Quadrant, Ross Bay Cemetery*, prepared by Pechet + Robb Design, proposed the placement of a female statue, the *Lady of the Sea*, at the southwest corner of Ross Bay Cemetery where Memorial Crescent meets Dallas Road. No action has been taken on this proposal yet.

Membership in fraternal organizations is often indicated by the symbols used on gravestones. For example, the graves of Masons are indicated with a compass and square, tools of the stone mason. The grave of Charles Moss indicates his membership in the Independent Order of Oddfellows (IOOF). His tombstone incorporates IOOF symbols, such as the three-link chain standing for friendship, love and truth. The all-seeing eye represents the eternal presence of god. The hand holding a heart symbolizes charity freely given. The grave is enclosed by a cast iron fence with harps, oak leaves and acorns, and on the corner posts are draped lamps. The harp suggests heavenly music, the oak leaves and acorn, strength.

Other tombstones incorporate individual aspects of the deceased. For example, Fred Medley was a firefighter who was killed on duty in 1925. His gravestone features a distinctive bronze fire helmet resting on a concrete pillow.

Over time, the decorative symbolism of the Victorian era gave way to greater simplicity. Modern grave markers may be as simple as flat plaques. They may reflect individuality, with computer-generated carvings showing the deceased's hobbies and interests.

Ross Bay Cemetery is a fusion of opposites: the sea meeting the land, the stone headstones under a canopy of green branches, life respecting death. Its trees speak to the strength of the Green Man, the embodiment of nature in vegetation. The ground, of course, is Mother Earth.

The trees of Ross Bay Cemetery are symbols of renewal. Presently, about fifty species of trees grow in the cemetery. For many years after the cemetery opened in 1873, the site lacked significant vegetation. Not only were trees vulnerable to the wind and sea spray blowing off Ross Bay, but people of the Victorian era had a fear of water filling graves. As a result, cemeteries were not watered. As ideas changed, people began to see cemeteries as memorial parks and as a way to connect with nature. The Parks Department of Victoria initiated a tree-planting program in the late 1930s to early 1940s that saw the planting of most of the trees in Ross Bay cemetery.

Yew trees, both English and Irish yews, were planted as traditional cemetery trees. Yews are common in churchyards and cemeteries in the British Isles. Gerald of Wales recorded their abundance as early as the twelfth century. Some scholars suggest that this practice is related to ancient funeral rites; others believe it reflects the use of the yew for longbows; still others consider the plantings to be related to the yew as a symbol of resurrection. In Roman times, European warriors committed suicide by using yew extracts to avoid capture by the Romans. The yew is both poisonous and evergreen, symbolizing death combined with immortality.

The mother of all Irish yews was found in Ireland in the 1780s. All Irish yews today are clones of this plant. British folklore tells that the red in the branches of the yew reflects the auburn hair of a woman murdered by a local priest who hid her head in a yew tree.

The pine tree also represents immortality and its cone represents renewal. The City of Victoria planted about 5,000 pines in the cemetery in 1936 and 1937. In fact, Ross Bay Cemetery contains the widest range of pine trees in Victoria. Now only 500 pine trees are left. In ancient times, Druids were said to have burned pine at the winter solstice to bring back the sun.

Only a few willows were planted in the cemetery and these were planted in the 1930s and 1940s. They symbolize weeping for the loss of the dead and their image is commonly used to decorate gravestones. Because of their requirements for water, however, their presence in cemeteries is rare. A different weeping tree species, a magnificent and rare Weeping Temple Juniper, is located by the maintenance shed in the cemetery. The species is often found in the gardens of Japanese temples where its weeping branches symbolize tears for the departed.

Underground streams flow through Ross Bay Cemetery. At one time, West Creek and East Creek ran over the land, emptying into Ross Bay. Sometime after 1909, the streams were forced into culverts and now pass under the property. After a rain, the rushing water of East Creek can be heard under the access covers to the culvert. The underground stream is a common motif in Greek mythology which describes how the deceased must cross a river to the underworld. When the souls of the deceased drank from the Lethe, the river of forgetfulness, they would forget their earthy lives.

As a place for the living, Ross Bay Cemetery is treasured by citizens and visitors alike. On any given day, people stroll through the park-like setting, pause to rest on the many benches, or pay their respect to their family graves or those of historical Victorians. The cemetery is history in concrete form and includes the graves of many of the people who made their mark on local history, including Sir James Douglas, the first governor of the Province of B.C., the Honourable John Hamilton, a Father of Confederation, and John Robson, B.C. Premier. The grave of Emily Carr is the most popular. Her plaque reads "author and artist, lover of nature" and usually is decorated by recent offerings such as pens and pencils stuck into notes or artwork, paintbrushes and pine cones. Visitors come to pay her the respect she did not receive in life and perhaps to seek creative inspiration.

Although most people respect and value the cemetery, some come to destroy the headstones and desecrate the graves. Concern about vandalism and overall decay of the cemetery resulted in the formation of the Old Cemeteries Society in 1990 to raise the profile of the cemeteries in the Victoria area to better protect them. There are so many stories about Ross Bay Cemetery that the Old Cemetery Society can hold weekly tours with special themes, such as the gold rush and gossip in the graveyard. The Society's most popular tour is its Halloween ghost tour.

Ghosts seen at Ross Bay Cemetery include a mysterious, elderly couple dressed in Victorian attire gliding along the western side of the cemetery. There have been reports of the ghost of Isabella Ross, the first woman in British Columbia to own land and the owner of the farm that stood on the present site of the cemetery. The ghost of David Fee, murdered by a Fenian assassin on the steps of St. Andrews Cathedral on Christmas Eve 1890, is often spotted as a white mist near his grave. Ross Bay Cemetery is becoming more popular with ghosts as evidenced by video recordings of ghostly orbs. Over the years, many a teenager has visited Ross Bay Cemetery after dark on Halloween for a thrill.

In 1980, Ross Bay Cemetery became notorious when the book, *Michelle Remembers*, by Lawrence Pazder and Michelle Smith was published. It purported to recount the memories of Michelle as a child when she was the victim of ritual satanic abuse in Victoria. Smith said that she was taken to Ross Bay Cemetery where a grave was opened and she was put in it. The book also noted that the Church of Satan held a ritual in the Helmcken Mausoleum for Smith's unsuccessful "rebirth into evil."

Ceremonies are held in the cemetery to respect the deceased. For example, starting in 2011, the Japanese community holds an annual festival by the Kakehashi monument. The monument was erected in 1999 to commemorate the 150 Victorians of Japanese descent buried in the cemetery. Kakehashi means "bridge," referring to the "bridge across the Pacific Ocean." In August, the Japanese community participates in an Obon memorial ceremony in the cemetery. Obon, the Japanese Buddhist "Feast of Lanterns," is held to honour the spirits of people's ancestors. It has been celebrated in Japan for over five centuries. The ceremony lasts for three days, and traditionally ends with a Bon dance in gratitude to the ancestors. The festival originated, it is said, when a disciple of the Buddha was distressed to see his mother suffering in the realm of hungry ghosts. He asked the Buddha for help, and was advised to make offerings to several Buddhist monks. He did so, and his mother was released. He was so happy about this that he did a dance of joy and that joy is repeated in the Obon ceremony.

The cemetery preserves the memories of Victoria residents of the past. The War Memorial in the cemetery states, "Gone but not forgotten. Their name liveth forever more." This sentiment captures the value of cemeteries – a place to remember those who went before us. A sun dial in the cemetery reminds us of the passage of time and suggests that as our life is finite, it should be lived in light.

Chinese Cemetery at Harling Point, Crescent Road

The Chinese Cemetery at Foul Point (now called Harling Point) opened in 1903 and was Victoria's first and only exclusively Chinese cemetery. Previously, Chinese burials had been located at the Old Burying Ground and then at Ross Bay Cemetery. The Chinese community had become concerned because the Chinese graves at

Ross Bay Cemetery were located so close to the ocean that storms often washed them away, so they acquired land for their own cemetery.

When the Chinese Cemetery opened, many of the graves were moved there from Ross Bay Cemetery. It was a common practice in North America for the remains of overseas Chinese to be interred for seven to ten years and then exhumed, cleaned, and shipped back to Hong Kong for distribution to their native villages for reburial. Many people believed that they would return to China after they had made their fortune in "Gold Mountain." They wanted to be buried next to the remains of their ancestors in their home villages where their descendants could ensure that their graves received the proper care. They believed that without a proper burial and proper care, the spirits of the deceased would wander forever unless their bones were returned to China.

Reburial was not a new practice as it had been practised in Guangzhou (Canton) for centuries. If families were experiencing problems that may have resulted from an unhappy ancestor, they initiated a reburial to ensure that the ancestor was content, thereby improving their own fortune. The separation of the flesh from bones had a symbolic function of separating the authority that, like flesh, the deceased relinquishes after death from the durability, like bone, that the deceased holds over his or her descendants.

At Harling Point, bones were stored in a bone house (no longer standing) on the site before transport to China. Remains were shipped from across Canada to Victoria's Chinese Cemetery. The first centralized shipment back to China took place in 1909. When the Japan-China War broke out in 1937, it was no longer possible to ship the bones to China, so the bones remained on site. In 1961, the remains of 820 people were buried in a mass grave, adding to the 400 burials on the site when it closed in 1950.

The Chinese Cemetery is sited following the ancient Chinese tradition of *feng shui* or geomancy. *Feng shui* (which means "wind and water") is the Chinese art of positioning structures, including graves, in a harmonious relationship with nature. It was used to locate the best sites for burial places to ensure that the ancestors would be content with their placement and ensure a harmonious life for their descendants. The choice of burial location of an ancestor could affect many aspects of a person's life, such as their wealth, their children and their longevity. A tale from the third century told how when a man had to decide on the aspects of a site for the burial of his father, he chose the place that would give him many grandchildren rather than the place that would result in his success and longevity.

The geomancer takes the natural landscape into account when selecting sites, assessing how the landscape affects the *qi*, or energy of the area. For example, hills and mountains provide barriers to noxious winds that might carry evil spirits while at the same time, they allow favourable winds to pass. The presence of water is important to provide feminine balance of the masculine mountains. The duality of the masculine yang energy must be balanced by the feminine yin energy throughout a site.

The principles of *feng shui* are evident at Harling Point. To the east of the cemetery is the higher elevation "Azure Dragon" that brings treasure. It is balanced on the west by the yin element, the "White Tiger." At its back is "Pillow Mountain" or Gonzales Hill which provides shelter from winds carrying evil spirits. It is here that the two cosmic forces of Dragon and Tiger come together. The underlying geology of the area, the point where two sections of the earth's crust meet, supports the fusion of two forces. At the front of the cemetery flows the "Living Water" of Gonzales Bay and Juan de Fuca Strait, balanced by the Olympic Mountains as a "Worshipping Mountain Range." Mountains are a symbol of eternal life and water a symbol of wealth. No trees are allowed to block the view from the graves. In recognition of the belief that evil spirits follow straight lines, there are no straight paths in the cemetery and no structures, such as roads, point directly to the site. The move to the cemetery at Harling Point reflected not only the flooding of the Chinese graves at Ross Bay Cemetery, but the need for good *feng shui* as people believed that the siting at Ross Bay lacked good *feng shui*, being featureless and low lying.

The site is dominated by twin burners separated by an altar. Built in 1909, the structures were used for burning spiritual offerings for use by the deceased in the shadowy spirit world. The Feast of the Dead offering food and alcohol was spread out on the altar between the burners to provide sustenance for the ancestors.

The Chinese Cemetery at Harling Point

The care of the graves of ancestors is considered to be a sacred duty. Ancestor worship is the only native religion to China, and dates back for thousands of years. Families still visit the graves at the Chinese Cemetery on *Ching Ming*, Grave Sweeping day, when people honour their ancestors. *Ching Ming*, meaning "pure brightness," is held on the 106th day after winter solstice, usually April 4th or 5th, celebrating the return of summer. Descendants clean the graves, provide food for the spirit of the deceased and burn imitation paper money for use in the afterlife. They burn incense and may light off fire crackers to frighten evil spirits.

The *feng shui* of the site proved to be auspicious to its continued preservation when it was designated a National Historic Site in 1995 by the Government of Canada.

Royal Oak Burial Park, 4673 Falaise Drive

The Royal Oak Burial Park in Saanich was officially opened on November 28, 1923. In 2008, the park opened an area for "green" burials. "Green" or natural burials allow for the remains of the deceased to decompose naturally. Although natural burials were the norm for thousands of years, in the last several hundred years, preservation of the remains was practised. Recently, interest in green burials is re-emerging. The first natural burial ground in the United Kingdom was created in 1993 and the first in North America in 1998.

Green burials allow the deceased to return to Mother Earth, echoing the sentiments recorded by Emily Carr over 100 years ago.

The cemeteries of Victoria capture the beliefs and culture of their time. The symbolism of the Victorian era has been replaced by more individual inscriptions on grave markers. Memorial benches or trees are in demand as replacements for gravestones as a way to remember loved ones. Practices such as green burials are emerging with the growth of the environmental movement. New myths may arise for the cemeteries of the future or perhaps the Gaia concept of Mother Earth will re-emerge as the central motif.

Secret Tunnels

Yes, there are secret tunnels in Victoria. The idea of labyrinths of secret tunnels running under Victoria has long been dismissed as an urban myth. But there are tunnels below the city. They attract urban explorers because they are dangerous and because they hold secrets. The idea of travelling under a busy city, unseen and undetected, has the appeal of the mythical cloak of invisibility. In myths, secret passages can take people to supernatural realms.

According to urban folklore, a person can travel underground through all of Victoria. Myths have suggested that in the early days of Victoria, miners drawn by the gold rush created the tunnel system. Stories about the use of the tunnels as escape routes, for smuggling, to store treasure, as homes, as crypts and for satanic rituals proliferate, as do conspiracy theories that serve to keep the tunnels secret. Some people have suggested that the tunnels follow ley lines, that is, lines of energy that link significant sites.

In the early days of Fort Victoria when ships unloaded in the Inner Harbour, tunnels were built to move the cargo to the Fort. Some end near the location of the present day Bay Center. Other tunnels are just urban myths, such as the bricked-in opening in the rock wall on the west side of Wharf Street. This wall once formed the basement of a Hudson's Bay Company warehouse. Over the years, many people thought the opening led to the fabled passage from the harbour to a secret location. However, it was actually just a niche for storage, later bricked in to minimize risks.

Heritage sidewalk prisms are embedded on many of the sidewalks in downtown Victoria, providing filtered light for the tunnel-like areaways under the streets. Once, hundreds of thousands of glass tiles were located on city sidewalks, now only about 11,000 remain. They can be found at several locations on the sidewalks in front of some buildings on Fort, Broughton, Johnson and Blanshard Streets. Beneath the tiles, now coloured purple with age, are the basements in which merchants stored their goods and received delivery of freight and fuel. Also found on downtown sidewalks are large metal grates, openings for freight elevators used to bring deliveries into the stores. Most are no longer in use. Some of the basements of the older buildings are connected to others, creating tunnels. In addition to the underground spaces for the storage and delivery of goods, many of tunnels in Victoria are storm drains and sewers. A brick storm drain at the foot of Johnson Street Bridge attracts many tunnel-seekers. Another storm drain runs the distance from Hillside Mall to Rock Bay.

The most persistent rumours relate to the network of tunnels under Chinatown that led to the Inner Harbour, allowing smugglers and opium dealers to escape from the police. In fact, there were escape routes in the Forbidden City of old Chinatown, but they ran between buildings and through courtyards and alleys such as Fan Tan Alley. Significant underground passageways have not been found.

Fan Tan Alley

It has been said that a tunnel runs from the Janion Hotel on Store Street to Chinatown. Located on the waterfront at Store Street, the Janion was opened in 1891 as a railroad hotel. Many believe that the basement of the Janion Hotel has a portal to a Victoria's secret underground.

There are many stories about tunnels under the Empress Hotel. A tunnel does run from the Empress Hotel under Douglas Street to a nearby lot. It was built to move laundry between the hotel and the steam laundry building. The entrance to the tunnel was sealed when it was no longer used. According to one account, when the tunnel was sealed, screams came from inside. The tunnel was reopened but only the marks of fingernails on concrete were found. Use of the tunnel continued as evidenced by a fire in 2007 started by a group of homeless people living in the passageway. Another tunnel ran from the basement of the Empress Hotel to the waters of James Bay. At high tide, its entrance would be flooded. Its original purpose is not known but it has been suggested that it might have been used for sewage. Another rumour is that a tunnel ran between the Empress Hotel and the old Union Club for the use of patrons to visit brothels unobserved.

A tunnel does run under Douglas Street from the Parliament Buildings to the Douglas Building, allowing confidential briefing material to be rushed between the two buildings. The tunnel has now been closed for security reasons.

Other rumours hold that there are hidden passageways under Craigdarroch Castle and tunnels under Tod House in Oak Bay. According to some, rum-runners during the Prohibition used tunnels that ran to the water's edge in areas such as Gonzales Bay.

Speculation about secret spaces under Ross Bay Cemetery continues. According to the book, *Michelle Remembers*, hidden places used for satanic rituals can be found under the cemetery. However, there is no evidence of either tunnels or satanic rituals in the cemetery. Its underground conduits were built to channel the flow of the creeks which ran through it. And there are underground vaults for graves, such as those for Sir James Douglas.

Some light on this fascination with secret tunnels can be shed with a look at ancient myths. The *Epic of Gilgamesh*, one of the oldest myths in the world, mentions a tunnel in a meaningful way. After the death of his friend, Gilgamesh sets out on a quest for the secret of immortality. After a long journey, he reaches two mountains called the Twin Peaks where the sun sets every night and then travels through a tunnel under the mountains to rise the next morning. The tunnel is guarded by two dreadful scorpion people but they allow Gilgamesh to enter the path of the sun. He had to run through the tunnel in total darkness in twelve hours before the sun entered the tunnel with its deadly fire. At the twelfth hour, he emerged from the tunnel at the Garden of the Gods, a paradise full of jewel-laden trees. The tunnel in this myth suggests a journey to the treasures of a rich afterlife. In psychological terms, a tunnel can be seen as the birth canal leading to the promise of life. The phrase, "the light at the end of the tunnel," captures the idea of spiritual illumination after time of darkness.

Victoria is a city of secrets, and tunnels are just one of them. No doubt many of the tunnels are urban myths, but the presence of the existing tunnels provides a fascinating allure.

CHAPTER 17
Creating Community

Community spirit grows when members have a strong sense of the place where they live. This sense is reinforced by the stories people tell about the place. The language of myth and symbols can help build community spirit in three ways. First, myth can create connections and provide perspective through shared understanding. Second, myth helps people identify what is important in their community. Through shared action such as rituals and ceremonies, people can work to preserve what is important, create change as needed and celebrate successes. Finally, through linking to the subconscious and archetypal images, myth and symbols gain potency, creating meaning throughout the landscape.

The Fremont Troll

An example of how choosing the myths and symbols that embody community values and identity can strengthen a community can be found in Fremont, a suburb of Seattle. In 1990, Fremont was having problems with crime and illegal dumping in the dark area under the Aurora Bridge. The Fremont Arts Council commissioned artists to develop five models, then the citizens voted at the Fremont Fair for their favourite. The winner was a hideous, one-eyed, two-ton troll.

Ever since the troll was built in 1991, it has inspired an amazing display of community spirit. Every October 31, the people celebrate Troll-A-Ween. Classes in making costumes and masks lead up to a masquerade ball followed the next day by the annual clean-up of the troll. The residents love their troll. The street was even renamed in honour of the troll, becoming Troll Avenue North in 2005. People are encouraged to interact with the troll and at any given time, visitors can be seen clamouring over the sculpture and posing for pictures.

The troll was a familiar symbol from fairy tales. Trolls represent the shadow side. In Scandinavian folklore, they are hairy monsters who live in hidden places, such as caves. The troll under the bridge was made famous in the fairy tale, Three Billy Goats Gruff. Fear of trolls was invoked to stop children from exploring dangerous places and keep them safe.

Mythological symbols can be unifying factors, serving to channel the energies of a group. Because myth captures the human condition, creatures of myth are as true to their roots today as they were centuries ago.

In Fremont, the motif of the troll has been modernized. The troll crushes a Volkswagen Beetle in its claws and its glaring silver eye is a hubcap. The choice of the menacing troll may have been an expression of the community's feelings toward the traffic in their neighbourhood. Kirby Lindsay, an iconologist for Fremont's History House, said that the historical and mythological relationship between trolls and bridges might have been part of the reason the Fremont Troll was installed under the bridge. The team researched behavioral information about trolls and learned that trolls are normally peaceful unless they are angered, and that their worst enemies are development and pollution. "That he decided to feast on a VW as a sample of the creatures that plagued him from above, before daylight turned him to stone, appears only natural," Lindsay said.

The Fremont troll shows the role of myth and art in building a sense of community and it shows how communities rally around their iconic projects.

Chestnut Trees

Boulevard chestnut trees contribute to the character of Cook Street Village. When the City announced the removal of five trees diseased with white mottled rot, residents became very concerned, expressing grief on local websites. A protestor had to be hauled from a tree when the removal started. Debates ensued about whether the chestnut trees (originating in southeastern Europe) should be replaced with native species not susceptible to fungus disease.

The City cut down the five old horse chestnut trees starting on January 18, 2010 and planted five new horse chestnut trees in their place. In late January, red cards decorated the twigs of a chestnut sapling planted in front of a coffee shop on Cook Street. Messages on the cards spoke to the saplings as sentient beings, wishing the saplings good growth and deep roots.

Clearly, the horse chestnut is a favourite tree for Victorians. Many residents carry memories of the chestnut trees along Cook Street in their various seasonal garbs. They may remember walking down Cook Street in May when the blossoms, like creamy-white candles, carried the scent of incense and the hint of promise of summer days. Or drinking coffee under the shade of the chestnut trees on a hot summer day, watching children climb the trunks, or seeing the filigree of snow-covered branches in winter. And who has not felt wealthier for collecting the glossy brown conkers that fall from the trees in autumn?

Why do people treasure these trees? Their age alone makes them important. The 100-year old chestnut trees are among the oldest in Victoria. Horse chestnuts are associated with good luck. It is said that carrying three conkers in your pocket will bring good luck. Although the chestnuts are not edible, they do have use as medicinal herbs, serving to increase blood circulation. Horse chestnut extract is used to treat varicose veins and a variety of other ailments. Good health is lucky. Although there is no agreement about why the tree is referred to as a "horse" chestnut, some have suggested that the name refers to the horse-shoe shaped stem or leaf scars, recalling the link between horse shoes and good luck.

Folklore holds that spiders are "conkerphobic." Putting conkers in the corners of your rooms will keep your place spider-free. Chestnut burrs are believed to predict weather. When the spines of the chestnut burrs are longer than usual and the burrs are thicker, a long cold winter is coming.

Communities do rally to save trees, such as the movement to save the Anne Frank tree. As she hid in Amsterdam from the Nazis in 1944, Anne Frank wrote in her diary that as long as she could see nature—sun, the sky, the birds and the chestnut tree—from her attic window, she could not be unhappy. When Amsterdam city officials announced that the tree should be removed as it was a hazard, the "Support the Anne Frank Tree" campaign garnered support from an international community to save the tree. The tree was recognized a symbol of hope and a remembrance of the Holocaust. Steel cables were installed in 2008 to prop up its fungus-infested trunk and limbs. Unfortunately, it wasn't enough. The Anne Frank tree is gone, toppled in a storm on August 23, 2010. However, the message of the tree lives on. Saplings from the horse chestnut tree by Anne Frank's house have been sent throughout the world where they grow as a symbol of hope, freedom and tolerance.

The flower spike of chestnut trees is known as a thyrse, a name derived from the staff carried by Dionysus, the Greek god of resurrection. The Cook Street chestnut trees were given new life as woodwork created by the Victoria Island Woodworkers Guild who received donations of the wood. And in 100 years, the new saplings should re-create the shade provided by the old trees. Until then, we can only send our best wishes to the spirits of the saplings for new growth.

Thyrse of the Chestnut Tree

Public Art

Public art provides an external representation of the values of a community. The City of Victoria Public Art Policy states, "Art in its many forms has the power to energize public spaces, make us think and transform where we work, live and play." Public art can serve to develop a sense of place, community pride and identity.

Public art may commemorate history, such as war memorials or historic figures. A statue of the first Prime Minister and Member of Parliament for Victoria from 1878 to 1882, Sir John A. MacDonald, stands outside Victoria's City Hall. A statue of explorer Captain James Cook can be found by the Inner Harbour.

Symbolic images expressing community values are also depicted through public art. A poignant example is the sculpture entitled *The Homecoming* by Nathan Scott that shows a sailor greeting a little girl. Real Admiral Tyrone Pile, commander of Maritime Forces Pacific, said that the image symbolizes, in one snapshot in time, the essence of the navy. Harmony between the different cultures in a community is portrayed in works such as the *Bright Pearl* sculpture located between Centennial Square and Chinatown to honor the people who immigrated to Victoria from the Pearl River Valley in China. The pearl is a symbol of wealth, good luck and prosperity.

Mythic themes inspire the work of many artists as they express the basic human condition and provide layers of meaning. The *Red Dragon* statue by Ping Tsing, located on Government and Pandora Avenues, is a beautiful representation of the mythic creature symbolizing strength and power. The dragon faces upwards so that it can ascend to the sky where it rules water-related weather.

First Nations myths are often expressed in public art in the Capital Region. In 2009, the District of Saanich held a public art competition for proposals for the new Gorge Waterway Park. The theme was knowledge of place and understanding the natural and cultural community along the Gorge. The judges chose Fred Dobbs' proposed statue of Camossung as it reflected both First Nations history and Saanich's goal of environmental stewardship. The statue captures the myth of the maiden Camossung who was responsible for the food resources of the Gorge. A plaque beneath the statue reads,

An ancient Songhees story tells of a young girl named Camossung, turned to stone by 'Hayls' the Transformer. Camossung is believed to have spirit powers and is associated with protecting the local food resources (Coho Salmon, Herring, Oysters and Ducks) of the Songhees people. The sculpture symbolizes the significance of this location. A unique place, where fresh and salt-water merge with each ebb and flow of the Gorge Waterway. A place where animals thrive, and historically, people sought food and a spiritual connection. The original sacred stone is located below the southern side of the Tillicum Bridge, viewable beneath the water at low tide. The Songhees people have participated in this project in good faith and co-operation. District of Saanich Public Art.

Camossung by Fred Dobbs

Artist Fred Dobbs explained his work, "In connecting the story of Camossung to the theme, 'Knowledge of Place' I was immediately inspired. I felt as if I could release an ancient story from the depths as a sculpture. Bringing to the surface a message from the past about how significant this area was to the people who lived here, and how similar the message is today in nurturing and caring for our environment."

A significant series of work honouring the First Nations people can be seen at seven sites around Victoria. The sculptures of giant spindle whorls, names *Signs of Lekwungen*, identify culturally significant sites to the Songhees and Esquimalt Nations, the Lekwungen people. The bronze casts, unveiled in 2008, were created by Songhees artist, Butch Dick. Symbolically, the spindle whorl was considered to be the foundation of the family. The spindle whorl was used by Coast Salish women to spin wool from which the women wove pieces such as blankets. As they took so long to make, the blankets were an important symbol of wealth. The spindle whorl may be seen as the essence of transformation—changing wool into wealth. Decorations were added by the men, perhaps to increase the power of the spindle whorls. Ritual words may have played a part in the spinning and weaving process. The transformation theme related to spinning and weaving is evident in the German fairy tale, Rumplestiltskin, in which the elf spins flax into gold. Like using ritual words, Rumplestiltskin sings as he spins, but his incantation reveals his own name and thus, he forfeits his reward of the queen's first child.

Spindle Whorl by Butch Dick at City Hall

Songhees artist Butch Dick, said, "Mythology is important to us, especially when we are young. It is important for capturing the spirit of different animals to enhance our own spirits. The highest order of mythical animal is the Thunderbird." A spindle whorl illustrating the legend of the Thunderbird and Orca created by artist Charles W. Elliot of the Tsartlip First Nations can be seen at Esquimalt Municipal Hall. The whorl shows the Thunderbird and Orca in a struggle, representing the balance of power between the physical and spiritual worlds.

In 2009, the *Land and Sea Mural—Na'Tsa'Maht*, (a Lekwungen phrase meaning Unity Wall)—was unveiled at Victoria's breakwater to honour the traditions and history of the Esquimalt and Songhees Nations. The mural transforms the sides of the breakwater into an enormous colourful depiction of First Nations traditions and stories. It is planned to be the longest in the world, stretching nearly 2.5 kilometres. Phase I and II of the five-phase project are now complete. Phase I incorporates images representing the sea, designed by Butch Dick of the Songhees Nation, and images representing the land, designed by Darlene Gait of Esquimalt Nation, all painted by a youth team. The images represent the iconic animals of the area, such as the wolf, the killer whale, the cougar, the salmon and the deer; mythical animals such as the sea serpent; and sacred places such as Harling Point. Phase II includes images of dance, nature, music, spirituality and landscapes. The project creates a bridge between cultures. The rationale for the rich traditional stories is provided in the Land and Sea Mural sign which notes, "Stories associated with each species were taught to the young so they would gain the respect that is essential to all life on earth." Sharing the images and stories of the First Nations people heightens the sense of place for all who view the mural.

Art in the City

Symbols also feature in community fund-raising. Inspired by public art projects in other cities, the B.C. Lions initiated the "Art in the City" project in 2004 in Victoria and Vancouver. Artists created unique designs on large fibreglass forms in the shape of a specific animal and the works were displayed in prominent public spaces around the city for a period of time after which they were auctioned to raise funds for the B.C. Lions Society's Easter Seal Services.

The symbols chosen by the Society reflect the provincial identity. In the first year, the Orca, representing the ocean, was selected. The Spirit Bear was the next choice in 2006. The Spirit Bear, a rare white phase of the black bear found on B.C.'s central and north coast, has inspired myths over the years. The Kitasoo/Xai'xais First Nation tell how Raven, the Creator, transformed one in every ten black bears to white to remind the people of the time when glaciers covered the earth and how they should be thankful for the bounty of the land today. In some areas, such as Princess Royal Island, one in ten black bears is indeed white. The Spirit Bear has become the icon of the endangered wilderness. In 2009, the element of air was represented by the "Eagles in the City" project, personifying freedom. The orca, the spirit bear and the eagle have great resonance throughout British Columbia because of their beauty and because of the values they personify. In comparison, Toronto featured "Moose in the City" and Chicago had "Cows on Parade." In addition to fund-raising, supporting the arts and celebrating diversity, "Art in the City" had a goal to capture the imagination of people. This is one of the powers of myth—it awakens the archetypes of the subconscious, firing up the imagination.

Killing The Unicorn

The power of a mythic element to consolidate community action can be seen in the unicorn. A *Saturday Night Live* show which first aired in 2007 included a sketch where citizens voted at a town hall meeting on whether to develop multi-million dollar mall in the forest where the unicorn lived. Even though the unicorn granted their wishes and made them rich, the townspeople were bored with it. Only one gnome-like creature, a self-styled protector of the unicorn, spoke in favour of preserving the forest. The majority voted for the mall as it saved them a ten minute drive to the mall in the next town. Of course, the result was disastrous. Like the killing of the proverbial goose that laid the golden eggs, destroying the unicorn in the forest cost the people their true wealth.

The unicorn also appears in the story of *Harry Potter and the Philosopher's Stone*. Harry encounters a unicorn in the Forbidden Forest, dying because the evil Voldemort has drunk its blood to save his own life. The unicorn, here, is a symbol of innocence and purity. But Voldemort, too, will have to pay the price because whoever drinks the blood of the unicorn will lead a cursed life.

What is it about the unicorn that makes it so magical? The unicorn is a powerful mythological symbol, common in ancient times and modern times, found in writings from Asia, Africa and Europe. As expected, the unicorn has layers of meaning.

In Asian folklore, the unicorn was a sensitive animal, so caring that it would walk silently to avoid hurting the grass. It foretold change, such as the birth of a great leader. The ancient Greeks believed that the unicorn was a real animal living in India. By the Middle Ages, the unicorn was a popular symbol commonly displayed in tapestries and religious art. The art was based on an allegory about the unicorn being trapped by a maiden, representing the Virgin Mary, then laying its head in her lap and going to sleep. Even Leonardo da Vinci noted the unicorn's propensity to be tamed by maidens, allowing hunters to kill it for its horn, believed to have healing properties. As late as the sixteenth century, people drank concoctions allegedly made from unicorn horns to neutralize poison.

At the town hall meeting on *Saturday Night Live*, the unicorn in the forest serves a powerful metaphor for the tension between preserving environmental values and introducing the values of development. Killing the unicorn represents the loss of innocence in a community where children no longer feel safe to walk to school or where distrust arises from yet one more development proposal. It has been written that if we do not allow unicorns to survive, there is little hope for our own survival. As Alice was asked in *Through the Looking Glass*, now that we have seen the unicorn, do we believe in it?

CHAPTER 18
Pursuing Paradise

Victoria has been described many times as a paradise with its luxuriant gardens and gentle sea breezes. But what is the spirit of this place? What is its identity? Landscape, history and people influence the spirit of the place. We can get clues about its identity by looking at the symbols, myths and rituals strewn about the place.

Canadian poet, Earle Birney, wrote in his work *Can. Lit.*, "It's only by our lack of ghosts we're haunted." It was challenging for early settlers to move to a new land where there was no continuity of culture. They could plant their gardens and build their homes, but they still yearned for a spiritual connection to the land, for the ghosts of their ancestors and of a shared history.

Tony Kushner captured this yearning in his 1991 play *Angels in America*, stating that there are no angels in America. "...this reaching out for a spiritual past in a country where no indigenous spirits exist – only the Indians, I mean Native American spirits and we killed them off so now, there are no gods here, no ghosts and spirits in America, there are no angels in America, no spiritual past, no racial past, there's only the political."

As Victoria has changed over the years, so have the mythic themes that define it. In the Victorian era, references to classical Greek and Roman mythology could be found in architecture, literature and art. In the modern era, we see abstraction. Buildings are anonymous. Today, symbolic representations refer to natural resources, the landscape, vegetation and animals. Local and regional symbols have replaced those from classical mythology.

The myths of the Indigenous people who occupied Victoria for thousands of years continue to express a connection with the place. Much of Victoria's new public art incorporates elements derived from Indigenous myths. The art includes totem poles, spindle whorls and murals such as the colourful mural on the breakwater. The new castle on Salt Spring Island illustrates this change, with the replacement of traditional medieval gargoyles on drain spouts with native symbols.

Another example of the change in the mythical themes for Victoria is illustrated by the Coat of Arms of the Victoria Police Department announced in June 2010. The new Coat of Arms features Neptune's trident, representing the Island, and a Coast Salish wolf designed by Butch Dick, representing protection in the Coast Salish tradition. The Coat of Arms includes a dogwood flower, symbolizing British Columbia, surrounded by a wreath of golden maple leaves, the national symbol. It replaces the old Victoria Police Department crest which depicted Greek goddesses, just as many images of classical mythology are being replaced by a new mythic language.

The rotunda in the Parliament Buildings displays layers of symbols, like the layers of an archaeological dig. The dome and mosaic floor recall Roman architecture. Royal lions of the Imperial age decorate the walls. Dogwoods, as the provincial emblem, blossom as a unifying decorative feature throughout the building. Memorial plaques speak to the sacrifice of individuals and groups. A temporary display in the center of the rotunda in 2012 was *Shxwtitöstel*, the traditional inland river canoe carved by former Lieutenant Governor Steven Point and Chief Tony Hunt. It, too, has a mythical element, taking the form of a sea serpent, the legendary monster Slahkum from Chilliwack's Cultus Lake.

Modern myth-making continues. The *Shxwtitöstel* canoe brings traditional Aboriginal culture alive. Spindle whorl sculptures provide footprints of the traditional and mythical sites of the Coast Salish peoples. When the town plaza at Uptown shopping centre was opened in 2012, Esquimalt First Nation dancers blessed the new square in the plaza. The centrepiece mosaic fountain, designed by artists Joe Wilson and Chris MacDonald, features Coast Salish artwork depicting four thunderbirds and two human heads.

The natural beauty of the area draws artists to make their homes here. Many artists try to capture the spirit of the place in their work, expressing it as seascape or landscape, embodying it as a goddess or a crow, or transforming found materials into a new form. With every work of art by a local artist, a story is told and preserved.

Sociologists believe that story-telling is a natural way to structure our experiences. Stories share with sacred myths the value of locating the individual within the broader context of meaning and identity. Stories serve not just to entertain but to help us identify where we are within the big picture of our culture. They express our values and beliefs. Furthermore, the stories that engage our hearts enhance our appreciation for our community.

Stories about people, places and events in Victoria continue to be told in walking tours, articles, books and performances. When Victoria celebrated its 150th Anniversary in 2012, it selected seven icons that highlighted the last 150 years of the city's history and culture. The icons took the form of characters that appeared at the numerous public anniversary celebrations. They included a historical person—Amor de Cosmos; a mythological monster—Caddy; two animals—an eagle and a monkey; two places—Chinatown and gardens; and a concept—Big News. Amor de Cosmos founded the *Daily British Colonist* newspaper in 1858, the grandparent of today's *Times-Colonist*, and he served as the second premier of British Columbia in 1872. The Cadborosaurus is the most famous of Victoria's cryptids. The eagle and the monkey characters evoke memories of Emily Carr. The eagle was featured in many of her paintings and the monkey represents Carr's pet monkey, Woo. In the anniversary celebrations of 2012, the figure of Emily Carr herself often appeared with the mischievous Woo. The eagle also refers to the traditional design of the Coast Salish people. The character, China Gate, symbolized Victoria's Chinatown and its Gate of Harmonious Interest. The Flower Dancer was a woman bedecked in flowers riding a bicycle, personifying Victoria as the City of Gardens as well as a popular cycling center. Big News was a stilt-walker, perhaps illustrating the importance of the precarious balance the news must take in presenting the stories of the city.

The environmental movement calls upon mythic elements. People respond to the concept of spirits of the streams, the trees and the rocks calling out for protection. Stream restoration activities are often accompanied by community celebrations. Memories about the removal of the Cook Street chestnuts in 2010 will be accompanied by stories of the ritual of hanging good wish cards on the new saplings. Some myths hold that rocks act as guardians of a place and are transformed spirits. When bedrock next to Moss Rock Park in Fairfield Gonzales was blasted in 2009 to allow for the construction of houses, concerned citizens held vigils to mourn the spirit of the blasted rock, the little sister of Moss Rock. With its panoramic views and lofty presence, Moss Rock has been described as magical. Indeed, many of the people who visit this park feel the spirit of the place.

Mythic creatures thrive in Victoria. In many neighbourhoods, little doors can be seen at the base of trees where residents have installed portals for fairies. It seems that fairies do live at the bottom of the gardens of Victoria. The Cadborosaurus appears at public events. Dragons represent the archetype for heroism. It has been said that if dragons did not exist, it would be necessary to invent them. No need in Victoria with its abundance of dragons appearing as sculptures and murals near Chinatown, speeding over the waves at annual Dragon Boat Races in the Inner Harbour and welcoming the New Year in Chinatown. Chinese dragons rule the element of water, as does the Greek god Poseidon, both appropriate symbols to highlight the impact of the sea on Victoria. Just as the Taoist priest dots the eye of the dragon to bring it to life at Dragon Boat races, myth brings the layers of Victoria to life in the imaginations of the people. And with a thrust of Merlin's wand, the wasteland vanishes as the landscape becomes enchanted.

Bibliography

Books about Victoria, B.C.

Adams, John. *Historic Guide to Ross Bay Cemetery, Victoria, B.C. Canada.* Victoria: Sono Nis Press, 1998.

Akrigg, G. P. V. and Helen B. Akrigg. *British Columbia Place Names.* Vancouver: University of British Columbia Press, 1997.

Allen, Daphne, Allen Dobb and Bob McMinn. *Beautiful Rocks: A History of the Highland District.* Edited by Pattie Whitehouse. Victoria: Highland Heritage Park Society, 2008.

Bancroft, Hubert Howe, William Nemos and Alfred Bates. *History of British Columbia: 1792–1887*, San Francisco: The History Company Publishers, 1887.

Barrett, Anthony A. and Rhodri Windsor Liscombe. *Francis Rattenbury and British Columbia: Architecture and Challenge in the Imperial Age.* Vancouver: University of British Columbia Press, 1983.

Baron, Nancy and Frances Backhouse. "Rare Butterflies of Southeastern Vancouver Island and the Gulf Islands." B.C. Ministry of Environment, Lands and Parks, March 1999.

Boas, Franz. *Indian Myths and Legends from the North Pacific Coast.* Edited by Randy Bouchard and Dorothy Kennedy. Translated by Deitrich Bertz. Vancouver: Talonbooks, 2002.

Bowen, Lynne. *Robert Dunsmuir: Laird of the Mines.* Quebec: XYZ Publishing, 1999.

Brown, Robert. *The Races of Mankind: Being a Popular Description of the Characteristics, Manners and Customs of the Principal Varieties of the Human Family.* London: Cassell, Petter & Galpin, 1873.

Carr, Emily. *The Book of Small.* Toronto: Irwin Publishing Inc., 1942.

Castle, Geoffrey, ed. *Hatley Park: An Illustrated Anthology.* Victoria: The Friends of Hatley Park Society, 1995.

Chamberlain, Paul G. *Victoria's Castles: A Brief History of Lovers, Madmen, Millionaires and Ghosts on Canada's Imperial Margins.* Victoria, Dingle House Press, 2005.

Clark, Ella E. *Indian Legends of the Pacific Northwest*. Illustrated by Robert Bruce Inverarity. Berkeley: University of California Press, 1953.

Cornwallis, Kinahan. *The New El Dorado (or British Columbia)*. London: Thomas Cautley Newby, 1858.

Crockford, Russ. *Victoria: The Unknown City*. Arsenal Pulp Press, 2006.

Duff, Wilson. *The Fort Victoria Treaties*. BC Studies 3: 3-57, 1969.

Glavin, Terry. *The Other River*, www.dooneyscafe.com, July 28, 2008, downloaded Feb. 18, 2012.

Hargrave, James. "James Douglas to James Hargrave, February 5, 1843." In *The Hargrave Correspondence*. Edited by G. P. de T. Glazebrook. Toronto: Champlain Society, 1938.

Hawker, Ronald W. *Monuments in the Nineteenth-Century Public Cemeteries in Victoria, British Columbia*. History Bulletin, Fall 1987, pp 19-26.

Hayman, John. *Robert Brown and the Vancouver Island Exploring Expedition*. Vancouver: University of British Columbia Press, 1989.

Higgins, D.W. *The Mystic Spring and Other Tales of Western Life*. Toronto: William Briggs, 1904.

Hodgson, Alan. "Restoring British Columbia's "Marble Palace." Canadian Parliamentary Review, Vol. 14, No. 2, 1991.

Holloway, Godfrey. *The Empress of Victoria*. Victoria: Key Pacific Publishers Co. Ltd., 1992.

Humphreys, Danda. *On the Street Where You Live: Victoria's Early Roads and Railways*. Surrey: Heritage House, 2000.

——. *On The Street Where You Live: Volume 3, Sailors, Solicitors, and Stargazers of Early Victoria*. Surrey: Heritage House, 2001.

——. *Building Victoria: Men, Myths, and Mortar*. Surrey: Heritage House, 2004.

Jenness, Diamond. *Faith of a Coast Salish Indian*. Edited by Wilson Duff. Victoria: British Columbia Provincial Museum Memoirs in Anthropology Number 3, 1955.

Keddie, Grant. *Songhees Pictorial: A History of the Songhees People as seen by Outsiders, 1790–1912*. Victoria: Royal B.C. Museum, 2003.

Kennel, Rebecca L. *Victoria–Bench by Bench: A Creative Guide to Over 60 Intriguing Sites*. Rebecca Kennel Publishing, 2010.

Lai, Chuen-yan David. *Chinatowns: Towns within Cities in Canada*. University of British Columbia Press, 1988.

Bibliography

Lai, David Chuen-yan. *The Chinese Cemetery in Victoria*. BC Studies, no. 75, Autumn 1987.

Lai, David Chuen-yan and Pamela Madoff. *Building and Rebuilding Harmony: The Gateway to Victoria's Chinatown*. Victoria: University of Victoria, Western Geographical Series, Volume 32, 1997.

Leblond, Paul H. and Edward L. Bousfield. *Cadborosaurus: Survivor from the Deep*. Victoria: Horsdal and Schubart Publishers, Ltd., 1995.

Lutz, John Sutton. 2008. *The Lekwungen*. In *Makuk: A New History of Aboriginal-White Relations*, pp 48-117. Vancouver: University of British Columbia Press.

Minaker, Dennis. *The Gorge of Summers Gone: A History of Victoria's Inland Waterway*. Victoria: Dennis Minaker, 1998.

Obee, Dave. *Making the News: A Times Colonist Look at 150 Years of History*. Victoria: Victoria Times Colonist, 2008.

Neering, Rosemary. *Government House: The Ceremonial Home of All British Columbians*. Photography by Tony Owen. Winlaw, BC: Sono Nis Press, 2007.

Nilsen, Christina Esther. *Possessing Eden: Victoria's Ghosts*. Master of Arts Thesis, University of Victoria, 2005.

Rayne, Aryana. *Labyrinths of British Columbia: A Guide for Your Journey*. Victoria: Somewhere on the Path Publishing, 2010.

Reksten, Terry. *Rattenbury*. Victoria: Sono Nis Press, 1978.

———. *More English than the English: A Very Social History of Victoria*. Victoria: Orca Publishing, 1986.

———. *Craigdarroch: The Story of Dunsmuir Castle*. Victoria: Orca, 1988.

———. *The Dunsmuir Saga*. Vancouver: Douglas & McIntyre, 1991.

Ringuette, Janis. *Beacon Hill Park History, 1842–2004*. Victoria: J. Ringuette, 2004.

Roueche, Ken. *A Fairfield History*. Victoria: Trafford, 2005.

Seemann, Berhold. *Narrative of the Voyage of H.M.S. Herald During the Years 1845–51 under the Command of Captain Henry Kellett, R.N., C.B., Being a Circumnavigation of the Globe*. Volume 1. London: Reeve and Co., 1853.

Scholefield, Ethelbert Olaf Stuart. *British Columbia from Earliest Times to The Present*. Vancouver: S.J. Clarke Publishing Company, 1914.

Segger, Martin, ed. *The British Columbia Parliament Buildings*. Vancouver: Arcon, 1979.

Segger, Martin. *Victoria: A Primer for Regional History in Architecture, 1843–1929*. Photographs by Douglas Franklin. New York: A Pilgrim Guide to Historic Architecture, 1979.

Smith, Michelle and Lawrence Pazder. *Michelle Remembers*. New York: Congdon & Lattès, 1980.

Suttles, Wayne. *Coast Salish Essays*. Vancouver: Talonbooks, 1987.

Ward, Robin. *Echoes of Empire: Victoria & Its Remarkable Buildings*. Madeira Park, B.C: Harbour, 1996.

Bibliography

Books about Mythology

Andrews, Tamra. *A Dictionary of Nature Myths: Legends of the Earth, Sea and Sky.* New York: Oxford University Press, 1998.

Bulfinch, Thomas. *Bulfinch's Mythology.* Edited by Richard Martin. New York: HarperCollins. 1991.

Campbell, Joseph with Bill Moyers. *The Power of Myth.* New York: Doubleday, 1988.

Green, Miranda J. *Dictionary of Celtic Myth and Legend.* London: Thames and Hudson, 1992.

Grimal, Pierre. *The Penguin Dictionary of Classical Mythology.* London: Penguin Books, 1990.

Grimm, Jakob. *Teutonic Mythologies.* Translated by James Steven Stallybrass. London: George Bell & Sons, Vol. 4, 1888.

Hogarth, Peter and Val Clery. *Dragons.* Toronto: Penguin Books, 1979

Homer. *The Odyssey.* Translated by George Herbert Palmer. New York: Dover Publications, 1999.

Jung, Carl G., ed. *Man and His Symbols.* New York: Dell Publishing Co., 1972.

Jung, C.G. *Memories, Dreams, Reflections.* New York: Vintage Books, 1965.

Lethaby, W.R. *Architecture, Mysticism and Myth.* London: Percival & Co., 1892.

Mackillop, James. *Dictionary of Celtic Mythology.* Oxford: Oxford University Press, 1998.

Mitchell, Stephen. *Gilgamesh: A New English Version.* New York: Free Press, 2004.

"Naiads." *Theoi Greek Mythology.* 2013. http://www.theoi.com.

Ovid. *The Metamorphoses.* Translated by David R. Slavitt. Baltimore: John Hopkins University Press, 1994.

Shearar, Cheryl. *Understanding Northwest Coast Art: A Guide to Crests, Beings and Symbols.* Vancouver: Douglas & McIntyre, 2000.

Willis, Roy. *Dictionary of World Myth: An A-Z reference guide to gods, goddesses, heroes, heroines and fabulous beasts.* London: Duncan Baird, 2000.

ABOUT THE AUTHOR

Linda Foubister searched for the myths and symbols in the island town of Victoria, B.C. and found them in abundance. This is Foubister's second book on mythology. Her first book, *Goddess in the Grass: Serpentine Mythology and the Great Goddess,* is available as an ebook. As a writer, researcher and public speaker, Foubister is interested in the interplay between mythology and popular culture. Her works include articles in community magazines, encyclopedias, ezines and anthologies.

www.ingramcontent.com/pod-product-compliance
Lightning Source LLC
Chambersburg PA
CBHW060022100426
42740CB00010B/1566